What people ar

China: The Super Predator

It is shocking and disturbing to read in this fine book about what has become of China and where it is heading. Pierre-Antoine has pulled together the whole story. One reads it with sadness but it paints a true picture.

Jasper Becker, journalist, author of *Why Communism Failed* and other books

In his latest book, Pierre-Antoine Donnet draws on 40-plus years of experience of China to provide insightful analysis of China's current place in a rapidly evolving world and the future challenges it poses for its neighbours and the West.

Peter Grout, formerly of the British Council, Beijing & Shanghai

Pierre-Antoine Donnet is a veteran journalist who speaks Mandarin and has been studying China for decades. He has a deep knowledge of the country, which makes this a most valuable book. He provides a meticulous analysis of the PRC today and describes the nature of its government and ambitions. I recommend it to anyone who wants to understand them.

Mark O'Neill, journalist, author and speaker

A provocative book that pulls no punches. While China's economic rise ought to have been welcomed as part of a new multipolar world order, President Xi and the CCP have turned it into an unwelcome bid for absolute global power.

George Cunningham, Chair, UK Liberal Democrats Subcommittee on China; former Strategic Adviser on Asia-Pacific, European External Action Service, EU

China:
The Super Predator

A Challenge for the Planet

China:
The Super Predator

A Challenge for the Planet

Pierre-Antoine Donnet

Translated by Richard Lein

CHANGEMAKERS
BOOKS

Winchester, UK
Washington, USA

JOHN HUNT PUBLISHING

First published by Changemakers Books, 2024
Changemakers Books is an imprint of John Hunt Publishing Ltd., No. 3 East Street,
Alresford, Hampshire SO24 9EE, UK
office@jhpbooks.com
www.johnhuntpublishing.com
www.changemakers-books.com

For distributor details and how to order please visit the 'Ordering' section on our website.

Text copyright: Pierre-Antoine Donnet 2023

ISBN: 978 1 80341 416 4
978 1 80341 417 1 (ebook)
Library of Congress Control Number: 2023934048

A CIP catalogue record for this book is available from the British Library.

Design: Lapiz Digital Services

UK: Printed and bound by CPI Group (UK) Ltd, Croydon, CR0 4YY
Printed and bound in the United Kingdom by TJ Books Limited, Padstow, Cornwall

MIX
Paper from
responsible sources
FSC® C013056

We operate a distinctive and ethical publishing philosophy in
all areas of our business, from our global network of authors to
production and worldwide distribution.

The original French version of this book:
Chine: le grand prédateur
Un défi pour la planète

Contents

I dedicate this book to Véronique, the widow of
French caricaturist Cabu, who was assassinated on
January 7, 2015, along with his friends at *Charlie Hebdo*.
I had the honor of working with him and we shared a
fascination for East Asia. His goodness and benevolence
remain etched in my heart. Perhaps unknowingly,
he gave me one hell of a life lesson.

Foreword

By Jean-Pierre Cabestan

This is both an important and essential book. It is important because Pierre-Antoine Donnet has drawn up a damning and worrying assessment of the current Chinese regime and its domestic and international projects. Essential because it is long overdue for us Europeans and French to draw the appropriate conclusions from our relationship with the People's Republic of China, on the diplomatic-strategic, economic and human levels. The title of this book—*China: The Super Predator*—is clearly inspired by the title of a recent book by François Heisbourg, *Le Temps des prédateurs* [The time of predators], Odile Jacob, 2020. Nevertheless, Pierre-Antoine Donnet rightly focuses his attention on China, not only because it is the country that he has been studying for more than 40 years and whose language he speaks, but also because the current Chinese political regime presents, in his eyes and as the subtitle of his essay indicates, "a challenge for the planet." I would add that it is this regime, that is the Chinese Communist Party (CP)—a huge machine of more than 90 million members, run with an iron fist and in total opacity by an elite leading cadre of fewer than 600,000—and not Chinese society that presents the main challenge for the planet today.

Pierre-Antoine Donnet analyzes here in five incisive chapters the reality of today's China, especially the inner workings that the Chinese CP tries to hide with its propaganda and disinformation campaigns. I am not going to repeat the arguments he develops, since we know them. The regime in Beijing, and especially the one honed and perfected by President Xi Jinping since 2012, is more toxic than ever to freedom. Having set up Orwellian surveillance systems thanks to modern technologies, it has managed to stay far ahead of any force that could threaten it. It has taken over Hong Kong, strangling the remnants of democracy and political freedom that have survived there since 2020. It has brutally repressed Tibet and even more so Xinjiang, painting all Muslims (Uyghurs, Kazakhs, Kyrgyz) who fight for real political autonomy or simply seek to preserve their culture and religion with the brush of "terrorism." Even more brutally than before, the regime nips in the bud any hint of democratization or even political reform. And it has openly stated its intention to remain in power—in undivided power—for "a thousand years" as China's Foreign Minister Wang Yi recently put it. In short, the Chinese regime and the "secret society" that presides over the country's destiny have become the number-one enemy of democracy. It is number one not because it is more opposed to democracy than other authoritarian governments. Putin's Russia, the recent military coup in Burma and even the seizure of the Capitol in Washington—an event unprecedented in the history of the United States of America—remind us how widespread authoritarianism is and how fragile democracy can be, and how quick and easy it is to move from democracy to dictatorship. No, China is number one because it is now the second-largest economic and military power in the world. It is likely to surpass the United States in terms of gross domestic product (GDP) before the end of this decade. And every day, it is in a better position to challenge the United States and its allies in its region, especially in the Taiwan Strait and the South China Sea. What might the future of our democracies be if American leadership were to give way to Chinese leadership? Democracy would inevitably be in a weaker position; our values would be more clearly at risk.

Those in the West who believed that our policies of engagement and "soft trade" would acculturate the People's Republic of China to democracy were quite mistaken. Pierre-Antoine Donnet is kind enough to quote from my book (2018). Sadly, three years after its publication, it is clear that my pessimistic conclusions remain valid. Moreover, as the author of *China: The Super Predator* clearly shows, the Beijing government no longer only criticizes what it calls "Western democracy" to protect its survival, that is, the Communist Party's dictatorship over Chinese society. Its economic strength now allows it to advance its pawns and to try to modify the balance of power between socialism and capitalism in its favor, between its highly authoritarian system and our democracies. While denying accusations that it seeks to export its "model," Beijing pushes its advantage by denouncing daily the universalist approach of human rights, by praising *urbi et orbi* the advantages of its system of governance and by developing, in particular in the UN system, an unprecedented entryism that allows it to impose its narrative, including Xi's message that humanity shares a common destiny...[1]

The predatory nature of the Beijing regime has many facets. The unprecedented development of the Chinese economy must be welcomed as the success of an element of Chinese society over which the Communist Party finally resolved to ease control in 1979, allowing it to do business and gain profits. But this unprecedented modernization has brought with it an unprecedented challenge as well: the environmental challenge. Xi Jinping's government is aware of this, but its opacity and its partial and unfinished integration into the international community have aggravated the problems it faces and that the world in turn must overcome: in China itself, the slow pace of decarbonizing electricity production and the large-scale pollution of water; on a global scale, the deforestation of the world's tropical regions and the organized plundering of the world's ocean fish stocks. It has long been known that the Chinese regime will stop at nothing to acquire and master the technologies that will enable it to overtake the technological leadership of the United States, and more broadly the developed countries. In recent years, this battle has intensified thanks to

3

the economic strategy introduced by Xi in 2020. In reality, this new "dual circulation" economic strategy, according to which the country must both stimulate domestic consumption and continue to globalize its economy, aims for the reduction of China's dependence on Western technologies. The real objective of the strategy is for China to develop its own technologies and standards and then to impose them upon as many countries as possible. First, upon the countries of the South that are the easiest prey to capture, and then on those of the North most dependent on the Chinese economy. In other words, the Chinese government is introducing its own strategy of economic decoupling from the West. Will China succeed in this endeavor? Will it succeed in becoming a leader in the technologies of the future? I am not certain it will. While China has acquired levels of excellence—missiles, rockets, satellites, drones, high-speed rail, online payments—it is still lagging far behind in many areas: microchips, aircraft engines, nanotechnology, medical research, to name a few.

China's international ambitions are well known: to reunify Taiwan at all costs; to take control of the maritime domain it claims as well as all the resources there; to impose its own international standards; and to reorganize the world economy so that the West is no longer its center but rather the Chinese economy itself. In this way, only the People's Republic can, in the eyes of the Chinese CP, knock the US off its pedestal. Those who refuse to see the strategic dimension of Xi Jinping's New Silk Roads are acting in bad faith. It is clear that the Belt and Road Initiative (BRI) pursues economic objectives: the internationalization of large Chinese groups, the conquest of new markets, the securing of supplies of raw materials. But by multiplying the links of economic and financial dependence between an ever-increasing number of countries in the South, China has set up new asymmetrical and, so to speak, dependent relations, constituting a new form of hegemony. The large number of states that have supported the Chinese government's policy in Xinjiang or Hong Kong in recent years at the insistence of the Chinese attests to this rise in power. Does this mean that these countries "love China"? No, of course not; it simply means that they are indebted to China and that the Chinese regime is keeping them on a leash.

The good news, if you will, is that the BRI is running out of steam, not only because countries in the South are finding it increasingly difficult to repay their debts to Chinese state banks, but also because Beijing needs more funding to support domestic growth, its own infrastructure projects, and research and development in advanced technologies. But this development is unlikely to mitigate the increasingly rough-and-tumble nature of Chinese diplomacy. Australia, Canada and now the European Union, who have dared to impose targeted sanctions against some of the most egregious human rights abusers in Xinjiang, are paying the price. And Beijing's threats against Taiwan are increasing. This is fueling fears of a military crisis, even an armed conflict which would inevitably pit China and the United States directly against each other and could quickly turn nuclear. And this in the context of a never-ending Covid-19 health crisis, where Europe's economy remains at half-mast while China and America are returning to sustained growth (between 6% and 8% in 2021), and populism and intolerance are on the rise in democratic countries.

In these circumstances, and given the worrying assessment that Pierre-Antoine Donnet has made with precision, what should we do? First, I believe that we must take measure of the geostrategic confrontation, the economic competition and the ideological rivalry that poses us against China. Personally, I believe that we have entered a new Cold War, not because we want to, but because the Chinese CP, through its discourse, policies and actions, has imposed it upon us. I understand very well the reasons that could lead the reader to disagree with my analysis because of the obvious differences that distinguish the current period from the old Cold War that I still remember. My first passage through Checkpoint Charlie in Berlin was in 1974 and my first trip to the Soviet Union was in 1977 when Brezhnev had just revised the country's constitution and become President of the Republic, in addition to his title of General Secretary of the Communist Party of the Soviet Union (CPSU). We are in a globalized world and China is part of it. But it has not fully integrated into it, taking liberties not only with the universal values we believe in, but also with the norms of the World Trade Organization, the law of the sea, and now the rules of politeness and courtesy of diplomatic life. And since it has become strong, it has fought these values and norms wherever it can.

Some Europeans tell me, echoing Beijing's arguments, that we have no strategic conflicts with China. They say we are far from the Asia-Pacific region, that our strategic concerns are on our doorstep: Islamic terrorism, the Sahel, Russia, the Middle East. They say we do not have the means to intervene militarily in the Far East, except to recall in a very symbolic way the principle of freedom of navigation, notably in the South China Sea. But in the event of a Sino-American conflict in the Taiwan Strait, for example, what policy will we adopt towards the People's Republic? As members of NATO, won't most European countries be forced to support their American ally, to impose a blockade on China and to severely curtail or even freeze our economic and human relations with China? We are not there yet, but we must be careful not to accept the likes of a Munich Accord with Beijing, giving in to this capital's will to impose its diktat upon Taiwan and to deny it any control over its destiny, or to gradually take control of the islets in the South China Sea or the East China Sea administered by other countries. Europe is better prepared for economic and especially technological competition with the People's Republic. However, it seems to me that it is now essential to reduce our economic dependence on this country as much as possible, by repatriating the most strategic industries and moving the others to countries that are less inclined to, or less able to, exploit this dependence at our expense. In doing so, we obviously risk losing market share in China itself. But hasn't the Chinese government's plan for several years been to marginalize the footprint of foreign groups in its domestic market? Doesn't it open up its economic sectors to foreigners only once it has ensured that its national champions are in a strong position?

Finally, more than ever before, we must defend democracy and its values. Because if we don't, no one will do it for us. In this regard, I would like to instill a dose of optimism into the discussion. I have been teaching at a Hong Kong university on the domestic and foreign policy of the People's Republic for 14 years. When I arrived in 2007, my students were generally not very political, not very interested in the affairs of the city. Then things changed; they got burned first during the Umbrella Movement in 2014 and then during the protests against the extradition bill and for the democratization of the territory in 2019. We know what happened. My students have obviously become more cautious. But we continue to cover all the topics that a political scientist must cover. Those of them who come from the mainland show a sensitivity to politics and an independence of mind that I would not have imagined even ten years ago. More generally, the interest of my students in the Taiwanese democratic experience is growing. And I don't need to push them, despite my known penchant for extolling the virtues of that island society and ignoring the other qualities of those there who still used the term "communist thugs" (*gongfei*) when I studied there in the late 1970s.

So Chinese society is changing, and the reader who knows little about China should not be taken in by Beijing's propaganda. It's true that the regime still enjoys an undeniable "legitimacy of result," to use a Weberian expression (Sintomer et al., 2014). The Chinese are in their majority nationalists; but few of them "love" the Chinese CP and fully believe what it tells them. Those who join do so out of careerism. And many mainland Chinese — and now Hong Kong Chinese — tend to keep their thoughts to themselves and their relatives. They remain aloof and defiant of the official discourse. They are well aware that the Party's propaganda embellishes reality and hides anything that might damage its image. Above all, they know that the Party is above the law and that power is the rule. Finally, among the elites, Xi Jinping is contentious. The personalization of his power, his authoritarianism and his aggressiveness on the international scene are all criticisms that are regularly heard in China. But this does not mean that Xi is in any danger, even if some people venture to predict his downfall following a palace revolution. It means even less that his regime is in the doldrums. But it does mean that Chinese society is becoming more autonomous, more global, and that a pluralism of ideas is emerging more and more. The Chinese are better educated and better informed than ever about the outside world and about their own country. They also aspire to more freedoms, especially freedom of information and opinion, as demonstrated by the Covid-19 crisis in the spring of 2020.

Let us also not forget that the Chinese government — any Chinese government, for that matter, regardless of its political color — will continue to face multiple domestic challenges. In addition to the worrying environmental situation, the rapid aging of the population, the dramatic reduction in arable land, the relative but persistent poverty of a good half of society (600 million Chinese earn less than 120 euros per month) and the ever-increasing expectations of an urbanized middle class in search of wellbeing. In other words, China is not as powerful as it wants everyone to believe. And as I try to show in a forthcoming essay, it will continue to hesitate to engage in armed conflict with the United States, preferring to use what strategists call "the grey zone" between war and peace to its advantage, including in dealing with Taiwan (2021). These are all reasons not to give in to the demands, threats and intimidation of the Chinese communist regime. We are engaged in an arm-wrestling match with the Chinese regime that is bound to last for a long time. We must therefore be better prepared.

This preparation does not prevent us from trying to cooperate with the Chinese government where our interests converge, such as in the fight against global warming, the management of the Covid-19 crisis, or the Iranian and North Korean nuclear programs. But we must not delude ourselves, either. Today's world structurally favors confrontation over cooperation.

China is of course not the only predator. Russia is another; but with the GDP of Italy, its capacity to cause harm is much more limited. Therefore, Pierre-Antoine Donnet, a faithful friend I first met in Beijing more than 30 years ago, is right to alert us. Enjoy your reading!

Jean-Pierre Cabestan is a French sinologist, specializing in the law and institutions of contemporary China and Taiwan. He is a senior researcher at France's National Scientific Research Center and since 2007 he has served as a professor and head of the Department of Political Science at Hong Kong Baptist University. He is also a research associate at the Asia Centre—Centre études Asie.

Notes

1   "No country in the world can enjoy absolute security. A country cannot have security while others are in turmoil, as threats facing other countries may haunt itself also. When neighbors are in trouble, instead of tightening his own fences, one should extend a helping hand to them. As a

saying goes, 'United we stand, divided we fall.' All countries should pursue common, comprehensive, cooperative and sustainable security." Xi Jinping's 2017 address to the United Nations in Geneva. Available at http://iq.china-embassy.gov.cn/eng/zygx/201701/t20170123_2309166.htm

Acknowledgments

I learned a lot during the writing of this book thanks to the enlightened advice of many friends. A Long March towards a bit more light. First, I would like to thank Manon Viard, editor of the Aube publishing house, and her father Jean Viard, a renowned sociologist, for their trust and support of a project that was not self-evident. This trust was surprising and it touched me deeply. The Aube publishing house calls itself a committed publisher, and I have certainly felt their commitment to me. A commitment that has provided the comfort for me to develop as a writer. I would also like to thank Jean-Pierre Cabestan for his foreword, which I consider an act of courage in these times. My thanks also go to Tim Ward, through whom this book was published by John Hunt Publishing, as well as to Richard Lein who translated my manuscript with speed and great talent. My gratitude also goes to my son Pierre-Arnaud for his editorial advice throughout the writing of this book. Thanks to Hubert Testard for his unfailing support in an undertaking that more than once raised doubts in me and for his careful rereading of the manuscript. His encouragements were very precious. Thanks for his luminous ideas to Thierry Dussard, an experienced reporter and faithful companion with whom I have often shared the joys of investigative journalism. Thanks also to Catherine Martel-Rousson for her precious contributions in the search for information, and to my sister Anne-Michèle who reviewed the manuscript and added some very constructive proposals to the debate, as did my old friend Hubert Villette. My gratitude also goes to my colleague Joëlle Garrus who knows China well and who, although her time is limited, took the bull by the horns and reread my manuscript. Thanks to Marie Holzman whose opinion on my manuscript was important to me. A friendly nod to Katia Buffetrille for her eagle eye that didn't miss a thing. Thank you to Nancy Li for an incredible sense of humor that was very helpful. Thanks again to Patrick Bonnassieux who, involuntarily no doubt, put me on the track of precious information. Thanks also to Didier Lacaze for his generous and faithful contributing of sources of information. Then there are also all those others who must remain anonymous but without whose support I might not have succeeded in completing my work. My deepest gratitude goes to my wife, Monika, my tireless muse who has so often shared her boundless energy when I had hardly any left and who accepted with good grace the hours stolen from our daily life to write this book.

Introduction

Today's China under President Xi Jinping is slowly heading towards a fascist dictatorship. China's absolute master is leading the country into a dead-end situation where it is now more isolated from the West than at any time since the death of Mao Zedong in 1976. Domestic clampdowns have been accumulating, with the savage crackdown on Uyghurs in Xinjiang and the crushing of all individual freedoms in Hong Kong the most serious. But China has also intensified its threats and intimidation against Taiwan, become more belligerent towards its neighbors and, most recently, begun a dangerous rapprochement with Moscow despite Russia's invasion of Ukraine.

These mistakes are leading to China becoming a pariah state on the international scene. Following the United States, many Western countries have become disillusioned with China and have realized that the ultimate goal of the Chinese leadership is to take control of the world, both commercially and politically. The European Union, which Beijing hoped to use as a counterweight to the United States, is gradually distancing itself from China. As for China's neighbors — Japan, South Korea, the Philippines, Indonesia, Australia, India and Vietnam — they too have come to realize not only that this large country will no longer be the motor of economic growth for the region, but that it is also an invasive rival to be wary of.

On the economic front, China is no longer the world's growth engine and will not be for a long time. Xi Jinping, who dreamed of seeing his country become the world's leading economic power, must now be disappointed because China will not achieve this for a very long time, if ever. A declining population is contributing to China's faltering economy. India will soon become the most populous country in the world, with China relegated to second place.

But now more than ever, Taiwan has become the epicenter of tensions in East Asia, with the Chinese president dreaming of "reunifying" the rebellious island with the Chinese mainland, by force if necessary. But here again, his goal is likely to be thwarted because not only has the Taiwanese army been greatly modernized, but Taiwan can now count on US military assistance in case the People's Liberation Army attempts to invade.

Taiwan has now become a bastion of Chinese democracy against the autocratic mainland. Taiwan is a living, daily demonstration that democracy suits China very well, contrary to what some self-proclaimed China experts have been professing for years.

The big question is whether Communist China will take the plunge and align itself militarily with Russia. Having become a beleaguered citadel because of its master's mistakes, China must now decide which path to take: either becoming a responsible great power accepted on the international scene or joining the club of totalitarian countries opposed to the Western powers.

It is to be hoped, of course, that China will choose the first option. Such a choice is likely to require a change of leadership. Xi Jinping's departure is probably not for the foreseeable future, as since coming to power in 2012 he has sidelined all rivals, declared or otherwise, and surrounded himself with loyal followers.

Regime change is unlikely to come from the Chinese people. Nor will it come from external pressures, which will further consolidate the nationalism that Xi Jinping uses to hold on to power. But it may well come from within the Chinese Communist Party as its elite gradually realizes the extent to which the party's General Secretary and head of the Central Military Commission is leading the country into disaster.

Let us hope that such a transition, if it takes place, will be carried out without violence, because such a regime change will call into question the very foundation of Chinese society since 1949. The end of the Chinese Communist Party is not for tomorrow, nor for the day after tomorrow. But, more than a century after its birth, the Party today projects the image of a regime that has reached its limits and not the vehicle to realize the Chinese Dream of national rejuvenation promoted by Xi Jinping when he came to power in 2012.

Chapter 1

The new *Homo sinicus*, the tragedy of the Uyghurs and Tibetans

Placed under the close and constant surveillance of the authorities, 1.4 billion human beings are evolving in a universe of conformity, obedience, discipline, and submission to the authorities, where free will is gradually disappearing in favor of an invasive societal mold. Subjected to a kind of collective confinement, the men and women of tomorrow in China are frightening. Do they foreshadow the future of human society? The tragedy of the Uyghurs and Tibetans calls out to us.

There are days when I despair of the human race.
—Robert Badinter (French philosopher and historian), speech on the abolition of the death penalty at the National Assembly on September 17, 1981

The world will not be destroyed by those who do evil, but by those who watch them without doing anything.
—Albert Einstein

The Chinese, the most watched humans in the world

The Chinese are the most monitored people in the world. An armada of cameras equipped with sophisticated facial recognition software follows their every move in public places in every major city in the country. The results are clear: 18 of the 20 most monitored cities in the world are in China. London and Hyderabad are the only non-Chinese cities to make it into the top 20, but they are ranked at the bottom. By 2021, a total of more than one billion surveillance cameras had been installed in cities around the world, large and small, and 54% of them in China alone (Bischoff, 2022). This means that in China, Big Brother is now watching you everywhere. And if a camera or a neighborhood commissioner detects bad behavior? You can no longer be a Party member or a representative of your neighborhood. Certain doors close to you. Throwing a paper on the ground, crossing the street outside of the crosswalk, not reading the water meter correctly, cutting down a tree, traveling by train without a valid ticket: in China, these incivilities can be costly. About 40 Chinese cities have been experimenting since 2019 with a so-called social credit system, which consists of rating citizens. Each citizen obtains, in essence, a credit score of their behavior, and it serves as a second ID card. "The aim of this system is to rebuild morality," says Lin Junyue, father of the social credit system. According to him, such a system allows the Chinese people to reach "the same level of civility as in developed countries." But beware those who do not obey all the rules of good conduct. China began rolling out the social credit system nationwide in 2020. This *blacklist,* accessible on the internet with people's names, addresses and sometimes even facial images, has been extended throughout the country. The list also includes citizens with financial problems.[1] These millions of surveillance cameras have become the active core of an omnipresent system of social control that has become a valuable tool for the Chinese Communist Party (CCP). As François Heisbourg (2020) notes, this system, like the one imagined by George Orwell in his prophetic book *1984*, will control access to employment, housing, education, and social security benefits, as well as limit freedom of movement, payments and communication. Although its implementation will undoubtedly not be easy, "it will nonetheless devastate countless lives and will allow the CCP to consolidate its power."

China is also a massive exporter of its surveillance equipment, including of course its cameras, in particular to developing and emerging countries where authoritarian regimes are attracted by these new possibilities of social control. The question we should ask ourselves is whether we accept the fact that China is exporting its Orwellian social model and that new surveillance societies are springing up in all these countries without any safeguards. Is Big Brother going to extend his grip all over the world? Oppressive governments are buying surveillance technology from China, US Assistant Secretary of State for Western Hemisphere Affairs Kimberly Breier said in a speech to the Council of the Americas on April 26, 2019. "China exports technological know-how that can help authoritarian governments track, reward, and punish citizens through a tyrannical system of digital surveillance," she said. China has introduced these technologies in Tibet and Xinjiang, among other places, to spy on Tibetans, Uyghurs, ethnic Kazakhs and members of other minority groups. Agreements to export such high-tech surveillance equipment are often included in its New Silk Roads program, according to a report by the Center for a New American Security entitled *Grading China's Belt and Road*. Zimbabwe, for example, as part of such a trade deal, signed a deal with a Chinese firm to implement facial recognition screening across the country. The system "risks entrenching Zimbabwe's authoritarianism," the report's authors say, while noting that all the facial data on all Zimbabweans is sent to China under the deal (Kliman et al., 2019). But it isn't a one-way street. According to a report by Amnesty International published in September 2020, several European companies have supplied China with surveillance equipment, including facial recognition technology. In its report, the NGO mentions the French giant Idemia, one of the world leaders in the biometrics sector with 15,000 employees and 2.3 billion euros in annual revenue, which sold a system to detect and recognize faces on video footage to the Shanghai Public Security Bureau.

Given that they live in a social and political straitjacket, the only freedom the Chinese people can still hope to enjoy is that of consumption. Here, the floodgates are wide open. The Chinese have been plunged into a world of unbridled consumerism that has made fortunes for big online sales platforms, such as the giant Alibaba.[2] A huge wave of materialism has swept over China, even though more and more Chinese people are seeking a spiritual life.[3] "Consumption is setting records each year. Black Friday, which is a one-day sale event invented in America, was imported by the Alibaba group in 2009 and called its November 11 event Singles' Day. In 2013 sales were 6 billion euros, while this year (2020) sales were 68 billion euros. So over seven years, we've seen this incredible progression, with records broken from one year to the next. To give you an idea of what this can represent, at the peak of sales on November 11, it was 585,000 orders per second. We can see this frightening acceleration of digital consumption in China. China is the second-largest digital consumer in the world behind South Korea. The fashion sector accounts for eight to ten percent of the world's CO_2 [carbon dioxide] emissions, which is more than international flights and maritime transport combined. It is also the second-largest consumer of water after the oil industry," noted Nathalie Bastianelli (2021), a specialist in environmental and consumer issues in China. Meanwhile, a recent report found that more than half of the Chinese population is now overweight. The report by the National Health Commission, published on December 23, 2020, also found 16.4% of Chinese to be obese. It blamed these rising levels on a profound change in lifestyle that now sees less than a quarter of the Chinese population being physically active at least once a week. It also blamed increased consumption of meat and a sharp decrease in the eating of fruits and vegetables (*BBC*, 2020).

Hong Kong joins Tibet under the boot

In Communist China, there is no room for different viewpoints. No space for any dissent. When a nail sticks out, you must hammer it in. On December 28, 2020, Zhang Zhan, a "citizen journalist" who had covered the Covid-19 epidemic in Wuhan, was sentenced to four years in prison. Her only crime: broadcasting videos that were not in line with official propaganda of the health situation in Wuhan and chronicling the lives of Wuhan residents, the first in China to be confined. Zhang was convicted of "picking quarrels and causing trouble," the term commonly used in China to condemn dissidents. She "looked very downcast when the verdict was announced," said one of her lawyers, Ren Quanniu, who added he was very worried about her psychological state. Zhang, who had gone on a hunger strike while awaiting trial and was force-fed in her cell, appeared before her judges in a wheelchair. Journalists and foreign diplomats were not allowed to enter the Shanghai court where the 37-year-old former lawyer was tried in a matter of hours. Police pushed back some of her supporters who had gathered for the opening of the trial. It has since emerged that the Chinese authorities lied to the world about the extent of the pandemic in Wuhan where the virus was first detected in December 2019. A study conducted by the Chinese Center for Disease Control and Prevention, whose findings were made public in late December 2020, showed that 4.4% of the city's 11 million population, or some 500,000 people, had antibodies to Covid-19 in their blood, ten times the official figure (50,008) (McCarthy and Zhuang, 2020). The official death toll of 4634 is also clearly questionable.

The day following Zhang's conviction, a young pro-democracy activist in Hong Kong was sentenced to four months in prison for "insulting the Chinese flag" and "illegal assembly." Tony Chung, head of a now-disbanded group that called for Hong Kong's independence, was convicted of throwing down a Chinese flag during clashes between protesters and law enforcement in front of the local parliament (Legislative Council, or Legco) in May 2019. Chung, 19, will wait in detention for another trial on secession charges that carry a life sentence under the national security law imposed by Beijing in June 2020 in the former British colony. A sadly routine snapshot of life in today's China. On the same day, ten young Hong Kong fugitives were tried behind closed doors in Shenzhen, a city bordering Hong Kong, after being arrested at the end of August while trying to leave the city to take refuge in Taiwan. Of the ten defendants, eight were accused of illegally crossing the Chinese border, an offense punishable by one year in prison, while two were accused of organizing the escape, a crime punishable by seven years in prison. They all pleaded guilty. Two minors from the group were tried separately. Two days later, the defendants were sentenced to between seven months and three years in prison. The trial was emblematic of the blanket of repression that has fallen upon the city since the massive protests of 2019 and the subsequent imposition in June 2020 of a "national security law" by Beijing. The law provides for sentences of up to life imprisonment for anyone convicted of secession, subversion, terrorism, or collusion with foreigners. As for press magnate Jimmy Lai Chee-ying, 73, the owner of the *Apple Daily* newspaper and fierce critic of the Chinese communist regime who is one of the few remaining voices for democracy in Hong Kong, he has been languishing in prison since the beginning of December 2020 while he awaits trial on charges of secession. He was convicted on April 1, 2021, on separate charges of organizing and attending two illegal gatherings in 2019 and sentenced to 14 months in prison on April 16. On the same day, prosecutors handed Lai an additional national security charge that could see him sentenced to life in prison (Mahtani and Yu, 2021). Joshua Wong, 24, and Agnes Chow, 24, arguably Hong Kong's best-known pro-democracy activists, are being held in solitary confinement in two high-security prisons, and have been classified as Class A prisoners, the most dangerous. Thousands of young activists, some of them very young, were arrested during the mass demonstrations that brought out onto the streets up to 2 million people, or more than one in four Hongkongers, including children and the elderly, in 2019. On January 6, 2021, police arrested 53 pro-democracy activists and opposition lawmakers on suspicion of "plotting to overthrow the government" in Hong Kong. They were rounded up in early morning raids on their homes by about 1000 law enforcement officers under the National Security Act. Just an ordinary day in Hong Kong. Until the autumn of 2020, the city was a haven for civil liberties that mainland Chinese do not enjoy. The city is now under the complete control of Beijing. At the end of February 2021, a new draft electoral law was proposed for Hong Kong. The draft law, which came from Beijing, will require candidates for the post of municipal councilor to swear allegiance to the Chinese nation, and any "dishonest" violators will be removed from their posts, according to Eric Tsang, Hong Kong's Minister for Mainland and Constitutional Affairs. This new procedure aims to have only "patriotic" candidates and elected officials at all levels of the local political system. It seems clearly aimed at disqualifying the 90% of pro-democracy local elected officials, who won seats in the November 2019 municipal elections in a vote that inflicted a stinging defeat on the pro-Beijing camp, from the legislative elections scheduled for September 2021. Hong Kong is now completely under lock and key.

On February 28, 2021, 47 leading figures in the democratic camp were charged with subversion under the new national security law for organizing, in 2020, primaries within their movement to select candidates for the September elections to the Legco, which were postponed by the authorities, ostensibly due to the Covid-19 pandemic. The following day hundreds of supporters of the accused activists lined up outside the court to attend the opening of their trial. Clad in black, the color of protest in Hong Kong, the activists were joined by diplomats from the consulates of the United Kingdom, Canada, Germany, the Netherlands, and the European Union. "The Chinese and Hong Kong authorities promised that the national security law would be used in a very narrow sense and it's clear that that is no longer the case and that is concerning to us," Jonathan Williams, head of political and communications at the British Consulate-General in Hong Kong, said outside the court (*Hong Kong Arrests: British Consulate Official Blasts China and the H.K. Authorities*, 2021). Meanwhile, US Secretary of State Antony Blinken condemned their detention and called for their immediate release. "Political participation and freedom of expression should not be crimes. The US stands with the people of Hong Kong," he tweeted. British Foreign Secretary Dominic Raab tweeted that the charges against the 47 demonstrated "in the starkest terms the NSL [national security law] being used to eliminate political dissent rather than restore order—contrary to what the Chinese Government promised."

This is perhaps the most serious blow to the democratic camp in Hong Kong since the 1997 handover, with key leaders of the Democratic and Civic Party among those indicted. Among them is Joshua Wong Chi-fung, 25, the tireless young activist for human rights and democracy in Hong Kong who has been involved in all the battles of recent years in the former colony, as well as journalist Claudia Mo Man-ching, a former *Agence France-Presse* correspondent who became a prominent politician and member of the pro-democracy group in the Hong Kong Legco. There is little difference now between Hong Kong and any other city on the mainland, even though Beijing had vowed to maintain a high degree of autonomy in Hong Kong for 50 years and had promised that it would be able to retain its own institutions, independent judiciary and way of life.

These moves mark the definitive end of the democratic movement that swept Hong Kong, which in 2019 had brought up to 2 million demonstrators onto the streets (out of a population of 7 million) to protest China's grip on this great port city. It also formalizes the death of the "One Country, Two Systems" (一国两制) concept that Deng Xiaoping used to wrest the UK's handover of Hong Kong from British Prime Minister Margaret Thatcher in 1984. Skeptical at first, the "Iron Lady" eventually relented when Beijing threatened to cut off water and electricity to Hong Kong and brandished other retaliatory measures. The handover was made effective and celebrated with great fanfare by Beijing 13 years later. Macao, a Portuguese colony, followed in 1999. These latest developments are also, last but not least, an extremely strong political message for Taiwan and its population, which was offered the same concept to reunify with the Chinese mainland. The 23 million inhabitants of Taiwan will see in this tragedy a telling lesson about the real meaning of Beijing's so-called smile diplomacy: China is one and indivisible under the leadership of the Chinese Communist Party; and, under its banner, there is no room for pluralism or any kind of dissent. As a result of the crackdown, the Heritage Foundation (2021) removed Hong Kong in March 2021 from its annual list of cities with the freest economies, where it had been consistently ranked first for 25 years up until 2019, saying it believed that the city is now "ultimately controlled from Beijing."

On March 11, 2021, China's National People's Congress closed its annual session by implementing its plan to radically transform Hong Kong's electoral code, ensuring that only "patriots" will be allowed to run the Special Administrative Region. From now on, candidates will have to be judged eligible by a committee chosen by Beijing. Delegates approved the decision with 2895 votes in favor, zero against and one abstention. "When the vote count was revealed, around 30 seconds of applause followed" (Ho, 2021). Beijing's systematic demolition of freedoms in Hong Kong is now complete. Reacting to the move, the G7 ministers said:

We, the G7 Foreign Ministers of Canada, France, Germany, Italy, Japan, the United Kingdom and the United States of America and the High Representative of the European Union, are united in expressing our grave concerns at the Chinese authorities' decision fundamentally to erode democratic elements of the electoral system in Hong Kong. Such a decision strongly indicates that the authorities in mainland China are determined to eliminate dissenting voices and opinions in Hong Kong. (Ministère de l'Europe et des Affaires étrangères, 2021)

From all these events, and in particular the massive protests of 2019, one major lesson emerges: the Chinese people, when free to do so, dare to stand up against the central power in Beijing, which is unbearable for the regime.

What is the real situation in Xinjiang?

Colonization and colonial wars are nothing new. A dominant culture intends to replace a dominated culture by claiming to bring it civilization. China is obviously not a trailblazer in this matter. The colonization of America by the Europeans and the extermination of the indigenous peoples from the end of the sixteenth century are just one earlier historical example.

The United Nations (UN) convention on genocide, adopted in December 1948 by the UN General Assembly and to which China is a signatory, defines genocide as acts perpetrated "with intent to destroy, in whole or in part, a national, ethnical, racial or religious group." Is a genocide underway in Xinjiang? History and horror are repeating themselves in China. Some 30 years ago, on June 4, 1989, on Beijing's Tiananmen Square, the Chinese army opened fire on pro-democracy demonstrators and killed hundreds, if not thousands of people. We will never know the real toll of that disaster, which the regime's propaganda machine has since erased from the collective memory. Since

2015, an even more abominable tragedy has been unfolding in Xinjiang, in the far west of the country, where the Chinese authorities have interned more than a million Uyghurs, a Muslim people who speak a Turkic language, and subjected them to inhumane treatment. It was in this region that the Chinese regime first experimented with the electronic surveillance of the population. Today, the mounting testimonies leave no room for doubt. According to multiple credible sources, more than 1 million Uyghurs, perhaps as many as 3 million, are interned in re-education camps, while more than 500,000 others are victims of forced labor. The Chinese authorities fiercely deny this and have called these camps "vocational training centers," a denial that is hardly credible in view of all the gathered information that all points in the same direction. Information unearthed by Xinjiang expert Adrian Zenz is particularly damning. According to a study he published under the auspices of the US think tank the Center for Global Policy (now known as the New Lines Institute) in December 2020, at least 570,000 Uyghurs had likely been coerced into service in the cotton fields of Xinjiang, a region that produces some 20% of the world's cotton. The numbers are frightening, even more so as Zenz[4] used official Chinese documents that estimated that at least half a million Uyghurs were forcibly conscripted to handpick cotton in three regions of Xinjiang Autonomous Province alone (Aksu, Hotan, and Kashgar). An assessment that could be much higher province-wide, according to the study. Asked about the issue of forced labor of Uyghurs at a press briefing in December 2020, Chinese Foreign Ministry spokesman Wang Wenbin said that these workers were free either to sign or not sign their labor contracts. He accused Zenz by name of "fabricating rumors and slanders" against China and being "a member of a far-right organization founded by the US government and a key member of [an] anti-China institute set up by the US intelligence agency" (MFAPRC, 2020). In September 2020, Zenz published separate research—

corroborated by the British news agency Reuters—on the forced labor imposed in Tibet for years.

Adrian Zenz explained the terrible logic at work in Xinjiang in an interview with the French media outlet *Mediapart*:

> The Uyghurs are culturally and spiritually closer to Istanbul than to Beijing. Decades of repression and the brutalities of the Cultural Revolution have led to a toxic mix in ethnic relations. More recently, Uyghurs have been able to search for their roots by listening to Turkish music and Islamic sermons via the Internet and their smartphones...Beijing emphasizes the Uyghurs' violent resistance, but the passive, non-violent resistance to assimilation and integration was probably the biggest problem. This inability to fully control their society has become a growing problem for Beijing. In 2013, Xinjiang was declared the core region of the Belt and Road Initiative. The region is rich in natural resources and of great geopolitical importance...In the end, Beijing felt it needed something like a 'final solution' to this situation. The lessons it is now learning in Xinjiang can be applied to other regions and other religious groups. Now Hong Kong is becoming another Xinjiang. Repression has become Beijing's main tool of governance. (El Azzouzi, 2020)

The latest report by the German researcher, published on March 2, 2021, contains unprecedented revelations about the forced labor of rural Uyghur youth. In December 2020, the researcher published a first article on the forced transfer of Uyghur workers, in which he established the existence of two types of forced labor in Xinjiang. The first concerns the inmates of re-education camps. Once they have "graduated," that is, are judged to have been "de-radicalized" and able to return to a "normal" life, these detainees are not released. They do not return to their families but are forced to work in nearby factories, sometimes adjacent to the camps. Or they are sent, by the hundreds of thousands, to pick cotton on state farms. It is this kind of forced labor that has led to a wave of denunciations around the world. The second, much less known, potentially concerns a much larger segment of the Uyghur population. This is what Chinese researchers call the "rural surplus laborers" of southern Xinjiang. In this hardscrabble rural region, where Uyghurs make up more than 90% of the population, there are many young people without steady employment who subsist on seasonal jobs and the cultivation of their families' land, according to *Obs* journalist Ursula Gauthier. These are the people that the Chinese government "recruits" to "train" before "placing" them in a job in a Chinese factory and organizing their "transfer" to their new workplace. In studying these programs, Adrian Zenz discovered that although they are not detainees, the "recruitment," "training," "placements," and "transfers" of these young workers are neither free nor voluntary. He believes that they constitute another type of forced labor, intended to enroll the entire youth of southern Xinjiang. He dedicated his latest article, published in March 2021 by the American think tank The Jamestown Foundation, to this group. The German researcher relied on public documents from official Chinese organizations, including the Nankai Report, a 2019 paper named after the prestigious university where its authors work. Zenz's article, entitled 'Coercive Labor and Forced Displacement in Xinjiang's Cross-Regional Labor Transfer Program' (2020), found that these increasingly massive transfers of rural Uyghur workers were not driven primarily by economic objectives, but by political and demographic objectives. Although repeatedly presented as "poverty alleviation" measures, Zenz discovered references in the Nankai Report that indicate the "labor transfers represent a long-term measure to promote 'assimilation' and 'reduce Uyghur population density'." Elsewhere it is acknowledged that the transfers are part of a plan to "optimize the population structure of southern Xinjiang." Zenz found other Chinese academic publications that "describe labor transfers as a crucial means to 'crack open the solidified [Uyghur] society' and to mitigate the negative impact of religion." He said Chinese academics consider that young Uyghurs are reluctant to voluntarily seek employment elsewhere because of "a) religious views, b) 'backward' [traditional] mindsets and c) the emotional cost of separation from family," when in fact Uyghurs had traveled widely before the crackdown on them and research shows that they are now motivated by fear of discrimination, not religious ties. He noted that another passage in the Nankai Report emphasizes that labor transfers can "comparatively quickly change poor people's views." Another passage in the Report states that the experience "allows for a gradual transformation of their thinking, knowledge, values, and outlook on life through their working as laborers and changing their environment and lifestyle."

Victims speak out

For those who are skeptical of the academic research, there is a growing number of accounts, such as the shocking story of Gulbahar Haitiwaji, a victim of a Machiavellian trap set by the Chinese security apparatus. This Uyghur woman based in France was forced to return to her native region, Xinjiang, in 2017, where she experienced the hell of the internment camps. A year and a half after her release, she told her story in a 2021 book, *Rescapée du goulag chinois*, co-written with journalist Rozenn Morgat. In an interview (Fallevoz, 2021) published on *Asialyst*, Haitiwaji recounted the torment she suffered after returning to Xinjiang where she had been ordered to return by the authorities to regularize her pension rights:

At the time, I was not very suspicious. I had never even heard of the internment camps in Xinjiang. During my previous visits, I had noticed a strengthening of the checkpoints and identity controls, but nothing abnormal. So, when my former employer called me and asks me to come quickly, I simply asked him if I can give someone power of attorney to do it. He refused. Ten days later, I was in Xinjiang with the idea to stay there for two weeks. Instead, my stay lasted two years and nine months...I was harassed with questions about my life in France and that of my family. Then I was shown a photo of my daughter, taken at a Uyghur demonstration in Paris. In the picture, she is holding up a flag of East Turkestan [a former self-proclaimed republic based in what is now Xinjiang]. Suddenly, I was a little angry with my daughter because I was not militant. The police released me but confiscated my passport. In mid-January, I was told to come back for it. Three State Security agents were waiting for me. I was taken to the Karamay detention center.

It was clear to Haitiwaji that she was targeted because of her husband's political activities.

You must know that at the time my husband was the vice president of the Association of Uyghurs in France. The previous times we had returned to Xinjiang, in 2012 and 2014, he had been summoned by the State Security service which had asked him to spy on our community in France. He had refused and I think the authorities wanted to take retaliatory measures. And since I was the only one in the family who did not have French nationality, it was easier to act against me...At first there were about ten of us in my cell, then about thirty. Uyghur prisoners had their feet chained all day. We wore a yellow uniform, much too thin to support the winter and its -30-degree temperatures, and small black slippers. We slept on benches with comforters that stank, under neon lights that were on day and night. On the floor, there are two squares drawn in red. Every hour, two inmates have to stand still in them, to 'stand guard'. On the rare occasions when they let us outside, it is onto a sort of screened terrace adjoining the cell. The cold was unbearable there and when we came back inside, they put the air conditioning on as cold as possible. It was terrible.

Haitiwaji said that in April 2017 the prison treatment became harsher when for three weeks she and three other cellmates were chained to the bar of their beds. They needed the help of their fellow prisoners to relieve themselves. They were never told why they received this treatment. Haitiwaji does not mince words when describing what she sees as China's objective: "They want to make us disappear, it is a cultural genocide, a total assimilation, but there is a resistance among the people, one does not suppress a whole culture in this way," she wrote in her book. Haitiwaji attributes her release to interventions by the French government (Fallevoz, 2021).

Another Uyghur woman who has spoken out about experience in a labor camp is Tursunay Ziawudun, who spent nine months in one in the Xiyuan (Kunes in Uyghur) district of Xinjiang. She told the BBC (Hill et al., 2021) that some nights after midnight, masked men would open her cell to select a woman and take her to a "black room" with no surveillance cameras. There, these men would then engage in a gang rape session. She said she was taken several nights. "Perhaps this is the most unforgettable scar on me forever," Ziawudun told the broadcaster. "I don't even want these words to spill from my mouth." After her release, Ziawudun fled to Kazakhstan, and then to the United States, where she has lived ever since. The BBC interviewed another former detainee, Gulzira Auelkhan, an ethnic Kazakh woman who spent 18 months in China's Xinjiang prison system. "My job was to remove their clothes above the waist and handcuff them so they cannot move," she said. "Then I would leave the women in the room and a man would enter—some Chinese man from outside or policeman. I sat silently next to the door, and when the man left the room I took the woman for a shower," Auelkhan told the BBC. She said the Chinese men paid money "to have the pick of the prettiest young inmates" and called it a system of organized rape. "It is designed to destroy everyone's spirit."

If more testimony is needed, here it is. Gulbahar Jalilova, a Kazakh citizen, was held in a detention camp in Urumqi from May 2017 to September 2018. She was freed thanks to UN intervention and has been living in France since January 2021. She said she was locked in a room of 25 square meters with about 40 other detainees aged 14 to 80 years, where she was tortured, raped, and subjected to forced contraception.

> We were standing in this room, chained at the foot with five kilogram chains. We could lie down on the floor, but not for more than two hours to allow other prisoners to lie down in turn. There were cameras set up in the four corners of the room. The police officers outside the room dictated orders to us over the loudspeaker. We had to sing songs in praise of Xi Jinping. Several times a week, we were given drugs, which resulted in that I didn't have my period anymore. I saw with my own eyes the torture inflicted on other prisoners. One day, a 23-year-old man who was interrogating me pulled down his pants and put his penis in my mouth. I told him, 'How can you do that, you could be my son.' I was able to survive that hell because we inmates supported one other. When I was finally released, they warned me: 'China is the most powerful country in the world. We have very, very long arms. If you talk, we'll find and kill you.' But my fellow prisoners begged me to tell the world about them. (El Azzouzi, 2020b)

For Dilnur Reyhan, president of the Uyghur Institute of Europe, "the heart of the matter is colonial" because of the mineral resources in Xinjiang and because of the region's geostrategic position. Reyhan is a Uyghur who has been a refugee in France for 16 years and teaches at the National Institute of Oriental Languages and Civilizations (INALCO), and who has become a whistleblower and a main spokesperson for Uyghurs in France. She said that for many of the sometimes-deadly attacks in China that have been attributed to Uyghurs there is in fact no evidence.[5] A certain level of tension should be expected between the colonized and their colonizers, she added.[6] However, the pressure that Uyghurs now find themselves under is immense. "Digital surveillance is everywhere. China also sends Chinese officials, often male, to live with the families of those imprisoned in camps to monitor the family very closely: to see if the family maintains Uyghur traditions, continues to speak the Uyghur language, continues to practice religion at home," Reyhan said. "China meets all the criteria of the UN definition of genocide. If the world allows Beijing to organize the 2022 Winter Olympics, it will be reminiscent of the Berlin Olympics in 1936. The world will have repeated the same mistake and Beijing will be able to continue the eradication of the Uyghurs," she added. (23h, 2021).

Uyghur women who dare to speak out are not safe from Chinese police even thousands of miles away from Xinjiang. Qelbinur Sedik was preparing breakfast in her new home in the Netherlands when a video call came in on her smartphone. The app identified the caller as Sedik's sister, who was still in Xinjiang. This immediately made Sedik very nervous as the two sisters had not spoken for several months—since she and three other Uyghur women gave interviews to the BBC, which was preparing a program about rape and torture in detention camps in Xinjiang where Sedik had previously worked as a teacher. When Sedik answered the call, it was not her sister's face that appeared but that of a policeman. "What are you up to, Qelbinur?" the policeman asked with a smile. It was not the first time that this policeman had called her. Sedik took a screenshot and, hearing the noise, the police officer hastily took off his jacket that had his identification number on it. When Sedik told the BBC about this incident, she broke down in tears. The police officer made not-so-subtle threats against Sedik's family still in China: "You have to remember that all your family and relatives are with us here. You have to think about this very seriously." He then tried to pressure her for information on other Uyghur exiles: "You have been living abroad for some time now. You must have friends. Can you give us their names?" The police officer then turned the camera to show Sedik's sister, who shouted, "Shut up. You should shut up from now on," followed by insults. The BBC posted a picture of this police officer online (Gunter, 2021).

Another example of the determination of Beijing to eradicate the cultural identity of Uyghurs was provided by my former colleagues at *Agence France-Presse* (Xiao et al., 2019), who despite constant surveillance were able to gather firsthand information about Chinese efforts to demolish Uyghur cemeteries to construct parking lots. I provide excerpts from the text of the story, but I also encourage readers to check out the video and interactive graphic which powerfully capture the changes over time.

China is destroying burial grounds where generations of Uyghur families have been laid to rest, leaving behind human bones and broken tombs in what activists call an effort to eradicate the ethnic group's identity in Xinjiang.

In just two years, dozens of cemeteries have been destroyed in the northwest region, according to an *AFP* investigation with satellite imagery analysts Earthrise Alliance.

Some of the graves were cleared with little care—in

Shayar County, *AFP* journalists saw unearthed human bones left discarded in three sites. In other sites tombs that were reduced to mounds of bricks lay scattered in cleared tracts of land.

While the official explanation ranges from urban development to the 'standardization' of old graves, overseas Uyghurs say the destruction is part of a state crackdown to control every element of their lives.

'This is all part of China's campaign to effectively eradicate any evidence of who we are, to effectively make us like the Han Chinese,' said Salih Hudayar, who said the graveyard where his great-grandparents were buried was demolished.

'That's why they're destroying all of these historical sites, these cemeteries, to disconnect us from our history, from our fathers and our ancestors,' he said...

According to satellite imagery analyzed by *AFP* and Earthrise Alliance, the Chinese government has, since 2014, exhumed and flattened at least 45 Uyghur cemeteries—including 30 in the past two years.

The Xinjiang government did not respond to a request for comment.

The destruction is 'not just about religious persecution,' said Nurgul Sawut, who has five generations of family buried in Yengisar, southwestern Xinjiang.

'It is much deeper than that,' said Sawut, who now lives in Australia and last visited Xinjiang in 2016 to attend her father's funeral.

'If you destroy that cemetery...you're uprooting whoever's on that land, whoever's connected to that land,' she explained.

Even sites featuring shrines, or the tombs of famous individuals were not spared.

In Aksu, local authorities turned an enormous graveyard where prominent Uyghur poet Lutpulla Mutellip was buried into 'Happiness Park,' with fake pandas, a children's ride, and a man-made lake.

Mutellip's grave was like 'a modern-day shrine for most nationalist Uyghurs, patriotic Uyghurs,' recalled Ilshat Kokbore, who visited the tomb in the early 90s and now resides in the US.

The 'Happiness Park' project saw graves moved to a new cemetery in an industrial zone out in the desert. The caretaker there said he had no knowledge of the fate of Mutellip's remains.

The Aksu government could not be reached for comment.

In China, urban growth and economic development has laid waste to innumerable cultural and historic sites, from traditional hutong neighborhoods in Beijing to segments of Dali's ancient city wall in southwestern Yunnan province. It is an issue Beijing itself has acknowledged.

The government has also been criticized for its irreverence towards burial traditions outside of Xinjiang, including the destruction of coffins in central Jiangxi last year to force locals to cremate...

'The destruction of the graveyards is very much part of the wider raft of policies that are going on,' said Rachel Harris, who researches Uyghur culture at the School of Oriental and African Studies University of London.

'From the destruction of holy shrines, the tombs of saints, to the destruction of tombs of families, all of this is disrupting the relationship between people and their history, and the relationship between the people and the land that they live on,' she said.

Tamar Mayer, a professor of geosciences at Middlebury College, who researches Uyghur shrines and cemeteries, described the new sites as homogeneous and tightly packed...

The Shayar government did not respond to *AFP*'s questions on the process of moving remains to new sites.

But it is clear that human remains have been left behind in the process.

On a trip to Xinjiang in September, *AFP* visited 13 destroyed cemeteries across four cities and saw bones in at least three Shayar sites.

Local officials dismissed the evidence—one even picked up a bone, held it next to his right shin, and declared it 'too big to be a human's'.

But seven forensic anthropologists who saw images taken by *AFP* identified a number of human remains, including a femur, feet, hand bones, and part of an elbow...

In Hotan, southern Xinjiang, residents were given just two days to claim their dead, according to a government notice photographed by *AFP* in May...

Carrying out such an investigation today would be impossible as surveillance of foreign journalists in Xinjiang has been considerably tightened. "Traveling to Xinjiang or Tibet is extremely difficult and the harassment from authorities makes working nearly impossible," says Frédéric Lemaître (2021), *Le Monde*'s correspondent in Beijing. I note in passing that the top official of the communist regime in Xinjiang is the Han (of Chinese descent, therefore) Chen Quanguo, 64, a member of the CCP Politburo. Chen is a former military officer who had already made a name for himself with his surveillance methods in Tibet. In Xinjiang, Chen has implemented the same policies that he applied in Tibet, beginning in August 2011, where cities are now dotted with police stations every 500 meters.

The West speaks out

On January 19, 2021, US Secretary of State Mike Pompeo accused China of carrying out genocide on the Uyghurs. "I believe this genocide is ongoing, and that we are witnessing the systematic attempt to destroy Uyghurs by the Chinese party-state," he said in a statement (Pompeo, 2021). He also referred to "crimes against humanity" carried out "since at least March 2017" by Chinese authorities against Uyghurs and "other members of ethnic and religious minority groups in Xinjiang." The very same day Pompeo's successor, Antony Blinken, echoed this accusation. So, are we seeing a large-scale predatory enterprise in Xinjiang? "At the end of the day, what we're looking at is a settler colonial project of Han settlers moving into the Uyghur region, taking the resources and then beginning, eventually, a process of eliminating and replacing Uyghur identity—trying to sort of assimilate them into the body politic of China," says American anthropologist Darren Byler at the University of Colorado, Boulder. "This settler colonialism in this case is, at least so far, less violent, in some ways, than American settler colonialism, you know, which produced a genocide. We haven't seen a genocide in terms of mass killing of Uyghurs yet, but it is a similar dynamic that's going on at this time," he added (Scahill, 2021).

France added its voice to the international chorus of condemnations on February 24 when Foreign Minister Jean-Yves Le Drian denounced an "institutionalized system of repression" against the Uyghurs before the UN Human Rights Council. "We have received from the Chinese region of Xinjiang testimonies and corroborating documents which report unjustifiable practices against Uyghurs, and a system of surveillance and institutionalized repression on a massive scale," he said during an intervention by video conference. On March 26, 2021, Le Drian went a step further. "The term 'genocide' deserves to be considered and we are ready to consider such a reflection," he said on the France Info radio station.

On February 22, 2021, the Canadian parliament unanimously passed a non-binding motion calling China's treatment of Uyghurs in Xinjiang "genocide." The Dutch parliament did the same on February 25, becoming the first European Union country to do so. "A genocide on the Uyghur minority is occurring in China," the Dutch motion said, stopping short of directly accusing the Chinese government of responsibility (*Reuters*, 2021). In the United Kingdom, several Holocaust survivors publicly declared in February 2021 that China's policy in Xinjiang constitutes genocide. China's Foreign Minister Wang Yi, on the other hand, described China's treatment of ethnic minorities in Xinjiang and Tibet as a "shining example" of the progress China has made in safeguarding human rights (*AFP*, 2021).

China, thanks to a very effective entryism strategy, has supporters in French universities to deny any idea of repression in Xinjiang. Take for example the participation of Christian Mestre, honorary dean of the Strasbourg Law School, in an "international seminar on Counter-terrorism, De-radicalization and Human Rights Protection" organized in September 2019 by the Chinese government in Urumqi, the capital of the "autonomous" Xinjiang region. His statements were reported by state media, including the official agency *Xinhua* and the CCP's English-language daily, the *Global Times*. For Beijing, they are worth their weight in gold. Mestre said the Xinjiang government had found "some answers" in using education to counter the effects of terrorist propaganda. "I hope that France and other European countries [haunted by terrorism] could take the answers given by Xinjiang," he told the *Global Times* (Xie et al., 2019). Mestre visited one of the camps in Kashgar. He said that the Chinese authorities are telling the truth: that no, they have not forcibly interned hundreds of thousands of Uyghurs, that these people are not in prison, but were sent for compulsory training. Mestre's participation in the seminar and comments were the subject of a February 2021 article in the French magazine *Le Point*. Sinologists at the University of Strasbourg were aghast. "This is of course not the position of the Chinese department of the University of Strasbourg," said its director,

Thomas Boutonnet. "It is not our role as academics to relay such a political message. Because it is not even naive to say that it is negationism," he added. Lecturer Marie Bizais-Lillig said she was "extremely shocked" by Mestre's comments. "It's worthy of Aragon's trips to the USSR, or of the collaborationists in Nazi Germany," she said (André, 2021).

The *Le Point* article also caused trouble for Mestre in his role as the ethics chief of the Strasbourg region government, Eurometropole. The day after the article appeared, the vice president of Eurometropole and first deputy mayor of Strasbourg, Syamak Agha Babaei, called on Mestre to explain himself. "This is a political statement about the way the Chinese government treats a political and religious minority. My group will ask him to explain himself. If what he is alleged to have said is true, that is problematic. I don't think we can say that the treatment of the Uyghurs is a matter of debate. If he admits the statements, it is incompatible with the function of ethics officer of Eurometropole," he said. Faced with a growing outcry, Mestre resigned later the same day.

On February 25, 2021, French President Emmanuel Macron spoke on the phone with his Chinese counterpart, but, according to an initial account from the Elysée Palace, without discussing the Uyghur situation with him. That immediately provoked criticism. "The concentration camps and the Uyghurs are therefore of no importance to our President, at least that is clear now. History will judge him and we will judge him before it. I am very angry this morning. I can't stand the cowardice and weakness of our leaders anymore. They have made cynicism and impotence a religion. They trample on our principles and strategic interests. They despise our past and our current mobilizations. France deserves so much better than this," said European Parliament deputy Raphaël Glucksmann (2021), one of the whistleblowers in France on the Uyghur tragedy. The omission was all the more glaring as US President Joe Biden had brought up the subject when he finally phoned his Chinese counterpart on February 10, more than three weeks after his inauguration. Biden expressed to Xi Jinping "his fundamental concerns about Beijing's coercive and unfair economic practices, crackdown in Hong Kong, human rights abuses in Xinjiang, and increasingly assertive actions in the region, including toward Taiwan," according to a White House (2021) readout of the call. Biden (2021) later said that in the phone call he told Xi that: "as long as you and your country continue to so blatantly violate human rights, we're going to continue, in an unrelenting way, to call to the attention of the world and make it clear—make it clear what's happening. And he understood that." In the face of mounting criticism in French political circles, the Élysée Palace issued a new summary of the call that said Macron had indeed raised the question of the Uyghurs. In what terms? We don't know.

Since the publication of their letter, a lot of credible information has come to light in support of their claims. On February 26, 2021, the United Nations High Commissioner for Human Rights, Michelle Bachelet, came out of her silence. "Activists, lawyers and human rights defenders—as well as some foreign nationals—face arbitrary criminal charges, detention or unfair trials" in China, she told the Human Rights Council, of which China is a full member. She said her office continues to assess "alleged patterns of human rights violations," including reports of arbitrary detention, ill-treatment, sexual violence and forced labor in Xinjiang, and expressed confidence that "mutually agreeable parameters" could be found with Chinese authorities for a visit there. These are cautious words, but they are courageous when one considers China's influence at the UN, where it is one of the five permanent members of the Security Council.[7]

Aside from Turkey, which has discreetly asked China for explanations about the situation in Xinjiang, no Muslim country has yet come forward to denounce Chinese practices against the Uyghurs. Why is this so? Slimane Zeghidour (*TV5 Monde*, 2019), a Franco-Algerian writer, researcher and journalist specializing in the Arab world, offers some explanations:

> The first thing to understand is that in Muslim countries, opinion is restricted by the regimes in place. There is not as much freedom of expression—as in the West—to go out and demonstrate. For the Uyghurs and others. There is no habit or culture of such demonstrations, protests and public solidarity in these countries. This is not to say that people don't feel it in their hearts. But there is a myth—which exists only among Islamists and Islamophobes—that there is a Muslim world that breathes with the same lungs, that has the same vision of the world and that vibrates in unison. This has never existed, from the time of the Prophet until today. States, contrary to what the Islamophobic or Islamist myth thinks, never react in the name of Islam. For example, Saudi Arabia, which has very good relations with China, or Iran, is careful not to embarrass Beijing. Public opinion in these countries must be outraged by what is being done to the Uyghurs, but their governments are playing politics. No government has ever been mobilized by Islamic solidarity, except that of Erdogan, the Turkish prime minister [*sic*]. Because the Uyghurs have a huge diaspora in Turkey, and so the Uyghur lobby in Turkey has pushed Erdogan to express his displeasure so that he asks China for an explanation.

> [Interviewer] Will Muslims ever wake up to what is going on?

> I don't think so. But you have to bear in mind that the presence of Islam in China goes back to the time of the Prophet, 15 centuries ago. It is a very old dimension of Chinese culture.

Muslim personalities have played a very important role in the history of Chinese empires. The influence of Chinese Muslims has been enormous in the history of their country. The greatest admiral in the history of the Chinese navy, for example, was a Muslim who lived in the 16th century. One must realize that the situation of Muslims in China is worse than it has ever been with any of the previous feudal empires. There are surely Chinese who would support the Uyghurs today, but the government's policy is the same as with the Tibetans. This Chinese regime, with its hyper-nationalism, considers Christianity and Islam as foreign pollution. The Uyghurs were the majority in Xinjiang, and a policy of colonization—with the massive arrival of non-Uyghur Chinese—has turned them into a minority. It is a policy of cultural suffocation. But there will be no awakening of Muslims abroad to support the Uyghurs or to support anyone or denounce anything: these Muslim countries are mostly dictatorships. That said, it is possible that countries like Saudi Arabia have quietly asked China to explain this problem. But not publicly.

The West takes action

On March 22, 2021, the European Union, the United Kingdom, Canada and the United States simultaneously adopted sanctions against Chinese officials in Xinjiang to denounce Beijing's policies against the Uyghurs. It was the first coordinated move of its kind since Joe Biden took office and left Beijing more isolated than ever. The European Union was the first to take the initiative, adopting its first sanctions against Chinese officials since the Tiananmen Square massacre, targeting four Chinese officials and one Chinese entity for active participation in the crackdown on Uyghurs. The four officials targeted were: Zhu Hailun, a former secretary of the Xinjiang Political and Legal Affairs Commission; Wang Junzheng, secretary of the Communist Party of Xinjiang Production and Construction Company and deputy secretary of the Xinjiang Party Commission; Wang Mingshan, a member of the Xinjiang Party Standing Committee; and Chen Mingguo, director of the Xinjiang Public Security Bureau. The targeted entity is the Public Security Bureau of the Xinjiang Production and Construction Company. The European Union has determined that these individuals and entity are responsible for "serious human rights violations in China, in particular large-scale arbitrary detentions inflicted upon Uyghurs and people from other Muslim ethnic minorities" (Council of the EU, 2021). The sanctions, which include an asset freeze and travel ban on EU soil, were adopted by the foreign ministers of the 27 EU member states and immediately enshrined in EU law.

The Chinese foreign ministry (MFAPRC, 2021) in Beijing denounced the action by Brussels as "based on nothing but lies and disinformation," and stated that it "disregards and distorts facts, grossly interferes in China's internal affairs, flagrantly breaches international law and basic norms governing international relations, and severely undermines China-EU relations." In a vitriolic article, the *Global Times* (2021), the Communist Party's English-language mouthpiece, indicated that Beijing would respond tit for tat. It derided Europe as seeing itself as a "teacher of human rights" that is "zealous to point at other countries' affairs with a condescending attitude" but at the same time "has caused countless unrests and tragedies worldwide." The *Global Times* stated that "'Genocide' is a label that can never be put on China" while noting that "In contrast, Germany which initiated the sanctions on China has had so many misdeeds that constitute genocide with ironclad evidence." The Chinese government immediately retaliated with the announcement of sanctions against ten European personalities, including five members of the European Parliament, one of whom was MEP Raphaël Glucksmann. Also targeted by these sanctions is the German anthropologist Adrian Zenz. These personalities and their families are now banned from Chinese territory, including Hong Kong and Macao. Also targeted were four European entities, including the Alliance for Democracies Foundation, a forum chaired by former NATO chief Anders Fogh Rasmussen (MFAPRC, 2021).

With its sanctions, the EU was following in the footsteps of the United States, which in July 2020 imposed sanctions against several Chinese leaders over their connections to human rights abuses against the Uyghur minority. Just before stepping down as secretary of state, Mike Pompeo compared the situation in Xinjiang to the Holocaust. "Since the Allied forces exposed the horrors of Nazi concentration camps, the refrain 'Never again' has become the civilized world's rallying cry against these horrors," Pompeo said. "The Nuremberg Tribunals at the end of World War II prosecuted perpetrators for crimes against humanity, the same crimes being perpetrated in Xinjiang" (Gehrke, 2021). With its March 2021 sanctions the United States added another layer by extending these sanctions to two new officials who are part of the list announced by the European Union. The coordinated sanctions appear to have been the result of US diplomatic contacts with its allies. Senior US administration officials cited by *Reuters* explained that they were in daily contact with governments in Europe on China-related issues. Those increased contacts also resulted in US Secretary of State Antony Blinken joining with his British and Canadian counterparts to condemn China's ongoing human rights abuses in Xinjiang. "China's extensive program of repression includes severe restrictions on religious freedoms, the use of forced labor, mass detention in internment camps, forced sterilizations, and the concerted destruction of Uyghur heritage," they said (US Department of State, 2021). The same week, Blinken made his first visit to Europe as America's top diplomat for meetings with his EU and NATO counterparts. Separately, Australia and New Zealand expressed their "grave concerns about the growing number of credible reports of severe human rights abuses against ethnic Uyghurs and other Muslim minorities in Xinjiang." Both welcomed the sanctions effort by their allies, although they didn't join in due to legal issues (Manch, 2021).

When a Dutch MP was sanctioned by Beijing, The Hague summoned the Chinese ambassador to the Netherlands to protest. "It's terrible. It's chilling to see that a dictatorial regime can attack a parliamentarian and his family in this way," Belgian MP Samuel Cogolati told *AFP* (2021b). "This intimidation, these threats, will not stop us, on the contrary! They strengthen our determination to fight for democracy in Hong Kong, Tibet or Xinjiang where we see that concentration camps are developing to lock up Uyghurs," he said. "It is time to break a European silence that has lasted too long, a silence that has become complicit over time," he added. MEP Raphaël Glucksmann (2021b) took the decision of the Chinese authorities in his stride: "So, I am on the Chinese sanction list: banned from entering China (my family too!), from having contacts with Chinese officials or companies...All of this because I stand for Uyghurs and human rights. Let us be clear: these sanctions are my Medal of Honour. The fight continues!" he said on his Twitter feed. On March 26, 2021, the Chinese government added nine British figures and four entities, including former Conservative Party leader Iain Duncan Smith. "It's our duty to call out the Chinese Govt's human rights abuse in #HongKong & the genocide of the #Uyghurs. Those of us who live free lives under the rule of law must speak for those who have no voice. If that brings the anger of China down on me, I'll wear that badge of honour," Smith said on Twitter (2021).

One of the likely consequences of this escalation is the death of the investment treaty—the Comprehensive Agreement on Investment—concluded in December 2020 after seven years of difficult negotiations between Beijing and Brussels. It would be a blow to China not only from a financial standpoint but a strategic one as well, as Beijing saw it as a possible wedge to divide the European Union and the United States. To come into force, the treaty must still be voted on in the European Parliament and ratified by all 27 EU member states, an increasingly unlikely prospect.

China's propaganda machine strikes back

When it comes to Chinese propaganda, I thought I had seen it all during my long career. But I was wrong. The anti-Semitic attack it mounted against MEP Raphaël Glucksmann after banning him from China was off the scale of sordid, despicable and abject. On March 24, 2021, Zheng Ruolin, the former Paris correspondent of the Shanghai newspaper *Wenhui Bao* who remains a journalist and widely-read blogger, publicly accused Raphaël Glucksmann and his father of stirring up hatred of China in the Muslim world and of having indirectly orchestrated the assassination of Samuel Paty![8] A history and geography teacher in a Paris suburb, Paty was stabbed and decapitated in October 2020 by a young Russian citizen of Chechen origin who had been granted refugee status in France when he was a minor. Zheng claimed that Glucksmann had "brought 'peaceful' Chechens into France to oppose (Vladimir) Putin's policies," knowingly doing so "to sow terrorism in France." He wrote that Glucksmann was continuing his father's policy of garnering the support of Muslim terrorists by defending the poor Uyghurs. Raphaël Glucksmann denounced Zheng's post as a classic smear attempt by an authoritarian regime:

> Further evidence that our mobilization is frightening them: the Chinese propaganda machine has been at full throttle since yesterday. Its objective? To sow doubt and to try to discredit our fight for the Uyghur people by pathetically trying to discredit the people who publicly support it (researchers, politicians, intellectuals, Uyghur activists, etc). This is a

classic method of authoritarian and fascist regimes. For the past few days, tens of thousands of messages have been stirring up the Chinese networks and this will very quickly arrive here. I am and will be presented as the architect of a worldwide Jewish plot against China, the friend of Islamist terrorists, an agent of the CIA and Mossad, the mastermind of the war in Iraq, of the revolution in Syria, the architect of the Great Replacement of the 'native French'...This will be relayed to us by the useful idiots of the tyrants. I am not going to waste time denying these idiocies one by one, nor even to point them out, but you can be certain that our mobilization disturbs them and that we will not win without fighting, without being attacked. Politics, as I understand it, is knowing how to take risks for what we think is right. Our leaders have forgotten this for too long. We will remind them together. (Glucksmann, 2021c)

On March 26, 2021, French Foreign Minister Jean-Yves Le Drian met with Glucksmann and expressed his solidarity with him following the anti-Semitic attack, which also included a post by Zheng of a picture of Glucksmann with a Star of David. Glucksmann (2021d) said he used the meeting to press the French government to enact measures banning Chinese goods made using slave labor and forcing French brands to respect human rights, noting that the European Parliament has already approved such moves and it is now for national governments to implement them.

China's propaganda machine has more than one trick up its sleeve. In December 2020, a book entitled *Ouïghours, pour en finir avec les fake news* [Uyghurs, stop the fake news] was published by the La Route de la Soie publishing house, written by a certain Maxime Vivas. This publishing house, founded in 2017 by the very discreet Sonia Bressler, presents itself as independent. However, part of its catalog is devoted to praising cooperation between France and China, and it co-publishes a magazine with a Chinese Communist Party publisher entitled *Chine-France Dialogue* [China-France Dialog]. A recent issue was entitled "A Chinese five-year plan (14th 5-year plan from 2021–2025)—What impact on Europe" and gives the floor at length to China's ambassador to France, Lu Shaye, as well as to several other Chinese officials. "Did you like the fake news about the betrayal of Captain Dreyfus, the mass graves of Timisoara in Romania, the contents of Colin Powell's vial at the UN, the disconnected incubators in Kuwait, the network of pedophiles in Outreau, the Chernobyl cloud at our borders, the arrest of Dupont de Ligonnès in Scotland, the invasion of the Salpêtrière hospital by the Gilets Jaunes? You will hate this book," warns the publisher on the back cover of a recent book by Maxime Vivas (2020). The author, who has made two chaperoned visits to Xinjiang that were carefully prepared and supervised by the Chinese authorities, denounces any idea of genocide in this region. "In truth, this autonomous region that is three times the size of France is pulling itself out of its backwardness and poverty with the help of China as a whole: financial aid, positive discrimination for students taking exams, vocational training, learning the national language (Mandarin) in vocational and educational training centers, without any of the fifty-six ethnic groups in Xinjiang being forced to give up their language, culture, beliefs or non-beliefs. At the same time, Beijing is waging a merciless struggle against the 'three scourges' (fundamentalism, separatism, terrorism) stirred up by Islamist fanatics, thousands of whom have trained in Syria with al-Qaeda and whose objective is to establish an independent caliphate on one-sixth of Chinese territory, where the law of the Republic would give way to Sharia law," wrote Vivas.

I will leave it to the reader to judge these words. His book, which failed to generate much, if any, interest in France, has on the other hand been abundantly quoted and used by official

Chinese media outlets such as *Xinhua* and the *People's Daily* as irrefutable proof that no genocide exists in Xinjiang. The same is true of Chinese Foreign Minister Wang Yi, who used it at a press conference on March 7, 2021, on the sidelines of the annual session of the National People's Congress.

Does what is happening in Xinjiang amount to genocide?
Does the situation in Xinjiang amount to genocide? That is the question the US think tank The New Lines Institute for Strategy and Policy sought to answer when it assembled more than 50 experts in international criminal law, including former members of the International Criminal Court, UN ambassadors, jurists, independent researchers, and human rights and war-crimes experts to review the available information. They concluded in a report (New Lines, 2021) released on March 8, 2021, "that the People's Republic of China (China) bears State responsibility for committing genocide against the Uyghurs in breach of the 1948 [UN] Convention on the Prevention and Punishment of the Crime of Genocide..." This is the first independent, expert analysis that concludes what is happening in Xinjiang constitutes genocide. The text of the UN Genocide Convention defines genocide as "acts committed with intent to destroy, in whole or in part, a national, ethnical, racial or religious group." The Convention goes on to define such acts as: killing members of the group; causing serious bodily or mental harm to members of the group; deliberately inflicting on the group conditions of life calculated to bring about its physical destruction in whole or in part; imposing measures intended to prevent births within the group; forcibly transferring children of the group to another group. The report found that China hasn't committed just one or more of these acts in Xinjiang, but all of them. Furthermore, it said there are plenty of statements from Chinese officials indicating that there was an intent to destroy the Uyghurs. "China's policies and practices targeting Uyghurs

in the region must be viewed in their totality, which amounts to an intent to destroy the Uyghurs as a group, in whole or in substantial part, as such," it stated. "While commission of any one of the Genocide Convention's enumerated acts with the requisite intent can sustain a finding of genocide, the evidence presented in this report supports a finding of genocide against the Uyghurs in breach of each and every act prohibited in" the Convention, the report stated.

What does a China specialist like Marie Holzman make of the plight of the Uyghurs? I put the question to her during an interview (2021). Here is what she answered:

I am divided between the pain from human compassion for these people who are experiencing unimaginably terrible moments. We can't imagine what they must be going through. That's one thing. The other thing is amazement. We all have Chinese friends who love life and have a sense of humor, who have sophisticated social and human relationships. But here again, we find it very difficult to imagine that it is Chinese people from the same nation who commit crimes against humanity as if this could be part of a perfectly acceptable policy. This is something that is beyond my imagination and understanding. It goes beyond indignation. Indignation is ordinary. You can't think the unthinkable.

[P.-A. Donnet] What is the goal of Chinese power in Xinjiang?

A comparison immediately comes to mind, even if it is not correct. It's what happened to the Manchus. They invaded China, as everyone knows. They dominated the whole period of the Qing dynasty (1644–1911) and they completely assimilated culturally and linguistically with the Han Chinese. And so, this Manchu culture disappeared. I don't know anyone who can still speak Manchu and read Manchu today. It is said that there are still two or three speakers, but this is obviously not an endangered species, but an extinct species. Without saying that the total Sinicization of the Manchu people within the Han people is a model for the Uyghurs, I would say that in the Chinese subconscious there is an awareness of this ability: the Chinese stomach is strong enough to swallow and digest the culture of an ethnic group and transform it into a form of perfect Chinese. I think that in the Chinese subconscious, there is this idea that Uyghurs would find it advantageous to integrate Chinese culture as it is so superior to Uyghur culture. I think that's in the consciousness of the leaders and in the subconscious of most Chinese citizens. On the other hand, those who are aware of the fact that these Uyghurs are different from Han culture seem to me to be a tiny minority in China.

[P.-A. Donnet] Is this tragedy a crisis of conscience for those who love China?

You can take out the second part of your sentence. I would say that I love the Chinese and that I respect them greatly. But to say that I love China, no. I don't like China and especially not the China of today, especially not the China of Xi Jinping. That is the first part of my answer. I don't like to make this comparison; I don't often make the comparison between the Nazi regime and the Chinese government. But on the other hand, I can imagine what it must have been like for a morally conscious and responsible German who was a real human during the Nazi regime. I can imagine the suffering it was for him to be a German national and I think that today, there is a very large number of Chinese people who are awake, aware of what is happening, aware of the situation. I can imagine what inner human and moral distress they find themselves in at this moment.

On March 7, 2021, Chinese Foreign Minister and State Councilor Wang Yi used his traditional press conference (MFAPRC, 2021b) on the sidelines of the annual session of the National People's Congress (NPC, Chinese parliament) to denounce accusations of genocide in Xinjiang. "The claim that there is genocide in Xinjiang couldn't be more preposterous. It is just a rumor fabricated with ulterior motives, and a lie through and through," he said. "Speaking of genocide, many people would have in their minds the native Americans of the 16th century, African slaves of the 19th century, the Jewish people of the 20th century, and the aboriginal Australians who are still struggling even today," he added. History will judge these words. The fact remains that the Chinese regime made a major error of judgment in thinking that it could carry out such acts in Xinjiang without the world eventually learning about the existence and scale of this total disaster. The consequences for the regime's image and credibility will be catastrophic and long-lasting. And the primary culprit will be Xi Jinping, who in 2014, after an attack on a train station by Uyghur militants that left 31 people dead, instructed local authorities in Xinjiang to show "absolutely no mercy" with the Uyghurs. In an article published on November 16, 2019, *The New York Times* demonstrated, based on more than 400 pages of official and classified Chinese documents leaked to the West, that it was indeed Xi and no one else in the Chinese apparatus who was the chief architect of the crackdown and the establishment of these hundreds of detention camps in Xinjiang (Austin et al., 2019). The Chinese people will undoubtedly have to long bear the stigma of this genocide carried out by the Communist regime, although they are hostage to decisions over which they have no control. It is sad they will have to carry this burden, a heavy one, for generations to come, as Germans have learned.

MEP and former Minister of European Affairs Nathalie Loiseau is a person close to Emmanuel Macron. She was kind enough to respond to some of my questions. What I find significant is the recognition today that China doesn't share our values and doesn't want to. Nevertheless, she argues for engagement with China:

> For too long, our country and more broadly the free world, but also the developing world, have been naive about the reality of China, its political system and its international ambitions. After the fall of the USSR, we were convinced that communism in China would take the same path. This was a big mistake: 1989 was the year of the fall of the Berlin Wall and the year of the Tiananmen Square crackdown. We have also paid insufficient attention to the rise to power of Xi Jinping and its consequences: the crushing of freedom in Hong Kong, the provocations towards Taiwan, the imperialism in the China Sea. Today there is a general awakening, but also an effect of stupefaction. The persecution of the Uyghurs in Xinjiang is an example. It can no longer remain hidden: testimonies, satellite images, leaked official documents, everything converges to describe the re-education camps, sterilizations, forced labor...Therefore, dialogue with China remains necessary but this dialogue takes place in a context that can no longer be ignored. We need to engage China on major global challenges such as the climate and health. But we know that this partner does not seek to approach anything resembling our values. We must therefore ensure that we strengthen our means to defend both these values and our interests. We are not powerless: let us never forget that China bases its power on its growth, and that its growth rests on two pillars: its exports and its innovations. We must therefore strengthen our industrial sovereignty and better protect our technologies. In this respect, it is the responsibility of the public authorities, but not only them: companies, consumers, researchers, academics. Let's be

aware that China has woken up. The goal is not to enter a new cold war, the goal is to avoid a tipping of the world towards an authoritarian regime. (Loiseau, 2021)

Revisiting Tibet in light of Xinjiang: Disconcerting parallels

The parallels with Tibet are striking as well as disconcerting. Everything is there: the labor camps, torture, rape, forced sterilizations, displacement of populations. Today, the Sinicization of Tibet continues at a forced march, whether you look at the cultural, linguistic, architectural, or economic fields. An additional step was taken at the start of 2020 with the implementation of a new program of forced labor. Independent researcher Adrian Zenz, Beijing's bête noire, wrote a report (2020) on the program for the Jamestown Foundation that found that the program is, in fact, being implemented by the military (*junlüshi*, 军旅式). It is supervised by officials and cadres of the People's Liberation Army (PLA). Photos published by the official Chinese media show Tibetans dressed in military uniforms being forced to work. PLA officers participating in the program have recruitment quotas that, if not met, could see them punished (*yange jiangcheng cuoshi*, 严格奖惩措施). The program aims to reform "backward ways of thinking" and includes training in "work discipline," law and the use of the Chinese language. It has fallen particularly hard on the Chamdo area in the "Tibetan Autonomous Region" where a so-called vocational training school is located. According to an official Chinese government website cited by Zenz in the report, half a million people were trained during the first seven months of 2020. Nearly 50,000 people were transferred to other parts of Tibet to work and more than 3000 were sent to other provinces. While ostensibly the goal of the program is the total elimination of extreme poverty in rural areas, it is being imposed in particular on the nomadic Tibetan populations. Nomadism is an age-old tradition in Tibet and hundreds of thousands still practice it. By forcing these people to settle, Beijing is mounting a major attack on the secular traditions of the Tibetan highlands. "This is now, in my opinion, the strongest, most clear and targeted attack on traditional Tibetan livelihoods that we have seen almost since the Cultural Revolution" of 1966 to 1976, Zenz said when the report was released (Cadell, 2020). While Zenz does note the differences between what is happening in Tibet and Xinjiang, his comparison has come in for criticism. Gabriel Lafitte, a Melbourne-based expert on Tibet who maintains the blog rukor. org, disputes the analysis, pointing to the fact that in Xinjiang, Beijing has millions of Han Chinese settlers who have already made the region their home for some generations while there are only a few non-Tibetans with roots in Tibet.

The Chinese central government has exercised absolute control over all the frontier regions of China, and Tibet has been no exception since the People's Liberation Army invaded that part of the roof of the world in October 1950. It tightened that control even further after March 1959, when an uprising against the Chinese broke out in Lhasa and the Dalai Lama fled into exile in India. In addition to the appalling atrocities and massive destruction carried out in Tibet during the Cultural Revolution, there has since been a turbocharged Sinicization policy that has hardly known any respite. The world has now become aware of the tragedy unfolding in Xinjiang, but the situation in Tibet is not much better. This Sinicization is leading to the gradual disappearance of the Tibetan language (which is very different from the Chinese language). It also poses multiple obstacles to religious freedom, as does the close surveillance of the activities of Tibetan monasteries. China's new consumerist society is also light years away from Tibet's ancestral traditions. The reality today is that Tibet is slowly dying, a victim of relentless steamrolling by the dominant Chinese culture. The Sinicization of the region continues at a forced march, whether in the cultural, linguistic, architectural or economic fields. Another turn of the screw: since the end of 2019, restrictions have been placed on freedom of worship. The Chinese government now forbids former employees of the local Tibetan government from practicing any form of traditional Tibetan worship, while those under 18 and members of the Chinese Communist Party are no longer allowed to enter monasteries on festival days. To add to this grim picture, the "Tibet Autonomous Region" (TAR) issued new regulations in early 2021 to encourage Tibetans to spy on each other and foreigners in the name of China's national security. The "Tibet Autonomous Region Counterintelligence Security Regulations," which went into effect on January 1, 2021, are regional-level regulations under the National Counterintelligence Law of the People's Republic of China (2014), which are part of Xi Jinping's "Overall National Security Outlook."

Despite the slow but inexorable death of his nation, the Dalai Lama[9] remains stubbornly opposed to the use of violence against aggressors. "I know that some Tibetans are thinking about violence. But I tell them they are wrong. Violence is immoral. For us Tibetans, it would also be suicide. Should the Tibetans go down the path of violence, the Chinese will take even more drastic measures. Basically, I think that violence is an inhuman act, unworthy of the human person. Human beings should instead cultivate the feeling of compassion that lies within each of us. How can men be attracted to blood? Furthermore, while I believe that by using violence it is certainly possible to achieve something, however this gain most certainly will not endure. Very often, rather than making a problem go away, violence adds to it. Look at us: there are six million of us against over a thousand million! Sometimes, when I explain this to young Tibetans, they start crying. They can't control their emotional reactions. But they have to accept it. Because whether they like it or not, this is the reality," he said. "I think China will one day become an open society, a genuine democracy that respects freedom of speech and freedom of religion. That will come. The truth is known outside, but also inside China and Tibet. And then, communism will fail. Dictatorial systems fail. Naturally, the voice of human rights is heard. The voice of freedom too. We are human beings. We only ask for more freedom, more democracy," added the Tibetan spiritual leader and Nobel Peace Prize winner (Donnet, 2019). For years he has been proposing, in vain, to open negotiations with China to agree on the principle of broad autonomy for Tibet, having renounced any idea of formal independence since 1988.

Katia Buffetrille[10] is probably the most knowledgeable Tibet specialist in France along with her colleague Matthew Kapstein. She explained to me why the restrictions against Tibetans practicing their religion and speaking their language are important attacks on their cultural identity:

Everything is being done to ensure that the Sinicization process advances rapidly and all areas of Tibetan life are affected: religion, language, way of life and even the environment. This process started a long time ago, but under Xi Jinping's reign it has taken on a magnitude not seen for a long time. One can only be amazed by the resilience of the Tibetans who have lived under colonial occupation for 70 years. While—or perhaps it should be said because of—the Buddhist religion is one of the foundations of Tibetan identity, the attacks against it are many and constant. Xi Jinping has clearly stated the need to 'merge religious doctrines with Chinese culture' and to 'guide the adaptation of religions to socialist society'. As a result, it has been ordered to Sinicize the scriptures (sutras), to put the Chinese flag on all religious buildings. Important clerics were strongly advised to become propagandists of the Chinese Communist Party. Monks trained in India were no longer allowed to teach and, since

2011, the 'democratic management committees' in charge of implementing the official directives in the monasteries are made up of Party members. Young people in the Tibet Autonomous Region (TAR) are now forbidden to participate in religious festivals, which are increasingly controlled and sometimes even banned under the pretext of Covid-19, as happened during the 2021 New Year celebrations. Another manifestation of this Sinicization: the teaching of the Tibetan language is constantly decreasing. In 2020, we learned that Tibetan has been banned in the TAR, even in kindergarten. More and more young people study in boarding schools where only Mandarin is allowed. The Kenyan writer Ngugi wa Thiong'o[11] described very well the consequences of replacing the language of the colonized with that of the colonizer: 'Language as culture is the collective memory bank of a people's experience in history. Culture is almost indistinguishable from the language that makes possible its genesis, growth, banking, articulation, and indeed its transmission from one generation to the next.'[12] Moreover, the forced urbanization of Tibetans is one of the phenomena that destroy the traditional way of life. The landscape, inhabited by the divine and therefore sacred world, is profaned, and then progressively destroyed by Chinese interference. (Buffetrille, 2021)

Buffetrille, who usually spends six months a year in the Tibetan region, also noted that in Tibet, like in Xinjiang, the authorities have used labor training as a means of imparting Chinese cultural values, and cited the recent reports of use of forced labor:

Adrian Zenz has recently shown that a similar process of forced labor seems to be taking place in the TAR. Of course, one should be cautious and wait for confirmation, knowing that it is difficult to verify information due to the ban on journalists and experts working in the TAR. However, since 2020, some 500,000 Tibetan farmers and nomads—about 15% of the population—have been sent for training in militarized camps under the pretext of eradicating poverty. This training aims to give them a 'real job' in a factory. It aims to teach them discipline, Mandarin and encourages the displacement of populations, thus cutting them off from their traditional environment. It should be kept in mind that for most Han people, so-called "minorities" such as Uyghurs or Tibetans are perceived as backward, lazy and ungrateful people who should be reformed. Only one model of culture and civilization is offered to them and imposed on them, that of the Han, since it is, according to the latter, the one and only valid model. (Buffetrille, 2021)

I asked her: is there still hope for the survival of Tibet's cultural identity?

This is a very difficult question. One can only be struck by and admire the resilience of the Tibetans. The country has been occupied since the 1950s. Tibetans were caught up in all the great Chinese catastrophic movements, whether it was the Great Leap Forward, the Cultural Revolution, etc., and to this day they continue to fight to exist as Tibetans. There have been different phenomena of resistance, the most tragic being the self-immolations. They began in 2009 but really took off from 2011, and then gradually stopped (the last self-immolation took place in November 2019), not because of an improvement in the situation, but because of the policy of punishing the relatives of the immolated who all ended up in prison. It should be noted that the exact number of those who burned themselves is still unknown. The number of 156 was recently corrected when it was learned in January 2021 that a Tibetan had immolated himself in 2015 in the Nagchukha region of the TAR. It's an unfair fight and the control is tightening further thanks to more and more advanced surveillance techniques that use artificial intelligence. With WeChat banned in India, contact between Tibetans in China and Tibetans in exile is becoming even more difficult than before. The threat to the survival of Tibet's cultural identity is very great. Therefore, it is our responsibility to make the world aware of the importance and greatness of Tibetan civilization, which, if it were to disappear, would be an immense loss for the world. (Buffetrille, 2021)

I am reminded of the luminous words of Robert Badinter, a former French justice minister, who addressed the European rally for Tibet at the Champs de Mars in Paris held in 2015 to mark the Lhasa uprising against the Chinese occupiers in March 1959:

Because the Dalai Lama saw his country Tibet invaded and crushed by a foreign power at the dawn of his life, he became, beyond the embodiment cause of the Tibetans which is so dear to us, a messenger of universal peace, this elementary condition for the happiness of the peoples. For the Dalai Lama, humanity is expressed in constant respect for the dignity and the rights of our other human brothers. For Tenzin Gyatso, human rights are the political charter of all humanity. They are the rights of all human beings everywhere in the world. History reminds us that these are precious and fragile rights. He tells us they can only be conceived as universal and indivisible. For what would human rights be if they belonged only to rich and developed societies while billions of other human beings live in misery, disease, ignorance?…The Dalai Lama believes in the power of law, and because, as we know, the cause of the Tibetans is just, it will eventually triumph.

What he asks for the Tibetan people (he does not even ask for independence, which sometimes I regret), [what] he asks for Tibet is only:

- the safeguarding of its cultural identity, so important in the concert of civilizations, and respect for the fundamental rights of all and thus of Tibetans;
- to put an end to a regime of oppression and cultural genocide;
- to establish self-government and the rule of law in Tibet.

There is nothing here that threatens the integrity of the Chinese Republic or its international sovereignty! Therefore, my friends, we will continue to tirelessly support the just cause of the Tibetans by lawful means and with the spiritual strength of justice. All of us together, without violence or provocation, but with resolution and steadfastness. (Badinter, 2015)

I add to the above lines the statement of Nancy Pelosi (2021), Speaker of the US House of Representatives, on the 62nd anniversary of the uprising of the Tibetan people in Lhasa against the Chinese occupier on March 10, 2021: "Sixty-two years ago, brave Tibetans rose up against the Chinese invasion to protect their way of life and culture. Today, we continue to stand with the Tibetan people and honor those who sacrificed all for their rights and freedom."

The steamroller of cultural colonization and forced assimilation operates elsewhere in China. There is another region where the Beijing regime intends to continue its policy of forced Sinicization: Inner Mongolia. In September 2020, thousands of Mongolian schoolchildren, pupils and students demonstrated in the streets for the preservation of their language. The epicenter of the unrest was in Tongliao prefecture in eastern

Inner Mongolia, where ethnic Mongolians make up 45% of the population, compared to about 16% for the Inner Mongolia autonomous region as a whole, alongside the dominant Han (ethnic Chinese) majority. New educational directives aimed, under the guise of a policy of "bilingualism," to substitute Mandarin for Mongolian in the teaching of almost all subjects other than language and literature. And to do it earlier, from the youngest grades. While information and official documents on the project had been leaked over the summer, on August 20 teachers were summoned for closed-door meetings on these reforms "decreed by the central government." The teachers had to sign a paper guaranteeing that they would not talk about or oppose the reforms. But soon calls for a boycott of the classes began to appear on the Mongolian-language messaging service Bainu, which the authorities temporarily shut down. Some parents refused to send their children to school. The protests then spread throughout the region. "There are at least tens of thousands of people protesting across Inner Mongolia," said one Hinggan region resident (Chen, L., 2020). Marie-Dominique Even, a specialist in Mongolian history at the French National Center for Scientific Research, said the region is one the most important places for the protesters. "This area is one of the oldest areas colonized by the Hans under the Manchus. It is a bit of a paradox, the natives do not speak the Mongolian language very well, they borrow a lot of Mandarin. But they are much more numerous than the others, and more integrated into the administrations. This is what gives them their strength. They seem to be all the more sensitive to what is left since they have lost much of their way of life and their identity," she said (Pedroletti, 2020).

The policy of "bilingualism" in Inner Mongolia has already been widely imposed over the past ten years in the regions of Tibet and Xinjiang, where Mandarin has replaced Tibetan and the Uyghur language in primary and secondary schools despite local resistance in the form of petitions and demonstrations. In early March 2021, President Xi Jinping instructed local authorities in Inner Mongolia to generalize the use of Chinese in schools to ease ethnic tensions. The Xinhua news agency reported that Xi told them that they should make more "solid and meticulous efforts in promoting ethnic unity to strengthen the sense of identity with the motherland, the Chinese nation, the Chinese culture, the Party and socialism with Chinese characteristics among people of all ethnic groups" (*Xinhua*, 2021). That includes using standard spoken and written Chinese language and use of state-compiled textbooks. "Cultural identity is the deepest form of identity. It is also the root and soul of ethnic unity and harmony," Xi said (Lua, 2021).

Notes

1   The surveillance of the Chinese population has deepened with the implementation since February 2019 of a "free" app dedicated to "Xi Jinping Thought" for owners of smartphones with Android software (80% of the smartphone market in China). On the surface, the "Study and strengthen the nation" (*Xuexi qianguo*) app quizzes users about their knowledge about their country and their leader Xi Jinping. The 90 million CCP members and government officials are instructed to use it on a nearly daily basis, and it has topped download lists. But the app contains a backdoor that allows the authorities to spy on all phone activities, including emails, photos, messages, contacts, and browsing history.

2   Including Alibaba's former boss Jack Ma, who is very popular in his country and is China's richest man.

3   Statistics show that the Chinese are very interested in religion, including Christianity and Buddhism, both of which are experiencing an extraordinary revival that is beginning to worry the Chinese Communist Party, which

has responded by imposing increasingly strict controls on religious practices in recent years.

4   The work of Adrian Zenz, based in part on Chinese official documents, cannot be easily dismissed. Marc Julienne, a researcher in sinology at the IFRI (French Institute of International Relations), considers the information published by Zenz on the internment camps in Xinjiang to be credible, although speculative. Based on satellite imagery, testimonies, data and official documents, Zenz proposes a figure of 1.2 million internees in 2018 and 1.8 million the following year. To discredit him, Chinese authorities describe Zenz as an "extreme right-wing fundamentalist Catholic" who believes he is "guided by God." Zenz himself confirmed this last point in an article in the *Wall Street Journal* which described him as a born-again Christian.

5   Between 1987 and 1990, more than 200 bombings were carried out in Xinjiang. Some of them were deadly, but most were directed against official buildings and birth control offices. In 1993, there were more than 17 explosions in Kashgar alone, and in 1994 there were three large explosions in Aksu. In 1996, the Chinese government launched a major anti-crime operation that resulted in a campaign of searches and arrests. On September 18, 2015, a group of Uyghurs, armed with cleavers and knives, killed dozens of Han Chinese working in a coal mine in the Aksu area. The police manhunt resulted in the death of 28 of the attackers. These attacks were and still are the main justification given by the Chinese government for its policy of repression in this so-called autonomous region.

6   For those who wish to learn more about this tragedy, we recommend reading the book by journalist Sylvie Lasserre, *Voyage au pays des Ouïghours* [Journey to the land of the

Uyghurs], published in 2020 by the Hesse publishing house.

7   The Chinese authorities invited Michelle Bachelet to visit Xinjiang but, sensing the trap, she asked for time to consider. It is obvious that she will not have access to what she wishes to visit on a trip that will certainly be carefully prepared by the Chinese regime. On the other hand, she will be eagerly shown all the grandiose achievements of socialist China in Xinjiang and receive vibrant testimonies of friendship between peoples.

8   Samuel Paty, a history and geography teacher in the Paris suburb of Conflans-Sainte-Honorine, was stabbed and decapitated on October 16, 2020, shortly after leaving his school, by Abdoullakh Anzorov. An 18-year-old Russian citizen of Chechen origin who had been granted refugee status in France when he was a minor, Anzorov was shot dead a few minutes after the attack by police.

9   It should be noted that if the Dalai Lama is the bête noire of Xi Jinping, this was not the case for his father Xi Zhongxun. The elder Xi was a veteran of the Long March at the side of Mao Zedong, who had taken a liking to the young Tibetan monk in the 1950s. The Dalai Lama gave Xi Zhongxun an Omega watch, which he wore on his wrist for a very long time. Xi Zhongxun is remembered as a man who was kind to minorities, especially Tibetans.

10   Katia Buffetrille is an anthropologist and Tibetologist, specializing in Tibetan culture. She has a doctorate in ethnology, is a researcher at the Ecole Pratique des Hautes Etudes (EPHE) and is the editor of the journal *Études mongoles et sibériennes, centrasiatiques et tibétaines*. She is the author, among other publications, of *Le Tibet est-il chinois?* [Is Tibet Chinese?] (with Anne-Marie Blondeau), Albin Michel, 2002; and *L'âge d'or du Tibet (XIIᵉ et XVIIIᵉ siècles)*

[The golden age of Tibet (17th and 18th centuries)], Belles Lettres, 2019.

11 Ngũgĩ wa Thiong'o, born January 5, 1938, in Kamiriithu, is a Kenyan writer who writes primarily in Kikuyu and English. He is a professor at the University of California, Irvine, and was the first director of its International Center for Writing & Translation.

12 The quote comes from Ngũgĩ wa Thiong'o's book *Decolonising the Mind*. It can be found on page 15 of the edition published in 1994 by Zimbabwe Publishing House.

Chapter 2

The environment: When China shakes up the planet

By far the biggest polluter on the planet, China has promised to become carbon neutral by 2060. Meeting this commitment is crucial because of the extreme environmental impact of ultra-fast growth in a country that will soon be the world's leading economic power. Its industrial and ecological choices today will weigh heavily on the world's destiny.

> Predators never die, unlike victims, because they are interchangeable. One monstrosity replaces another and we start again.
> —Andrea H. Japp (pseudonym of Lionelle Nugon-Baudon, French scientist and author), *The Reason of Women*

Carbon neutrality by 2060: Far-sighted or fantasy?

On September 22, 2020, Chinese President Xi Jinping made a bombshell announcement before the United Nations General Assembly in New York that his country had now set a goal of achieving carbon neutrality "by 2060." On December 12 of the same year, he followed up with a statement to a virtual world summit on climate change that China was "committed to further contribute" to the goals of the Paris Agreement by reducing its greenhouse gas emissions by "at least" 65% of carbon intensity per unit of GDP (gross domestic product) by 2030 compared to their 2005 level. China, he added, is committed to increasing the extent of its forests by 6 billion cubic meters and increasing the share of non-fossil fuels in its energy mix to 25% by bringing installed solar and wind capacity to at least 1.2 billion kilowatts per hour over the next decade. In the wake of these sensational announcements, the official press agency New China published a commentary on the same day stating that China's new commitments reflected "the ambition and determination of a responsible great power," while the spokeswoman for the Chinese Ministry of Foreign Affairs, Hua Chunying, declared that China would "honor its commitments" and "contribute even more to the fight against climate change." These are fine promises and nice gestures from the all-powerful president of a country that alone accounts for 30% of all global greenhouse gas emissions, making it by far the biggest polluter on the planet. Should we take these promises seriously? Aware of the need for it to further fulfill its responsibilities as a major power in this area, China signed the Paris Agreement on December 12, 2015. This agreement, signed by 195 countries, aims to limit global warming to 2°C by the end of the twenty-first century. Since the signing of the Paris climate pact, Chinese authorities have made real efforts, which will be detailed below, but which are largely insufficient to meet their commitments. Concerning coal-fired power plants, the Chinese government has even acted contrary to its stated goals by authorizing the construction of more coal-fired power plants in the first half of 2020 than in 2018 and 2019 combined (Pearl, 2020).

China's coal consumption alone accounts for 50.6% of global consumption. This is 4 times the consumption of the United States, 18 times that of Japan, 24 times that of Germany and 128 times that of France (Huchet, 2016, pp. 85–86). China currently has some 1400 coal-fired power plants (compared to 647 in the United States) that release 375 million tons of coal ash into the air annually, the equivalent of an Olympic-sized swimming pool every 2.5 minutes! Thirty countries have now joined an alliance promising to stop the construction of coal-fired power plants from 2020. But not China. The number of such plants under construction is declining around the world, except in China (and India), where capacity will further increase rapidly by 2030. China's Electricity Board, the country's power-sector umbrella organization, plans to increase its power-plant capacity by 30% over the next decade. It has proposed increasing capacity to 1300 gigawatts (GW) by 2030, "which is 290 GW more than current levels and more than the total capacity of the United States," notes Christine Shearer, a researcher at the Global Energy Monitor, a San Francisco-based nongovernmental organization (NGO) (Gradt, 2019). The country alone holds nearly half of the world's coal-fired capacity with nearly 1000 gigawatts, followed by the US (259 GW) and India (221 GW). According to projections by the International Energy Agency and the US Energy Information Administration, China's economy is expected to remain heavily dependent on coal well beyond 2030, with nearly 50% of its energy mix relying on coal by 2040. Moreover, Chinese companies are building many coal-fired power plants overseas. In 2018 alone, Beijing invested $36 billion in self-built coal plants in developing countries.

The air pollution these coal-fired power plants create, in addition to affecting urban areas in mainland China, also affects neighboring countries, including the two Koreas, Japan, Taiwan, and even North America, mainly in the spring when sandstorms are most intense in northwestern China due to the soil erosion and land desertification that has accelerated significantly since the early 1980s. The rapid increase in ground-level ozone in China is mirrored on the West Coast of the United States. "Asian" ozone is estimated to account for 20% of the ozone level in California (Main, 2012). China is expected to be responsible for nearly three-quarters of the increase in GHGs (greenhouse gases) in the world by 2030, according to projections by the International Energy Agency (2009). In addition to this air pollution, there is a cruel lack of water. Of the 660 major cities in China, 440 suffer from severe water shortages. The water supply of half of Chinese cities doesn't meet World Health Organization (WHO) standards for human consumption.

On the same day that Xi Jinping addressed the United Nations General Assembly, its Secretary General, Antonio Guterres, invited all the countries of the world to declare "a state of climate emergency." He stressed that the international community faces "a catastrophic rise in temperatures" if the current trend is not reversed. For China to meet its ambitious targets will require a huge effort that experts agree is unlikely to be achieved. Experts at Boston Consulting group (Chen et al., 2020) estimated the cost of doing so over the next three decades at more than 100 trillion yuan ($15 trillion), or the equivalent of about 2% of China's cumulative GDP from 2020 to 2050. China "must adopt, starting immediately, a 1.5°C pathway to carbon reduction of 75% to 85% by 2050," said the report's authors. One of those actions to be taken immediately is to stop building new coal-fired power plants for good. A goal almost impossible to keep, knowing that in 2019 coal accounted for about 58% of primary energy consumption in the country, with gas, nuclear and renewable energy constituting the rest. Why will it be so difficult? Because China's per capita energy consumption still lags behind that of other developed countries. It was 2236 kilograms (kg) oil equivalent in 2020, compared to 3470 kg in Japan and 636 kg in India, but it has literally exploded since the early 2000s and has increased by 381% in 43 years! Per capita consumption will likely increase further in coming years and China will be under intense pressure to increase production capacity as well, upping the challenge to stop building more coal-fired power plants. China is making an enormous effort to add nuclear capacity, hoping to double its share in the energy mix to 10% by 2035, building six to eight reactors per year, or nearly 100 over 15 years! To achieve the ambitious goal of carbon neutrality by 2060, China should increase renewable energy from solar and wind power by about 100 gigawatts each year from 2021 to 2025. Faced with these pressures, coal is shaping up to be a litmus test for determining whether China's top priority remains economic development at all costs or sustainable development with better protection of the environment.

Of course, the Chinese government is making some efforts that deserve to be highlighted in the fight against global warming. For example, China has become the largest manufacturer of solar panels and lithium-ion batteries in the world. China produces more than half of the world's electric cars and almost all the electric buses (*South China Morning Post*, 2020). In most major Chinese cities, cabs, buses and scooters all run on electricity. This reduces the volume of toxic emissions put into the atmosphere, although these same cities are still facing dramatic air pollution caused by traffic and surrounding industrial manufacturing facilities. But the flip side of the coin is that all these electric vehicles consume energy almost entirely produced by coal-fired power plants! In addition, a standard electric car battery contains an average of 16 kg of nickel, a rare metal whose production generates mountains of waste. It also contains 15 kg of lithium, which contributes to soil pollution during its extraction. There are also 10 kg of cobalt, whose extraction in Africa is associated with child labor, generally paid at a rate of two dollars a day (*Le Canard Enchaîné*, 2020). But as President Joe Biden's climate plan points out, during the first year of Donald Trump's presidency, for every dollar spent on renewables in the United States, China was spending three. China is by far the largest investor in clean energy. It alone attracts 29% of the total global investment in 2014 in clean energy (solar, wind, biomass and hydro) with nearly $90 billion invested (Crooks, 2015).

The fight for environmental protection and global warming has been enshrined in Chinese law since January 2015 with the recognition in its principles of the need to reconcile economic activity and environmental protection. This law allows the authorities to shut down companies that seriously violate pollution standards. The previous system only provided for fines, which companies preferred to pay and continue polluting. The new law protects whistleblowers, while the list of people who can file lawsuits over environmental violations has been expanded to include victims of pollution and NGOs. "China thus has a vast legal and regulatory framework which, in theory, should make it possible to protect the country against environmental damage," points out sinologist Jean-François Huchet (2016, p. 105). But, he adds, "as in many areas in China (human rights, economic and social rights), there are abysmal differences between the laws and their application on the ground" (p. 109). Indeed, all too often, the objectives of local authorities remain focused on maintaining employment, developing local industry and achieving growth at all costs. Plant closures remain the exception.

What are China's and Asia's share of global CO_2 emissions? In 2019, Chinese emissions were more than twice as high as US emissions and nearly three times higher than those of the European Union. Overall, Asia now accounts for over 50% of global emissions. 2019 was not a good year for Chinese emissions, which rose another 3.4%, a difference greater than all French emissions in the same year. During the pandemic, China's share of global emissions continued to grow, as its emissions shrank much less than the global average in 2020. They fell by 1.4% compared to a global decline of 6.3%, according to Carbon Monitor. This difference reflects the greater resilience of the Chinese economy to the health shock. Its strong rebound anticipated for 2021 will also cause a jump in CO_2 emissions, and China could account for a third of global emissions by the end of the year. China's renewable energy ambitions are nevertheless strong. The installed capacity in this area (solar, wind, hydro) has doubled between 2014 and 2019, reaching 820 gigawatts in 2019. However, the share of renewable energy in the country's overall primary energy demand remained slightly below 13% in 2019. The goal of increasing this share to 25% by

2030 is clearly more ambitious than those for energy efficiency or forest preservation. The current increase in the share of renewable energy in overall demand is 0.6% per year. This rate would have to be almost doubled to reach the target of 25% in 2030 (Testard, 2021).

Dramatic air pollution

All of China's big cities are now confronted with dramatic air pollution. In Beijing, the sun hardly appears in a hopelessly gray sky: the inhabitants of the Chinese capital live in an almost permanent smog. Breathing the air in Beijing is like living in the smoking area of an American airport (*Bloomberg*, 2013). China ranked 118th out of 174 countries in the air-pollution ranking made by Yale University's Center for Environmental Law and Policy, which uses 20 criteria for judging countries' pollution levels and trends (Huchet, 2016, p. 10). The thick layer of pollution covering Beijing on satellite images almost completely disappeared in spring 2020 when the capital was under Covid lockdown. But it has since returned, thicker and denser than ever, as economic activity and automobile traffic resumed. This pollution causes an estimated 1.6 million premature deaths per year (Rohde et al., 2015), at an annual cost of 5.8% of GDP. In 2001, a World Bank report stated that 16 Chinese cities were among the 20 most polluted cities in the world. This pollution is directly responsible for a rapid increase in lung cancer: a 465% increase over 30 years for the whole of China and 60% over ten years in Beijing, according to some studies (Huang, Y., 2013). China is now responsible for emissions totaling 9.7 gigatons, or 28% of the world total (compared with 5.9 gigatons for the United States and 2 gigatons for India). Air pollution also causes acid rain. Nearly 40% of Chinese territory is affected, especially the southeast of the country. Vegetation is a top victim, with forests taking first place, followed by arable land (Huchet, 2016, p. 38), leading to a considerable economic impact.

Greenhouse gas emissions are not the only aspect of China's pollutant releases. For years, China has been the world's largest producer of plastics. China discharges more than 200 million cubic meters of waste annually—mostly plastics—directly into the sea, according to the Ministry of Ecology and Environment (Xu et al., 2019). China is the world's largest producer of waste, generating some 1 billion tons of waste per year. The Chinese government responded by announcing on January 20, 2020, a ban on the use of single-use plastic bags in major cities by the end of 2020 and nationwide by 2022. The authorities have also inaugurated plastic-waste processing plants. According to a study by the organization Greenpeace published on December 17, 2020, 36 companies founded in the country in 2020 intend to build plastic-waste processing facilities with a total annual capacity of 4.4 million tons of such waste, a sevenfold increase in capacity in the space of one year. But this is still a long way from meeting the estimated national biodegradable plastic waste production of 5 million tons per year in 2025 for the e-commerce sector alone (Greenpeace, 2020), and the shift in China's plastics production to biodegradable plastics does not make up for everything. "Switching from one type of plastic to another cannot solve the plastics pollution crisis that we're facing," said Dr. Molly Zhongnan Jia, a researcher at Greenpeace East Asia.

What about tomorrow?

"We can explain the situation by an analogy with a roller coaster. You start out going up very high, then you're at a peak and you go downhill. And Xi Jinping would like to go down the slope to zero in 2060. The problem is that for the moment we are still going up. In 1990, China accounted for a little more than 10% of global production and 40% of Asian emissions. In 2019, we've gone from 10% to just over 30% and China's share of Asia's emissions has gone from 40% to 60%. Basically, China is exploding in terms of emissions. For overall greenhouse gas emissions, it's about the same. In 2020, its emissions have been reduced a little bit, but not much. And in 2021, there will be a very strong economic growth and therefore these emissions will jump again. At the end of 2021, we will probably have 33% of global emissions. China alone accounts for a colossal increase in global emissions," explained Hubert Testard, a specialist in East Asia and a professor at Sciences Po Paris, at a January 2021 webinar organized by *Asialyst* and France's National Institute of Oriental Languages and Civilizations. "In 2019, the increase of China's emissions represented more than France's total emissions. There are Chinese commitments to redress the balance. But in terms of the energy mix, it is still coal that dominates. We were at more than 70%, and today we are down to just under 60%. This is still huge. Coal still accounts for two-thirds of China's electricity production. We are now back to the 2013 level, that is, we are back to the peak of Chinese coal demand because China has launched a whole series of new coal-fired power plants. So, we are not at all out of China's addiction to coal, which represents half of the world's coal production," he said. "2060: are the commitments in line with this objective? For the moment it is not clear. We are more likely in an evolutionary situation, where a series of commitments have been made, but not a revolution. So, in my opinion, we are very far from being at a level that allows us to be sure that China will reach this objective. For renewable energies, they are more ambitious, but despite all the efforts made, we are still only at 13% of the primary energy demand in China made with renewable energy. So, it's still quite limited. Massive investments in renewable energy are needed to change the picture. In 2009, China committed to a 15% share of renewable energy in primary energy demand, then in 2015 it committed to 20% and now it has just committed to 25%. It doesn't sound like much to go from 20 to 25%, but it requires huge investments," he said (Zylberman, 2021).

Sinologist Jean-François Huchet, president of the National Institute of Oriental Languages and Civilizations (INALCO) and author of the 2015 book *La crise environnementale en Chine* [The environmental crisis in China], was equally skeptical when he spoke at the same webinar:

China for a long time had no environmental policy at all. Not until 2013. Why? Because coal was, and still is, at the center of its energy resource policy. We have more or less the same energy mix between 1978 and 2014, except that consumption has literally exploded. China burns about 4.2 billion tons of coal, which is more than the rest of the world. It has the third largest coal reserves in the world and, even at the current rate, it is estimated that China could still have two centuries of coal resources available to maintain this level of consumption. It is important to realize the sheer size of the numbers in China. Between 2006 and 2009, about one and a half 1000 MW [megawatt] thermal power plants were being built every week. Then it slowed down a bit, and then it went up to three plants between 2009 and 2013. So, it's colossal. From 2006 onwards, the equivalent of the French industrial electricity park has been installed in China every year. It's colossal! The changes have really occurred from 2013 to 2014, for reasons that have to do with the deterioration of air quality mainly. So, there was this inability for China to continue at the pace of pollution that was affecting major Chinese cities from 2013. People termed them 'airpocalyptic' episodes, particularly in northern cities and especially Beijing. But what have been the results? The biggest result was certainly the considerable increase in renewable energy. At a certain point, around 2015–2016, we had the impression that we had really reached a plateau in terms of coal consumption, in particular, and that we were certainly going to reach a peak much earlier than 2030. The additional electricity needed to meet economic growth could be satisfied by adding new renewable energy capacity instead of fossil fuel power plants. We took these as very encouraging signs, in around 2015–2016, and then we gradually realized that with each rebound in the economy, in fact we were dealing with a recovery of the conventional economy: infrastructure, real estate that needs a lot of cement, steel that requires a lot of energy, especially electricity produced from coal. For many years to come, we will have a 'green China' and a 'brown China' that will coexist with a kind of schizophrenia as China continues to pollute with disastrous consequences for public health. We are going to continue to have very significant degradation in many areas. And then, alongside this, we have a 'green China' that is moving forward out of necessity because 'brown China' cannot continue to dominate the Chinese production model, which has reached its physical limits in terms of industrial development and its environmental footprint. So, we have a China that is investing heavily in green industries and trying to reduce the impact of environmental degradation. We have these two Chinas and, on the international level, it goes without saying that China is trying to promote the green China narrative. Perhaps a peak will be reached in 2030. But in any case, as far as carbon neutrality in 2060 is concerned, I think it is still very, very far away and that for China it is more of a political statement in order to appear like a good student on the international stage. (Zylberman, 2021)

The ravages of deforestation, water pollution and soil depletion

Another scourge that is affecting the environment in China is deforestation. More than half of the world's forests (54%) are located in just five countries: Russia, Brazil, Canada, the United States and China. An assessment conducted in 2015 showed that there were about 3.4 trillion trees on our planet, a number that is decreasing significantly due to ongoing deforestation. The authors of the study point out that about 15.3 billion trees are cut down each year, particularly in tropical areas (notre-planete.info, n.d.). But while deforestation in the Amazon is a great tragedy, it is not the only one. China has been engaged in massive deforestation for the past 40 years, the result of industrialization and the inexorable expansion of urban areas, but also of illegal logging, particularly in Tibet.[1] Although this phenomenon has slowed down in recent years due to the undeniable awareness of the authorities that it accelerates desertification, deforestation continues. According to the NGO Global Forest Watch (n.d.), between 2002 and 2019 China lost a total of 74,900 hectares of rainforest, or 0.77% of the country's total forest cover. During the same period, the area of primary forests was reduced by 4.3%. From 2001 to 2019, China lost 9.92 million hectares of vegetation cover, which is equivalent to a 6.1% decrease in vegetation cover since 2000 and 3.18 gigatons of CO_2 equivalent. The mapping of China shows persistent and rapid deforestation in coastal areas due to the growth of urbanization in these regions where economic development is most rapid. Of course, we must mention here China's gigantic reforestation efforts in recent years, with the planting of billions of trees to combat desertification.

On the other hand, China is proving to be a formidable predator when it comes to deforestation in many developing countries, particularly in Africa and Southeast Asia, where millions of trees are cut down to satisfy China's voracious need for wood, including rare species threatened with extinction. In Laos, in the 1990s, the forest covered more than two-thirds of the country's surface. Today, it covers only 40%. This deforestation has been mostly illegal, and 98% of the wood was destined for China and Vietnam (*Le Bois International*, 2020). In Cambodia, the situation is even worse. This country experienced the highest rate of deforestation in the world between 2001 and

2014 at 14.4%. This rapid deforestation, which benefits mainly China, has had devastating effects on both the environment and ethnic minorities. Deforestation has also been a problem in Indonesia where forests are cut down to make way for palm oil cultivation.[2] Deforestation is also a problem in Africa, where China is an active participant. The Food and Agriculture Organization of the United Nations (FAO) noted in a May 2020 report that Africa now has the largest annual rate of net forest loss at 3.9 million hectares.

The pollution in China also affects its soils and its rivers. The Yangtze River (Chang Jiang), the longest in the country and the third longest in the world after the Amazon and the Nile, stretches 6300 kilometers from the Tibetan plateau to the East China Sea and is also one of the most threatened rivers. In order to preserve the biodiversity of the Yangtze, a ten-year fishing ban was decreed in early 2020 (WWF, n.d.). More than 230,000 fishermen were forced to find a new profession in the 19 Chinese provinces and autonomous municipalities that the "mother of rivers" and its tributaries irrigate, according to Ministry of Agriculture figures published in early December 2020 (Sureau, 2010). But this does not solve the problems of industrial pollution. The Yangtze River provides one-third of China's water resources but receives more than 40% of wastewater discharges (Yan, 2020). Riddled with over 50,000 dams, the Yangtze is overexploited and needs to recuperate. Sand extraction will be "severely limited" in the river basin, and the relocation of chemical factories away from its banks should also be accelerated, the state press reported, to ensure the "green development" of the "blue river" (*CGTN*, 2020, and *Radio France Internationale*, 2020). The flow of the Yangtze River is gradually decreasing. Scientific measurements have shown that this decline has averaged 2 centimeters every five years since the 1980s, the *South China Morning Post* reported. This drop in water level could have a huge impact on the environment and the economy in the Yangtze River basin, where 460 million people live. Nie Ning and his colleagues from the Geographic Information Laboratory of the Chinese Ministry of Education attribute this phenomenon to human activities and the numerous dams built on the river, without excluding the effect of global warming. More than 1000 natural lakes along the river have already disappeared (Chen, S., 2021).

The Yellow River, considered the cradle of Chinese civilization and the sixth longest river in the world, has dried up several times since 1972, for increasingly long periods of up to two to three months during the winter. This drying up lasted nearly 330 days in 1997. The Yellow River, as well as other large rivers that cross China and then irrigate other Asian countries such as the Mekong (Laos, Myanmar, Thailand, Cambodia, Vietnam) or the Brahmaputra (India, Bangladesh), are also seriously threatened by global warming and desertification (Huchet, 2016, p. 48). Note that in 40 years, 13% of China's lakes have disappeared from the map. And water is severely polluted throughout China. A study by the Organization for Economic Cooperation and Development (OECD) (2007) found that in half of China's major cities, the quality of tap water did not meet national standards. For over half of its course, the water of the Yellow River is unfit for human use. Nearly 60% of the groundwater in northern China is polluted to a level that makes it unsafe for consumption (Huchet, 2016, p. 51). In addition, the discharge of pollutants and other industrial wastes into waterways causes damage that will last for many years. Some damage is virtually irreversible (Xhie et al., 2013).

Another source of concern is the dams built by China on its rivers that impact neighbors. This is the case with the Red River, which originates in China's Yunnan Province, where dam construction is having a huge impact on the environment and economic life downstream in Vietnam. "Chinese Red River dams are causing repeated alluvium shortages, floods as well as droughts in Vietnam," experts told the Vietnamese newspaper *VnExpress*. The 1149-kilometer-long Red River flows through several northern Vietnamese cities, including Hanoi, that are home to 26 million people. Dams built by China upstream have lowered the water level of the river, preventing the flow of water into rice fields that is important for irrigation. "Consequently, agriculture activities in the Red River delta are strongly affected," Dao Trong Tu, head of the board of directors of the Vietnam River Network, told the newspaper. During the rainy season, the dams are of little help to Vietnamese farmers as Chinese authorities are forced to release water to ensure the safety of the reservoirs. "This creates the situation where Vietnam is constantly bombarded by floods," he added (Viet, 2021).

China has already built 11 mega-dams on the Mekong River, causing significant changes in the river's water levels as it flows downstream through Myanmar, Laos, Thailand, Cambodia and Vietnam.

In December 2020, China announced its intention to build a gigantic dam on the Yarlung Tsangpo (or Yarlung Zangbo) River in Tibet, the highest river in the world, which becomes the Brahmaputra River downstream and then irrigates India and Bangladesh. The dam will serve a 60-gigawatt (GW) hydroelectric power plant. At an energy conference, Yan Zhiyong, president of China's state-owned Power Construction Corporation, called the project a "historic opportunity." He said the project will help China solve its clean energy needs and is expected to improve the security of its water supply. This was reported by *China Energy News*, a publication linked to the *People's Daily*. When the construction was announced, environmental groups and Tibetan rights activists expressed concern as the project could have an impact on water resources downstream. According to associations opposed to these projects, China's rivers have already reached a critical point, with the construction of the

Three Gorges Dam as well as many other hydroelectric power plants on the Yangtze River and its tributaries. In response to the concerns, the Chinese Embassy in India said: "China has always taken a responsible attitude towards the development and use of transboundary rivers, following a policy that protection goes hand in hand with development." Embassy spokesman Counselor Ji Rong said each project will undergo scientific planning and assessment taking into full consideration the impact on downstream regions and the interests of upstream and downstream countries (*Chine Magazine*, 2020). But just three months later, Che Dalha, deputy Communist Party chief for China's "Tibet Autonomous Region," announced that local authorities should "strive to begin construction [of the dams] this year...Comprehensive planning and environmental impact assessments for the project should be approved as soon as possible" (Lo, 2021).

Another dramatic reality is soil pollution: 19.4% of arable land and 16.1% of soils are polluted, as well as 10% of forests and 10.4% of grasslands, mainly due to industrial and agricultural activity. This phenomenon now risks contaminating the food chain with all its repercussions on public health. In addition to this, intensive livestock farming and the cutting down of forests for firewood and construction accelerate soil erosion and promote desertification, particularly in the northwest of the country. Studies conducted by the Chinese authorities show that, despite the beginning of an improvement at the turn of the century, nearly a quarter of the Chinese territory is desertified or degraded due to a combination of climatic and human factors such as overexploitation of agriculture, livestock farming in fragile areas and overexploitation of water resources (Watts, 2011). Nearly 1.7 million square kilometers (three times the size of France), or 17% of China's territory, is now covered by deserts. These phenomena, as well as deforestation, have been accelerated by the demographic pressure, industrialization and urbanization that have exploded since the early 1980s. The rate of urbanization is expected to reach 65% of the population by 2030, with nearly 1 billion people living in cities. Urbanization is expected to continue for several decades and thus to continue to have massive environmental impacts (Huchet, 2016, p. 81).

Faced with this catastrophic situation, a collective awareness is gradually emerging and gaining importance among the Chinese on this subject that could potentially become a real political time bomb for the authorities. Nathalie Bastianelli, a specialist on civil society in China and president of the NGO We Belong, which organizes events on social networks in the country about social and environmental topics, says this environmental awareness is real and social networks have been very important in its development:

> I can give you the example of tourism...Studies show that 80% of Chinese city dwellers say they are willing to pay more for their travel if it protects wildlife. When you also look at surveys on meat consumption, you have 82% of people surveyed who say they are willing to not eat meat once a week and 63% who are willing to not eat meat twice or more a week. That gives you some indication. There is the health aspect of course, and then there is also the impact on the climate. There are now a lot of studies that show that there is more and more awareness. But of course, the official media don't talk about it much. It is rather on social networks that young people can get information, especially through bloggers. There is this famous blogger, Li Ziqi, who even if it is said that she is manipulated by the government, gathers as many followers as Lady Gaga. So it's phenomenal! Li Ziqi shows how to make her own cosmetics, how to wear clothes dyed with natural dyes to reduce the impact on the environment. She is a YouTuber who appeared in 2010 and so the impact is huge. In terms of views, I think on YouTube it

was ten million at the end of June 2020. There are a few stars in China right now who are often asked by the government to participate in awareness campaigns on the subject. Also consider the explosion of vegetarian or vegan dishes. We can see that everyone is taking up the subject. Just as the trend is emerging in Europe, in the United States, it is arriving in the same way in China. Meatless Monday arrived in China three or four years earlier than in France. These are things that are taking hold. When I was in Shanghai myself, in 2016, when I bought a vegetarian dish (I am a vegetarian) in a takeout restaurant, a second dish was offered free because I was buying vegetarian on a Monday. So there is an incentive. It's a private incentive, but you can see that there's an overall movement in society to reduce meat consumption everywhere. (Bastianelli, 2021b)

But Chinese civil society has few possibilities to organize and express itself in the current political landscape with the enormous political hold of President Xi Jinping on all the wheels of society, Bastianelli noted. And yet, sometimes, this civil society makes the authorities back down:

When there were major waves of pollution in January 2013, the population was in the streets! There had never been so many demonstrations in the streets, and the population pushed back projects to build chemical plants. Even if there were no authorizations to demonstrate, there was an arm wrestling between the population who could not stand it anymore and suffocated and the political power. And that, in all the cities of China. At that time, you couldn't see further than a meter. In Harbin (northeast of the country), cars that ran red lights were not ticketed because in fact they could not see the color of the lights! (Bastianelli, 2021b)

In 2018, Bastianelli organized an event that brought together several well-known personalities and a dozen bloggers. All the speeches were filmed and posted on social networks:

> It immediately went viral. Without any publicity, the event generated more than 4.2 million views. This gives you an indication of the fact that there is a youth, a chosen population that is totally open and wants to participate in many things...Because, first of all, they are worried about their health, and that we don't talk about it enough. There is air pollution, which is visible, which is now measured and more or less controlled, but this phenomenon remains very anxiety-provoking. But you have the invisible pollution of the water and land...what they drink and what they eat. And that is a major concern. Everything that has to do with health, with the body, worries them. That's why, when you offer them opportunities to understand and learn about the innovations that are going on, they mobilize immediately. (Bastianelli, 2021b)

Beijing wants to make it rain and make the sun shine

In December 2020, the Chinese government announced the launch of an extraordinary project aimed at controlling the elements to counter global warming and desertification[3] through the deployment of a weather-modification program over half of its territory. In a statement, Beijing said it plans to deploy a massive cloud-seeding program, previously used in a very targeted way to control the weather, over half of its territory by 2025. This would mean making rain fall on command over an area of 5.5 million square kilometers, more than half the size of the country (and 1.5 times the size of India). And all this without considering too much the repercussions that such a project could have on neighboring countries. Indeed, forcing it to rain in one place obviously leads to less rain elsewhere. The first "weather modification" experiments were carried out by the Chinese Communist Party in the 1960s. This involved seeding clouds with high humidity with small amounts of silver iodide (using aircraft or anti-aircraft guns), causing the water particles to condense and eventually cause precipitation. However, it was only in the summer of 2008 that the world discovered China's progress in this area. It fired hundreds of shells loaded with silver iodide to make it rain ahead of the opening ceremony of the Olympic Games and ensure dry weather for the events. Since then, many big events have been held under a radiant sun, ordered beforehand by the Chinese government. Cloud seeding is also regularly used to counter drought or hail. The first application of this technique was carried out in 1958 in Jilin Province, in the north of the country, which had just experienced its worst drought period in 60 years. According to the official New China News Agency, the country invested more than $1.34 billion in various weather-modification programs between 2012 and 2017, which resulted in an additional 233.5 billion cubic meters of rainfall, or three times the capacity of Qinghai Lake, China's largest inland saltwater lake (Mu, 2017). In 2017, the country made a new investment of $168 million to fund a program that is supposed to allow the deployment of aircraft, rocket launchers and numerical control devices to intervene meteorologically on 10% of China's territory (Anglade, 2020). We should add here that in Europe, the use of silver iodide by farmers dates back to the 1960s. The problem is therefore the extent of its use rather than its principle.

China: The world's top consumer and importer of raw materials

China is by far the world's largest consumer and importer of raw materials. It is also a very thirsty consumer of energy. It has become the world's largest oil-importing country, at an average total of 423 million tons per year, taking the title from the United

States in 2017. Imports accounted for 72% of total consumption in 2019, the highest rate on record. Pipeline imports from Russia and Central Asia amounted to more than 840,000 barrels per day in March 2020, which at that rate put it at just under 10% of total annual imports. While China remains highly dependent on coal, the share of oil in China's energy mix has been growing. Renewables and natural gas are expected to eventually expand their shares, but the growth in oil consumption will still be significant in the coming years. If supply struggles to keep up with this increase in demand, China's oil consumption could therefore lead to higher oil prices and fuel oil prices.

The Chinese economy's dependence on foreign countries for raw materials (iron, copper, zinc, aluminum, coal, rare earths) continues to grow. China is courting all suppliers to satisfy its voracious appetite. Both the enemies of the United States (Iran, Russia, Sudan) as well as its closest allies (Saudi Arabia, the United Arab Emirates, Australia, Brazil), not to mention many African countries, are all ready to meet its immense needs. In 2019, the last year before the Covid-19 pandemic upended the global economy, China paid $305.4 billion to import semiconductors, $238.7 billion for oil and oil products, $95.9 billion for iron ore, $45.3 billion for computer accessories and $41.1 billion for unwrought gold (World Bank, n.d.). With an annual total spend of $1.61 trillion, China is the world's second-largest importer after the United States (Commodity.com, n.d.).

China is also a large consumer of gas, which it mainly imports from its neighbor Russia. On December 2, 2019, Beijing and Moscow inaugurated the Power of Siberia gas pipeline with great fanfare. It will eventually stretch some 3000 kilometers from eastern Siberia to China's northeastern provinces. The new pipeline will be able to export up to 38 billion cubic meters of Russian gas per year to China when it reaches full capacity in 2025. The contract, signed for 30 years, is worth $400 billion. It is the biggest ever won by Gazprom, the company close to the Kremlin that has a monopoly on gas exports by pipeline from Russia. For China, it is a crucial piece of infrastructure that will meet the growing demand for gas, a source of energy pushed by Beijing for heating and industry to replace the more polluting coal. Demand has already tripled in less than ten years, but gas still accounts for only 8% of the country's energy consumption, compared with an average of 23% worldwide. The potential is therefore enormous. China produces its own gas, but not enough: imports account for more than 40% of its needs, a proportion that continues to grow (Collen, 2019). China is already connected by pipeline to Turkmenistan, Kazakhstan and Myanmar (Burma). It also imports gas in liquefied form (LNG) on a massive scale from Australia, Indonesia and Qatar. As for coal, which is essential to power its 1400 active thermal power plants, China produced 3.7 billion tons and imported 300 million tons in 2019, mainly from Australia but also from Colombia, South Africa and Indonesia (Tan, 2021).

Another largely unknown aspect of the predatory nature of China's economic hypergrowth is sand consumption. The construction sector is the main cause of sand-resource depletion. Every year, 40 billion tons of sand are extracted from the seabed, mines, rivers and lakes to feed the construction industry. Concrete is made up of two-thirds sand, and unfortunately our sand resources are not infinite. The consequences of the massive extraction of sand from the seabed are numerous. When it is extracted from offshore, beach sand fills the void. Little by little, it slides towards the seabed, and the beach finally disappears. Coastal sand also constitutes a natural barrier against the elements. Finally, massive extraction puts many underwater species in danger. In short, the environmental consequences of our overconsumption of sand are disastrous (Combe, 2018). China alone accounts for 57% of the world's consumption of sand, mostly to manufacture the large amount of concrete used in the frenzy of residential construction over the past two decades. So much so that over two years (2016–2017), China consumed as much sand as the United States did in a hundred years (1901–2000)! Over the past 30 years, the global demand for sand has increased by 360% and this momentum is expected to continue, mainly due to China's further rapid urbanization. China's urbanization rate is expected to reach 65% by 2030 with nearly 1 billion people living in cities. The construction sector has boomed along with urbanization. Construction volume rose from 125 million square meters built in 1980 to 230 million in 1990, 700 million in 2000, and a staggering peak of 1.8 billion square meters built in 2012! The accelerated development of sprawling cities such as Shanghai, Shenzhen and Chongqing, mega-projects such as the Three Gorges Dam and the hundreds of thousands of kilometers of roads and highways built in China over the past 20 years: all these need gigantic quantities of sand for concrete.

According to figures from the United States Geological Survey, China produced 2400 million tons of cement in 2017, far more than the entire rest of the world (Boittiaux, 2018). Most of the sand used in China is extracted locally.[4] Imports are mainly from Southeast Asia, where it is mostly extracted from rivers and streams, with serious environmental consequences. Nevertheless, some Asian countries (Cambodia, Myanmar, Bangladesh, Sri Lanka, the Philippines) have turned it into an export industry. This choice has serious consequences for their inhabitants and their ecosystems. According to researchers who monitor the Mekong, the crisis that has been brewing on the river for years has turned into an imminent threat. They blame two human-related phenomena: sand mining and the construction of new dams upstream in Laos and China, which are changing the river's flow, sediment content and even its color. "Mining boats are everywhere in the delta. Sand is in brisk demand for the concrete needed to build Ho Chi Minh City's high rises and for land reclamation across the sea in

Singapore," wrote *Financial Times* journalist John Reed (2020). This low-cost sand mining obscures the increasingly high price of sand, which is the subject of an extremely juicy but highly opaque and unregulated trade. "What's at risk is not an untrammeled eco-paradise, but an economically vital, densely populated region that the Vietnamese call their 'rice bowl'. Equivalent in size and population to the Netherlands, the delta is the garden of Ho Chi Minh City and the country's biggest inland fishery—a leading source of shellfish, fish and fruit," Reed wrote. American freelance journalist Vince Beiser (2018), who has made a specialty of investigating this issue, said:

> In towns and villages all along the Mekong River and many other rivers around the country, banks undermined by dredging are collapsing into the water, taking with them farm fields, fish ponds, shops, and homes. In recent years, thousands of acres of rice farms have been lost…Government officials estimate some 500,000 people in the Mekong Delta area alone need to be moved out of such landslide zones.

China is the world's top agricultural importer, with imports rising 13.9% year-on-year in 2020 to $171.9 billion. Feed grains such as soybeans (100.31 million tons, +13.2%) and corn (11.3 million tons, +136%) topped imports (China International Import Expo, 2022). "On corn, we are seeing prices at their highest since 2014; it is China's demand that is upsetting the face of world trade," said Marc Zribi, head of the grains and sugar unit at FranceAgriMer. The principal reason for China's increased imports of cereals, particularly from Europe, "is Trump's trade policy; that's what made China want to diversify its origins," a broker who requested anonymity told *AFP*. The "much faster than expected" rebuilding of the Chinese pig herd, decimated by the African swine-fever epidemic, is another reason (Gubert et al., 2020). Another factor was uncertainty related to the health crisis. "It is clear that for the Chinese government, it was necessary to minimize the risks" of a food shortage, said Sébastien Abis, director of the Demeter agricultural think tank and researcher at the Iris Institute of International and Strategic Relations in Paris. Chinese wheat imports nearly doubled in 2020 to 10.6 million tons (indexmundi, n.d.), sending prices soaring in international markets. Concerns about shortages are all the greater because of the "great famine" of the Maoist era, between 1959 and 1961, that "traumatized the generation that is in power today in China." If China has now become a top producer of many agricultural commodities, it has also become a leading if not the top importer of these same products, and "the 5 to 10% of commodities it lacks very quickly represent significant volumes on the international level," thus shaking up agricultural markets quickly, Abis said. While it is difficult to predict the extent to which China's buying fever will continue, it is a given, according to Abis, that Beijing "will never give in on the issue of its national security and will automatically have to rely on the world market to supplement its domestic production" (Pleinchamp, 2020).

Jean-François Huchet (2016, p. 146) summarizes China's environmental situation as follows:

> China is going through an environmental crisis unprecedented in the history of economic development [worldwide, but] despite the strong political will displayed in recent years, China is still far from implementing a long-term sustainable growth in environmental terms. [It should therefore] continue in the years to come to live in a schizophrenic and precarious situation: it will be both the largest laboratory and investor in the world in green energies, while remaining the country that consumes more coal than the rest of the

planet and which is experiencing very serious degradation in its ecosystem.

For this expert on Chinese environmental issues, President Xi Jinping's announcement that China will become carbon neutral by 2060 is little more than a publicity stunt to present his country in a good light, as the model student that intends to honor its international responsibilities:

The objective of carbon neutrality is really a deadline so far away that it seems to me too easy an objective to announce today, yet we are dealing in China with an economy that still depends heavily on coal, even if China, unlike India, is making great efforts...By 2040 China will still be burning around 4 billion tons of coal per year and, on the other hand, as we know, China is also exporting a lot of technology abroad on the coal-fired power plants that it is building very quickly now. It has acquired such a developed know-how and we can see this in the New Silk Roads projects. Unfortunately, there is still a very large number of coal-fired power plants being built...But even if this objective is achievable, we are very, very, very far from carbon neutrality in 2060. And thirty years is not much time. Given what we know about technologies and given the trajectories. If we look at China's trajectory from 2000 to 2030, there are obviously changes, but they are more inflections than sudden shifts in energy use patterns...If Beijing's objective of reducing greenhouse gases by 65% by 2030 seems achievable, on the other hand, as far as the objective of carbon neutrality is concerned, I am much more skeptical about China's ability to achieve it...It doesn't take much to make these kinds of grand declarations. In any case, in fifty years, we'll all be dead and we won't be around to check. He also has a lot of political ulterior motives behind this statement. (Huchet, 2021)

However, the situation is much more encouraging when it comes to air pollution, an area where the Chinese authorities have made great efforts:

> I think that an effort has really been made [in the face of a situation that was becoming catastrophic]. There is, on this subject, a stronger ecological awareness in all sectors of society, including in the political spheres. I think it is now more accepted in the thinking. This shows that China is now more aware of these issues and it has gone fast, as in everything, it has picked up positive results in a much more compact and much shorter period than what we have experienced [in Western countries, a bit like Japan in the 1970s and 1980s, when it experienced, as in China, a period of hyper-industrialization]. In the space of ten years, there has been, I think, a revolution in the way of thinking. (Huchet, 2021)

Chinese fishing: Organized plunder

The Chinese are big eaters of seafood. Accounting for one-sixth of the world's population, they consume one-third of the catch of the world's fisheries. China's appetite for seafood has become a source of tension as the country's fleet of fishing vessels has moved further from home and they fail to respect sustainable fishing practices. The exact size of the Chinese fishing fleet is unknown, although estimates put the number of vessels with the capacity to fish outside Chinese territorial waters at 17,000, making it the largest in the world (Clover, 2020). Chinese fishing vessels can be found fishing not only all the way across the Pacific off the South American coast, but also in the Atlantic off the coast of Africa, sometimes under bilateral agreements, sometimes not.

An article by Martine Valo (2013) in *Le Monde* provides some indication of the scale of Chinese fishing and underreporting of catches:

The plundering of the seas by Chinese fishing vessels has reached gigantic proportions, according to an international study coordinated by renowned biologist Daniel Pauly of the University of British Columbia, which quantifies for the first time the Chinese stranglehold on a rapidly declining fisheries resource. This research, first published in the specialized journal *Fish and Fisheries* and then reprinted in the scientific journal *Nature* on April 4, 2013, concludes that Chinese fishing vessels siphoned off between 3.4 million and 6.1 million tons of fish per year from their coasts between 2000 and 2011. At the same time, Beijing declared only 368,000 tons of fish on average to the United Nations Food and Agriculture Organization (FAO). Twelve times less than the reality estimated by specialists in fisheries resources. The value of fish landed from abroad by China is estimated at 8.9 billion euros each year.

Many Chinese fishing vessels practice bottom trawling, where the nets are dragged along the seafloor, damaging the natural habitat. This is the case for the several hundred large Chinese trawlers regularly fishing off West Africa in recent years, where they have become the largest fleet. "China has found off the coast of West Africa waters that are very rich in fish and very little surveillance. This has encouraged the proliferation of foreign fishing vessels in this region, where they sometimes operate in a totally illegal manner. Overfishing has therefore quickly become a reality," said Frédéric Le Manach, scientific director of the NGO Bloom, which works for marine conservation (Mateso, 2018).

However, to be fair, China has also developed extensively its aquaculture industry, which now accounts for a considerable part of overall consumption.

Notes

1   According to the Central Tibetan Administration-in-Exile's White Paper on Ecology published in December 2018, Tibet's forested areas dropped from 25.2 million hectares in 1950, when the Chinese army invaded Tibet, to 13.57 million hectares in 1985 due to massive deforestation by the Chinese authorities in Tibet, which was traditionally Asia's great reservoir of primary forests.

2   One can certainly argue that it is not China that is responsible and that it is the Indonesian, Malaysian and Singaporean business groups.

3   This is the case for the Gobi Desert in the north and northwest of China, which is expanding by thousands of square kilometers every year. To try to stop the sandy expanse, the Beijing authorities have also decided to plant the world's largest artificial forest, the Great Green Wall. In fact, the sandy areas that cover 27% of the country are growing rapidly—in 2006 they were gaining ground on arable land at a rate of 260,000 hectares per year (the size of Luxembourg), compared with 155,000 hectares in the 1950s.

4   The weekly magazine *Le Point* devoted an investigation into this matter in its January 28, 2021, issue entitled *La Chine lance la guerre du sable* [China launches a sand war], in which its special envoy in Taiwan, Jérémy André, found that on some days, more than 100 Chinese dredging boats were extracting sand in the Taiwan Strait, a few miles from the island of Matsu, controlled by Taiwan. In 2017, only two incursions of Chinese dredgers had been observed off Matsu, then 71 in 2018 and 600 in 2019. In 2020, 3987 dredge passes were recorded.

Chapter 3

The technologies of the future: China shifts from being the world's workshop to being its laboratory

In just a few decades, China has become one of the world's major centers of gravity, along with the United States, Europe and Japan-Korea, for research into the new technologies that will shape our way of life in the twenty-first century. A review of a new laboratory for tomorrow's world. The current state of innovation and its prospects.

> You can teach a computer to say: "I love you," but you can't teach it to love.
> —Albert Jacquard, geneticist

Made in China 2025: China's high-tech ambitions

The global stakes in terms of technological innovation are considerable. China, which is making enormous investments in this sector, is on the way to taking over the world's leading position from the United States. High technology will be the engine of human progress in this century. Whoever masters it will probably dominate the world tomorrow. This is why China is making colossal efforts to take control of all the key areas of high technology, whether it be aeronautics, the conquest of space, electric and hydrogen-powered vehicles, telecommunications, artificial intelligence, microprocessors, quantum supercomputers, rare-earth elements, robotics, or high-speed trains. If there is an emblem of the merciless industrial war being waged in this field, it is certainly the Chinese giant Huawei, the world's leading telecommunications equipment and smartphone manufacturer, against which the United States is concentrating the bulk of its retaliatory measures, aware as it is of what is being played out on a global scale for the takeover of a vital sector of economic and social life. The Chinese government is not hiding its ambitions. In May 2015, it adopted its "Made in China 2025" plan, which selected ten sectors deemed crucial to the country's future: information technology (IT), robotics, aerospace, advanced ship and rail industries, sustainable vehicles, energy, agricultural equipment, new materials and biomedicine. Xi Jinping himself set the goal for these sectors: to help China become "one of the most innovative countries" by 2030 and "the most innovative country" by 2049, the 100th anniversary of the Chinese Communist Party coming to power. To achieve this, Beijing is working hard. Over the decade ending in 2017, China's R&D (research and development) spending increased by 900%. China's total R&D spending reached 2.214 trillion yuan (about $321.3 billion) in 2019, up 12.5% from 2018, according to a joint report from the State Bureau of Statistics (BES), the Ministry of Science and Technology, and the Ministry of Finance. The figure saw double-digit growth for the fourth consecutive year (*Xinhua*, 2020).

On July 1, 2020, the US Federal Communications Commission (FCC) officially declared Huawei and ZTE, the other major Chinese telecommunications group, a threat to US national security. The FCC believes the two Chinese manufacturers are likely to share sensitive information with the government and the Chinese military. This was the first time that an official US entity agreed with the Trump administration. In addition, the FCC is asking US carriers to dismantle and replace any Huawei or ZTE-supplied network equipment already installed in the United States. "With this decision, we are sending a clear message: the U.S. Government, and this @FCC in particular, cannot and will not allow the Chinese Communist Party to exploit vulnerabilities in U.S. communications networks and compromise our critical communications infrastructure,"

FCC Chairman Ajit Pai tweeted. Since May 2019, Huawei and ZTE have been excluded from the US market. Despite several reprieves, the two firms cannot conduct business with companies located on US soil. Against the backdrop of the trade war, Donald Trump openly accused the two groups of working for the Chinese government and collecting sensitive data for the Chinese secret services. Accusations that have since been taken up by Joe Biden. Recall that a law, enacted in 2017, legally compels companies based in China to collaborate with the country's intelligence services.[1] So far, Huawei and ZTE have strongly denied all accusations of spying. Ren Zhengfei, Huawei's founder and a former Chinese People's Liberation Army (PLA) officer, has sought to reassure clients that Chinese authorities do not interfere with the company's activities. "I love my country; I support the Chinese Communist Party. But I will never do anything to harm any country in the world," he said. According to the Chinese group, Chinese law does not require the manufacturer to spy on foreign countries on behalf of the government. But Ren's assurances have been to no avail. The list of nations that have blacklisted Huawei has continued to grow. The United Kingdom, Australia, New Zealand, Canada, France, Israel, Poland, the Czech Republic, India, Sweden, Japan, Taiwan and many others have followed suit.[2] On March 12, 2021, the FCC listed Huawei as a national security threat among Chinese telecom equipment companies, dashing hopes of an easing of relations after Joe Biden took office as president. The FCC considers Huawei to pose an "unacceptable risk" to national security, along with other Chinese groups ZTE, Hytera Communications, Hangzhou Hikvision Digital Technology and Dahua Technology.

Why such exclusionary measures? US authorities are convinced that by installing their telecommunications equipment, especially for new 5G networks, Huawei and ZTE would have access through software backdoors to a lot of sensitive information that concerns all parts of society, including government agencies. On the other hand, and even more seriously, having become the absolute master of the control of these networks as well as of "big data," China and its intelligence services would be able to block the entire functioning of a country by cutting off access to telecommunications networks in the event of a serious crisis or open war with Beijing. Not only telecommunications services themselves would be paralyzed, but also air, road, and rail transport, hospitals, a good part of public services, and many other areas of the economic life of a country. Such an event would constitute a direct and immediate threat to the economic and social stability of a country. Nothing less, nothing more. The gravity of the threat explains why so many Western governments have followed the United States and banned the use of Huawei and ZTE network equipment on their soil.

In his book entitled *France-Chine: Les liaisons dangereuses* [France-China: Dangerous liaisons], journalist Antoine Izambard (2019) carried out an in-depth analysis into Huawei's impressive rise to power in Europe, and particularly in France. He highlighted intensive lobbying operations and systematic entry into French power circles and the networks of major universities, and the role of pro-China political figures such as former prime ministers Jean-Pierre Raffarin and Laurent Fabius or politician Jean-Louis Borloo. Izambard also traced Huawei's rise on the world markets thanks to the unconditional and massive support of Chinese banks. For example, between 2005 and 2009, the China Development Bank (CBC) provided Huawei with $30 billion in credit lines to facilitate its expansion around the world. The author also examined the links of some of the group's employees with the Chinese intelligence services. Peeling back the résumés of 25,000 Huawei employees shows "that many employees work for both the telecom giant and the Chinese military or intelligence services," he wrote (p. 40). In June

2019, *Bloomberg* also revealed that several Huawei employees had collaborated with the Chinese military on research projects. "Over the past decade, Huawei workers have teamed with members of various organs of the People's Liberation Army on at least 10 research endeavors spanning artificial intelligence to radio communications," it stated (*Bloomberg*, 2019).

The war for semiconductor global supremacy

Smartphones, autonomous cars, the cloud, artificial intelligence, connected objects, or simply the internet, digital technology and computers. So many objects and industries that define the third industrial revolution that we have been witnessing since the end of the twentieth century and that will continue to shape the coming decades. This new technological revolution originated with the invention of the bipolar transistor on December 23, 1947, by Nobel Prize-winning Americans John Bardeen, William Shockley and Walter Brattain, followed by the field-effect transistor (MOSFET) by Mohamed M. Atalla and Dawon Kahng two years later. A fundamental component of electronics, the transistor is a switch that controls the flow of electric current without the use of mechanical action. It is the transistor that allows the miniaturization of electronics in the form of integrated circuits better known as microchips or computer chips. As for the tremendous acceleration of technological progress that characterizes this third industrial revolution, it is described by Moore's Law. In 1975 the CEO and co-founder of Intel Gordon Moore posited a doubling of the number of transistors packed onto microchips every two years. A prediction that has largely held true. Today, electronic chips are made from semiconductor materials such as silicon. They are smaller than a postage stamp, thinner than a hair, and contain hundreds of millions of transistors. The semiconductor industry is the engine of most technological innovation. It is therefore not unreasonable to call it the most strategic industry in the world.

It has naturally become a key battleground between China, the United States and the island of Taiwan, which is caught between these two giants. The stakes are high. For the United States it is its national security at play, while China, which starts far behind, is concerned about its sovereignty.

When, in 1985, after a brilliant career in the United States, Morris Chang decided to leave everything behind and move to the small island of Taiwan, he could reasonably have been called crazy. An immigrant who left China in 1949 in search of a better future in the United States of America, Chang had succeeded in everything: he went through Harvard and MIT to finally obtain his doctorate in electrical engineering at Stanford, and 25 years later became vice president of Texas Instruments, then one of the most successful semiconductor companies. But the American dream of "one house, two cars, three dogs" was not enough for him. He dreamed of greatness. At that time, the semiconductor industry was dominated by a few big names: Intel and Texas Instruments in the United States, Samsung in Korea, Toshiba and NEC in Japan. They all used a "vertical integration" model: they controlled all stages, from design to manufacturing of electronic chips. Morris Chang saw an opportunity. He created Taiwan Semiconductor Manufacturing Company (TSMC) with the idea of setting up a chip-manufacturing plant (also called a foundry) that he would put at the service of customers who would take charge of the design of their integrated circuits. He had the intuition that the great complexity of chip manufacturing and the vertical-integration model prevented new players from emerging and stifled innovation. His intuition proved to be right: in the years and decades that followed, the vertical model broke down and new players emerged. These so-called 'fabless' players focus on research and development of new semiconductor designs without worrying about manufacturing, which is handled by TSMC. This is how Apple, Broadcom, AMD, Nvidia, Qualcomm (to name only the American ones) emerged and prospered. They design chips with various functions, and TSMC manufactures them and innovates by doing so. In 2004, TSMC developed a new lithography technique called immersion. It was so revolutionary that the giants of lithography, Japan's Canon and Nikon, refused to try it. TSMC was mocked. Only the small Dutch company ASML agreed to help the Taiwanese. Immersion proved to be a major technological breakthrough that propelled ASML to the top of lithography machine manufacturers, overturning the Japanese hegemony and giving TSMC a crucial technological advance.

Today, TSMC controls nearly a third of the global semiconductor-manufacturing market. Moreover, thanks to its mastery of 5-nanometer and soon 3-nanometer lithography, the company is between five and ten years ahead of its biggest competitors, such as Intel and Samsung, which are still stuck at the 7-nanometer technology "node." These technological nodes, characterized by their nanometric scale, represent the miniaturization capacity of a foundry. A nanometer (nm) is equal to one-billionth of a meter, and a microprocessor etched at 7 nanometers contains billions of transistors. The smaller a microprocessor is, the less energy it consumes and the less heat it generates, two essential qualities for any integrated circuit. TSMC's position as leader is a major asset for Taiwan, which is engaged in real semiconductor diplomacy to avoid getting caught up in the troubled waters of the new Sino-American economic war.

Indeed, when in 2020 the Trump administration added Huawei and then SMIC to the "Entity List," America was firing upon Chinese semiconductors. Huawei, then the world's largest smartphone manufacturer, is one of the main consumers of Qualcomm chips made at TSMC. As for Semiconductor Manufacturing International Corporation, or simply SMIC, it is the spearhead of chip manufacturing in mainland China.

Founded in 2000, SMIC's ambition is to be on par with TSMC and its sister companies. When a company is added to the Entity List, it must apply for a license from the US Department of Commerce to import and use products containing 25% or more US technology. In a globalized economy with multinational supply chains, such a restriction is highly disabling for SMIC, which is deprived of components, chemicals and tools essential to the design and manufacture of microchips. In an official statement, SMIC warned that its addition to the Entity List "will have significant negative impacts on research and development of advanced processes smaller than 10 nanometre [based] upon our initial assessment" (Pan, 2020). Similarly, the United States has put strong pressure on the Netherlands to block the delivery of EUV (extreme ultraviolet) lithography machines, critical to the development of sub-10-nm solutions and whose sole supplier is the Dutch company ASML (Alper et al., 2020). These geo-economic maneuvers undertaken by the Trump administration and continued by the Biden administration are part of a more global strategy of repatriating strategic supply chains, including semiconductors, to the United States, as well as slowing down China's technological development. Thus, in the second month of his presidency, Joe Biden (2021b) signed an executive order asking the Department of Commerce to issue a report on the vulnerabilities of supply chains, particularly semiconductors and rare earths, "so that our supply chains can't be used against us as leverage." In its final report submitted to the US Congress in March 2021, the National Security Commission on Artificial Intelligence chaired by Eric Schmidt, the former head of Google, recommended various regulatory actions to the Biden administration to keep Chinese semiconductors two generations behind the United States. Among the recommendations were also measures to encourage chip manufacturing on American soil after decades of outsourcing to Korea or Taiwan.

The corollary of this new American strategy is the need for China to achieve its own technological sovereignty. American efforts to contain Chinese innovation have made Beijing more determined than ever to accelerate its efforts to achieve self-sufficiency. In this logic of *decoupling* the two economies, the moves by Washington and Beijing in the semiconductor sector are tantamount to signing a divorce agreement.

China suffers from a significant imbalance between its domestic demand for microchips and its domestic manufacturing capacity. According to a report by the specialized firm IC Insights (2021), in 2020 only 5.9% of Chinese demand for microchips was manufactured by Chinese companies. If we add to this the microchips manufactured on Chinese territory by foreign companies, the proportion increases to 15.9%. This deficit highlights China's heavy reliance on imported microchips and helps us understand the significant efforts Beijing is making to close the gap. In a communiqué from the fifth plenary of the 19th Central Committee of the Chinese Communist Party held in October 2020, Beijing announced that by 2035 the Chinese economy will have made major advances in strategic technology sectors, including semiconductors. Already in 2015, as part of its ten-year Made in China 2025 reform, Beijing announced its intention to increase the share of domestic semiconductor manufacturing to 40% by 2020 and 70% by 2025. Although far from the mark in terms of results, the ambition for a major national development is there.

In 1958, Mao Zedong implemented a campaign to restructure agriculture that he called the Great Leap Forward. He mobilized the state apparatus and propaganda and forced the people to follow him in this reform. Unrealistic, the reform was such a fiasco that it led to the *great famine* that claimed the lives of tens of millions of Chinese. Thirty years later, Deng Xiaoping undertook the economic opening of China. He liberalized foreign trade, reformed state-owned enterprises and stimulated agriculture. Through his reforms, he lifted 200 million Chinese above the poverty line. This was an undeniable success. In its implementation of major national reforms, the Chinese Communist Party is capable of the best and the worst. What will happen to the semiconductor industry?

To help the nation achieve its goals, an investment fund called the China Integrated Circuit Industry Investment Fund was established in 2014 to provide $150 billion in funding to the sector over ten years. Douglas Fuller (2021), professor of political science at City University of Hong Kong and an expert on innovation policy issues in China, said "no government has invested so much money in the sector." This "mega project," as he described it, has triggered a nationwide silicon rush. But the results may disappoint, he warned: "There was a lot of waste in the semiconductor industry in China, especially on the manufacturing side. Every local government hoped to have a manufacturing plant in its township." Indeed, the national drive is not without its failures. One example is the misadventure involving HSMC, which, after receiving nearly $20 billion in investment between 2018 and 2019, eventually had to be put under state supervision due to payment defaults. In the summer of 2020, its CEO Chiang Shang-yi, poached from TSMC to take over the struggling company, threw in the towel and described his time at HSMC as a "nightmare" (Leng, 2020). Mansun Chan (2021), director of research at the prestigious Hong Kong University of Science and Technology, believes part of the problem is how the drive has been managed:

China is investing a lot of money, but so far we don't see major progress. The problem is the bureaucrats who never stay in their positions of responsibility very long. Their objective is not to build a new national industry but to put forward their personal contribution. They find a piece of land, put up a nice building, add a sign and take a picture. It's all about showcasing themselves.

In the end, nearly a dozen large-scale projects, heavily sponsored by the Chinese state, ended in failure, prompting the National Development and Reform Commission to tighten controls on new projects in what it called a "chaotic" industry (Lee, 2020). According to Mansun Chan (2021), money alone will not be enough:

> In this sector, it takes time, you have to accumulate the necessary experience. This is a process that the United States, Japan and Korea have already done and that China will have to catch up with. The Chinese government's approach is to set a course, a supposedly forward-looking vision. But they don't define a roadmap. Many times the goals are unattainable.

The road to self-sufficiency is long and full of potholes.

At the crossroads is SMIC. As the centerpiece of China's foundries, the company must decide its future. At the top of the company, several managers are jockeying for position and imposing their vision. After his misadventure at HSMC, Chiang Shang-yi joined SMIC at the end of 2020 as vice president. This appointment was not to the liking of Liang Mong-song, co-CEO of SMIC, who resigned. This game of musical chairs reflects a battle of ideas where the future of the company is at stake. The loser, Liang Mong-song, embodied a technophile management and wanted to invest more in research and development to try to produce 10 nm chips and then 7 nm chips. The winner, Chiang Shang-yi, wanted to focus on developing less technologically advanced but more commercially viable products (Cheng, 2020). Mansun Chan is not surprised by this strategic choice. As the director of his university's nanotechnology manufacturing laboratory, he knows the importance of production-line efficiency. Even if SMIC has the capacity to manufacture 14 nm chips, the yield is low with a high scrap rate that does not allow for generating considerable revenue: "Improving the yield of a 14 nm production line is not an easy task! It takes years of feedback and learning," Chan said (2021). The SMIC case is certainly a good indicator of what lies ahead for China in this highly competitive semiconductor-manufacturing sector. Both Fuller and Chan believe that China, handicapped by US restrictions on the acquisition of EUV lithography machines and other equipment, will certainly miss its production targets and find itself years if not decades away from truly mastering the technology nodes below 14 nm. The country will likely focus on less cutting-edge technologies and gradually increase its market share there.

Several reports from the consulting firm BCG have recently looked at the thorny issue of the cost of decoupling the US and Chinese economies. Their conclusions are edifying. The firm estimates that American companies have $400 billion in exposure to the Chinese market. Although this represents only 5% of their global revenues, the loss of these revenues would translate into a loss of nearly 15% of their market capitalization, i.e. $2.5 trillion! This is a big bill. In comparison, the cost would be three to four times less for Chinese companies (Varadarajan et al., 2020). In a case study of the repatriation of semiconductor foundries, the firm estimates the operating cost of an American foundry to be around 30% higher than a Taiwanese or Korean foundry and between 37 and 50% higher than a Chinese foundry. A difference that makes all the difference when you know that the initial investment and operating cost over ten years for a modern foundry can climb to $40 billion (Varas et al., 2020). If semiconductors do in fact represent the divorce agreement between China and the United States, it will be the most expensive divorce settlement in history, especially for the Americans!

Douglas Fuller describes a more realistic scenario. According to him, the proportion of microchips that is truly strategic for American national security represents only a tiny portion of world production. We can cite the example of the chips used in Tomahawk missiles or in the F-35 fighter planes, which are currently manufactured by TSMC. For Fuller, and in view of the prohibitive costs involved, it is in the interest of the Americans to identify the truly strategic technologies and repatriate only these, leaving the rest of the market largely unchanged. This scenario seems to be borne out by a recent announcement by TSMC that it is investing $12 billion in the construction of a new state-of-the-art foundry in the US state of Arizona (*Reuters*, 2020). When asked about the reasons for this decision, Mansun Chan didn't equivocate: "Obviously for military reasons! The Americans cannot continue to manufacture their military equipment abroad! I think China will do the same with SMIC. It is certain that China will not ask Taiwan to manufacture its military chips." A decoupling, yes, but targeted on the most crucial technologies.

Caught between the Americans and Asians and starved by the shortage of chips that has affected the sector since the start of the Covid-19 pandemic, the European Union is becoming aware of the stakes. "Without an autonomous European capacity in microelectronics, there can be no European digital sovereignty," said European Industry Commissioner Thierry Breton. Europe still holds 10% of the global semiconductor market and aims to double its market share by 2030. Currently, the American company GlobalFoundries, which operates a factory in Germany, is the main manufacturer of integrated circuits in Europe and typically produces 28 nm chips. According to *Bloomberg*'s sources, however, the Europeans have called on TSMC and Samsung to help them develop production capacities below 10 nm (Drozdiak et al., 2021). This is a technological challenge that will be very difficult to meet for years to come. Of the 27 EU member states, 19 have already declared their interest in the project and their willingness to participate in its financing. The European Commission has announced an initial public-private investment of up to 30 billion euros. This is more than TSMC's budget of 21 billion euros for the year 2021.

Finally, the race for silicon supremacy is above all a race to control the supply chain. Controlling the supply chain does not necessarily mean repatriating all of it. Ensuring that the supply chain is in the hands of allies is a sufficient guarantee of security, as it has proven itself for decades. Today, the supply chain is shared between the United States, Europe, Japan, South Korea and Taiwan—an allied bloc. China, on the other hand, seems to be isolated.

In light of the semiconductor race, how can we not wonder about the relationship between China and Taiwan and the potential for military conflict? On January 2, 2019, Xi Jinping proclaimed into the microphones lined up in front of him: "Taiwan must and will be reunited with China." Xi proposed to Taiwan a "one country, two systems" model based on Hong Kong's reunification, but did not rule out the use of force if necessary. Since then, the repression of the huge popular demonstrations in Hong Kong in 2019, the introduction of the national security law by force in 2020, and finally the arrest of the Hong Kong democrats in 2021 have definitively buried the "one country, two systems" model. With the only model of peaceful integration "officially dead" according to former Taiwanese president Ma Ying-jeou (Cheng, 2021), and in view of Taiwan's growing importance in the strategic semiconductor sector, tensions have risen. But on the other side of the Pacific, the United States is keeping an eye on things. With this new lens on the semiconductor industry, we can better understand some of the reasons why the United States is defending TSMC's home.

"TSMC is certainly one of the reasons why the US is defending Taiwan. Imagine the loss to the Western world if the company fell to the Chinese!" said Mansun Chan (2021). By inviting the Taiwanese ambassador to the inauguration ceremony for the first time in history, President Biden reaffirmed his desire to strengthen ties with Taiwan. In this context, it is unlikely that China will risk a military attack against the island. For Douglas Fuller (2021), an attack is even less likely because there are more optimal solutions to achieve its ends. He points to a study by Linda Jakobson, a writer and founder of China Matters, an Australian think tank that specializes in studying China and advising lawmakers. According to Jakobson (2021), China will use "'all means short of war' to force the Taiwanese leadership to start negotiating...These range from economic pressure or an embargo, via intimidation, cyberattacks, and covert actions and subversion, to assassination and the limited use of military force..." China did not wait for Jakobson's analysis to begin its offensive against TSMC: between 2019 and 2020, nearly 100 TSMC engineers were poached to join the ranks of Chinese companies (Borak, 2021). SMIC's co-CEO Liang Mong-song, as well as its vice president Chiang Shang-yi, are also Taiwanese former senior managers at TSMC. The battle has only just begun.

The colonization of space: China's new frontier

The conquest of space is another area of excellence where China is working hard to catch up with the United States and to demonstrate to the world the know-how of its best engineers and technicians, Europe and Russia having already been long overtaken. In November and December 2020, the Chinese space industry achieved a feat hailed worldwide with the return to Earth of a capsule containing 1.7 kg of lunar soil samples after an epic three-week mission. The Chang'e-5 mission (named after the goddess of the moon in Chinese mythology) went off without a hitch. It included the landing of a rover (near the

Rümker Mountains and the Ocean of Storms, an area chosen because it is one of the most recent on a geological scale, i.e. three billion years), the drilling of the lunar soil by an articulated arm with a drill capable of taking samples up to 2 meters deep, the module's take-off from the moon's surface, then the rendezvous with an orbiter, this last stage being the most risky technologically of the whole mission. After the United States and Russia, China has become the third country to achieve such a feat. This mission is one of the greatest achievements of the Chinese space industry in the field of robotic exploration. Beyond the technical feat and the firsts achieved during this mission (relaunch from the moon, rendezvous and transfer to lunar orbit), the scientific interest is very great. The chemical composition of the samples brought back to Earth will reinforce the knowledge we have of the moon's history, or even improve it. But above all, the samples will provide information on concentration levels of rare earths on the moon, possibly turning it into a lunar El Dorado. The speed and apparent ease with which China has recovered these lunar samples and brought them back to Earth is very impressive. They show the level of maturity reached in the mastery of robotic techniques and Chinese space technologies. Even more surprising is the fact that those in charge of the mission announced in advance the dates and times of each phase of the mission—something never seen on previous missions! It also broadcast them live, displaying a level of confidence rarely revealed to the public. After this historic lunar mission, "today, the only credible 'competitor' to this 'Chinese lunar activism' is of course the United States, which already federates several Western nations in the framework of the Artemis program," said Philippe Coué (2021), an expert on the Chinese space program, author of several books on the subject and member of the International Academy of Astronautics. "Not since Luna-24 (USSR) in 1976 has such a complex mission been carried out," he said.

Chang'e-5 was launched by a Long March 5 rocket, or CZ-5, a heavy launcher capable of placing a payload of 25 tons in low orbit and 13 tons in geostationary transfer orbit. For the next ten years, the CZ-5 will be the spearhead of Chinese space transportation. With it, China will be able to put into low earth orbit heavy satellites such as the modules of the future CSS/Tiangong-3 orbital station, which it will begin to assemble in 2021, and the Xuntian telescope, the "Chinese Hubble." "It will also be the launcher par excellence for planetary exploration, which promises to be ambitious with several targeted destinations in the Solar System," noted Coué (2021). The next mission, Chang'e-6, will target a landing site, certainly difficult to access, located either on the far side of the moon or at the South Pole, and, if so, it will be with a view to a future Chinese manned mission. Its launch is planned for 2024, or even 2023 (*Futura Sciences*, 2020). China's plan is to soon install a permanent manned lunar station. Just five days after the return to Earth of the lunar capsule in the steppes of Inner Mongolia, China launched into space the first model of its new Long March 8, an ultra-modern rocket whose first stage and boosters will soon be reusable to reduce costs. The goal is to carry out about 20 launches of the Long March 8 per year in a simplified mode. The program's commander-in-chief, Xiao Yun, explained that China wants to simplify and speed up its launch capability so that a team of some three dozen people could prepare a launch within seven to ten days.

The Long March 8 is intended to compete in the global satellite-launch market with the Ariane 6, the European Space Agency's new medium-to-heavy-payload launcher to replace its Ariane 5 heavy rocket as soon as 2022. The other competitor to the Long March 8 will be the US Vega rocket. In 2019, China became the world's leading country for the number of satellite launches, with 34 launches (32 successful), ahead of the United States (27).

On January 3, 2019, China had already become the first country in the world to land on the far side of the moon, ten years after the first spacewalk of a taikonaut.

Another major achievement: on July 23, 2020, China successfully launched a probe to Mars. Tianwen-1 (which translates as Questions to Heaven) arrived in Mars orbit in February 2021. That same month, NASA demonstrated its perfect mastery of the high technologies used in the race to the stars with the successful landing of its probe and rover Perseverance on the surface of Mars.

Just several weeks after the landing of Perseverance, China did the same. On May 15, 2021, it put down its own rover, Zhu Rong, the first non-American robot to land on Mars. The achievement is a technological feat that demonstrates that, little by little, China is catching up with the United States. The mission took seven months to travel 319 million kilometers to reach Mars. Before starting its descent to the surface, the Chinese probe spent three months in orbit taking high-resolution photos to determine precisely the least risky place to land.

Tianwen-1, which carried the rover, then went through the "nine minutes of terror" during which no communication with Earth was possible as it descended through the Martian atmosphere and when the chances of a catastrophic failure were high. But after these nine minutes, the Chinese scientists could shout for joy: Tianwen-1 had landed undamaged on the Utopia Plain. The Zhu Rong rover, which bears the name of the mythical Chinese goddess of fire and war, could start its three-month mission.

It then took 17 minutes for Zhu Rong to deploy its solar panels and send a first signal towards Earth. The radio messages take almost 18 minutes to reach the Earth. As soon as the first message was received from Zhu Rong, Chinese President Xi Jinping immediately wrote to congratulate the engineers and scientists of the Chinese National Space Administration (CNSA).

The successful landing represents "an incredible achievement," he said. "You have been brave enough to rise to the challenge and pursue excellence, placing our country at the forefront of the exploration of the planets."

For the Chinese people, this epic journey to Mars will undoubtedly be a source of immense pride, which will further sharpen the nationalist sentiment which the Sino-American rivalry has already been stoking. And this is what it is all about. For this rivalry, present in the economic, scientific, technological and military theaters, is now being teleported to Mars. The race to the stars has only just begun.

If Zhu Rong succeeds in collecting Martian soil samples as planned and sending them back to Earth, China will become the second country to accomplish this feat after the United States. The Soviet Union succeeded in landing its Mars 3 rover on the Red Planet in 1971, but it stopped sending signals to Earth shortly afterwards. As for the European Union, it is still far from succeeding. But it is the Soviets who have paid the highest price: 19 attempts to reach Mars, but without ever having a mission that succeeded in fulfilling all its initial objectives. Vladimir Putin's Russia hasn't dared to try.

The Perseverance mission was not the first time the United States had been to Mars: previously there was Curiosity and, in total, no fewer than ten successful expeditions. China, however, has been making rapid progress for years in its conquest of space. Its Jade Rabbit rover landed on the moon in 2013. But the technical difficulties were much less than for Zhu Rong, due to a much shorter distance that made communications with Earth easier and the lack of atmosphere. Entry through an atmosphere exposes a lander to high temperatures and violent shocks, increasing the chances of damage (Zheng, W. et al., 2021).

But compared to Perseverance, Zhu Rong is more modest. It weighs only 240 kg compared with more than 1 ton for Perseverance. It will not try to produce oxygen. No helicopter like Ingenuity will rise into the air. And so, of course, the curious public on Earth will never be able to hear the sounds made by the Martian winds.

The United States and China have become fierce competitors in the field of high technology and are now engaged in a similar rivalry in space, even if the means at Beijing's disposal are not the same. The OECD estimates China's space budget at more than $8.4 billion, compared to the US budget of $47.17 billion.

The United States was successful in space long before China. How can we not marvel at the extraordinary epic of NASA's twin probes, Voyager 1 and Voyager 2, launched on September 5, 1977? After flying past Jupiter, Saturn, Uranus and Neptune and leaving the solar system, they have now reached interstellar space, continuing to transmit valuable scientific data to this day.

Since the Bush administration arrived in power in 2001, the United States has made new efforts to make space a place of American domination. Space has become a major element of US national security and supremacy, both military and technological. But today, China is not to be outdone. It has proclaimed its intention to become the top space power in the world by 2030. Jonathan McDowell, an astronomer at the Harvard-Smithsonian Center for Astrophysics in the United States, calls Tianwen-1 a milestone for the Chinese as it is the first time they have ventured deep into the solar system. Their success demonstrates the rapid progress that has been made in just a few short years, whereas it took decades of effort for the United States. But this achievement leaves me with mixed feelings. If the United States and China had made common cause in the exploration of planets, much more could have been accomplished.

Supercomputers: China on the front line

Another spectacular advance by China in the competition with the United States in the field of advanced technologies:

on December 3, 2020, researchers from the Hefei University of Technology (East) announced that they had carried out a calculation almost impossible to perform on a conventional supercomputer. The operation was completed in three minutes by their quantum computer Jiuzhang, while the time it would have taken for one of the most powerful traditional supercomputers in the world was…2.5 billion years. To carry out their experiment, the Chinese scientists developed a highly complex optical device: a table of 3 square meters, equipped with 300 beam splitters and 75 mirrors. Powered by photon generators (which must be cooled to about -270°C), the system observes the trajectory and quantum state of the particles to predict their behavior. This photonic quantum computer, which exploits particles of light, or photons, performed a calculation that no conventional computer can do, according to Chinese researchers. This milestone, known as quantum supremacy, has only been achieved once before, in 2019, by Google's Sycamore quantum computer, which had previously been the fastest in the world. Google's computer, however, is based on superconducting materials, which conduct energy without resistance. While faster, Jiuzhang (named after *Jiuzhang suanshu* or the *Nine Chapters on the Art of Calculation*, a Chinese work on mathematics from 200 BC) has a major drawback. Its complex network of optical devices that carry photons around was designed to solve a specific mathematical problem and it cannot be reprogrammed to perform different calculations. The researchers are therefore working on a new, programmable version of their machine, similar to one developed by the Canadian company Xanadu (Lunil, 2020).

Nuclear fusion: The holy grail of clean energy
China has also achieved many successes in the very closed circle of countries engaged in research on nuclear fusion. This is a technology under development not to be confused with nuclear

fission, the method used in our nuclear power plants. Nuclear fusion is considered the holy grail of renewable energies since it produces neither waste nor greenhouse gases. Producing energy by bringing atomic nuclei closer together—as the sun naturally does—is done without producing greenhouse gas emissions or radioactive waste, and there are fewer risks of accidents. China's most efficient experimental tokamak nuclear fusion reactor, the HL-2M Tokamak, became operational in December 2020. It is affectionately known as the "artificial sun." Eventually, its magnetic confinement chamber should generate a phenomenal heat of over 200 million degrees Celsius. That is more than ten times the temperature at the core of our star. This artificial sun is expected to provide useful data to the teams developing the ITER project, a much larger international nuclear fusion reactor based in southern France. Launched in 2006, ITER brings together 35 countries, including EU nations, China, Russia and the United States, and is expected to be completed by the end of 2025—more than five years late and at a total estimated cost of nearly 20 billion euros or more than three times the original budget. But the project's director recently cast doubt on this target, warning of "years" of further delay (*AFP*, 2023). China had already achieved a world first in this field in November 2018 by maintaining for more than 100 seconds the conditions necessary for nuclear fusion, in its experimental reactor installed in Hefei (Anhui, eastern China). In 2017, the Chinese device had already broken the world record for maintaining the conditions necessary for the fusion of atomic nuclei. Then, in November 2019, it shattered its own record by reaching a temperature of 100 million degrees, which is six times the heat produced in the core of the sun. "We are hoping to expand international cooperation through this device...and make Chinese contributions to mankind's future use of nuclear fusion," said Song Yuntao, one of the top officials involved with the experimental reactor project (Wang, K., 2019).

However, China is no longer alone in the race for records in this discipline. At the end of 2020, a new significant advance was achieved in South Korea. At the end of November, the KSTAR (Korea Superconducting Tokamak Advanced Research) device succeeded in generating and maintaining plasma at 100 million degrees for 20 seconds. Never before had a nuclear fusion reaction managed to last so long at this temperature level (Lausson, 2020).

But as important as these records were, they still failed to generate net energy. They had all consumed more energy to produce the high temperatures than the energy generated by the reactions. It was US scientists who crossed this hurdle, called *ignition*, when researchers at the Livermore National Laboratory in California in December 2022 got back 1.5 times as much energy as they had put in, using a different type of reactor. Instead of a tokamak, which uses magnets to create super-hot plasma, the US scientists used lasers to force the fusion of heavy forms of hydrogen contained in a small pellet. "This is such a wonderful example of a possibility realized, a scientific milestone achieved, and a road ahead to the possibilities for clean energy," White House science adviser Arati Prabhakar said at a Washington news conference to announce the breakthrough. Much work remains ahead, however, to get this method to a point where it becomes a commercially viable method to generate power (Chang, 2022).

China dominates the critical rare-earths sector. These strategically important metals are made up of 17 elements that have become very important with the emergence of new technologies in sectors as innovative as magnets, hybrid motors, communication technologies, plasma and LCD screens, satellites, guidance and telecommunication systems, missile defense systems, aerospace and, more generally, all dual technologies (for civilian and military use). The People's Republic of China (PRC) has gradually acquired a monopoly in the exploitation and production of rare earths. Although its territory contains only 50% of the world's known reserves, China currently controls 97.3% of the world's rare-earth production. Reserves also exist in Russia (17% of the world's known reserves), the United States (12%), India (2.8%) and Australia (1.5%), but these are currently exploited on a small scale, or not at all. Indeed, the 'price advantage' held by China has led to the closure of almost all exploitation areas, mainly in developed countries where public opinion is particularly hostile to the most polluting extraction industries. In this context, the PRC started to implement exploitation quotas in 2004, with the aim of guaranteeing the supply of its own companies and — officially — reducing the environmental costs of this production. Since 2006, Chinese exports of rare earths have been cut in half, while world market prices have risen 300% since 2008. In 2010, China's rare-earth production quotas were cut by 72%, and in 2011, while exploration and mining licenses were officially frozen until 2012, Chinese exports were further reduced by 35% (Niquet, 2011).[3]

The United States was once one of the world's largest producers of rare earths. Today, it is nearly 80% dependent on Chinese imports. Beijing has already implicitly threatened to use this political weapon several times. In 2010, China first used the rare-earths weapon against Japan by abruptly suspending its deliveries to obtain the release of a Chinese fishing vessel accused of having collided with two Japanese patrol boats off the Senkaku Islands (also claimed by Beijing as Diaoyu) in the Sea of Japan. Overnight, dozens of Japanese high-tech companies stopped receiving deliveries, causing panic in the archipelago. On May 20, 2019, President Xi Jinping and his vice premier and chief negotiator Liu He made a high-profile visit to the site of JL Mag Rare-Earth, a leading rare-earth producer in central Jiangxi. The message was clear: remind the United States and the world that China controls these strategic metals.[4]

In what is apparently a sign of goodwill towards the United States, China decided in early February 2021 to increase its rare-earth production by more than 25% in the first half of 2021, from 66,000 tons to 84,000 tons. Meanwhile, the United States decided to revive domestic production of rare earths to reduce its dependence on China (*Reuters*, 2020b).

Industrial espionage: China in the dock

China's extraordinary success in the strategic field of high technology raises a key question: how has China been able to compete so quickly with, and even surpass, the United States and Europe in many advanced technologies, when it took them decades of hard work and considerable investment in research and development (R&D)? Many suspect the Chinese did it by industrial espionage—plundering the intellectual property of Western firms.

For American economist and analyst David Goldman (2020), who is known for his column in the *Asia Times Online* published under the pseudonym Spengler, the case is clear:

China has begged, borrowed and stolen the technologies that have propelled its economy to become as large as that of the United States. China pays $36 billion a year in royalties for its use of intellectual property, but the bill should be much higher. Much of it is in fact simply stolen.

In his February 2019 State of the Union address, then President Donald Trump dotted the I's in his intended economic and trade war with China by saying: "We are now making it clear to China that after years of targeting our industries and stealing our intellectual property, the theft of American jobs and wealth has come to an end."

In July 2020, Federal Bureau of Investigation (FBI) Director Christopher Wray reported a "1,300 percent increase in economic espionage cases involving China" over the previous ten years. The FBI opened a new counterintelligence investigation related to China "every ten hours," according to Wray, who sees in these campaigns coordinated by the Chinese Communist Party "the greatest long-term threat" to the security of the United States. In July 2019, speaking before the US Senate Judiciary Committee, Wray said there were more than a thousand open investigations into cases of suspected theft of intellectual property by Chinese companies, institutions and universities. "I would say that there is no country that poses a more severe counterintelligence threat to this country right now than China," he told lawmakers. China, through its Foreign Ministry spokespersons, categorically and systematically denies all these accusations. The US Attorney General Bill Barr targeted the big names of Hollywood and Silicon Valley, such as Disney, Google, Microsoft, Apple and Yahoo, as being "too quick to collaborate with the Chinese Communist Party" for fear of losing access to the vast market of the Asian giant. The US administration estimates the damage caused by intellectual property theft at $1.2 trillion for the 2014–2017 period alone (Commission on the Theft of Intellectual Property, 2017). Former French lawmaker Bernard Carayon points to the fact that under the intelligence law passed by the Chinese parliament in 2017, all Chinese organizations and companies "must support, assist and cooperate with the intelligence services."

That is to say, any Chinese, whether a member of the Communist Party or not, is de facto the obliged collaborator of the intelligence services of his country...When one knows the attachment of the Chinese to enforcing their legislation, especially when it comes to defending their strategic interests, one can understand the significance of this law, which has not been perceived by the West in its true light. (*Sputnik News*, 2020)

On December 12, 2020, a consortium of newspapers, including the *Daily Mail*, *De Standaard*, *The Australian*, and a Swedish publisher, revealed a massive leak of 1.95 million names of Chinese Communist Party members taken from a Shanghai computer server in 2016. The list was passed to the Inter-Parliamentary Alliance on China (IPAC),[5] a Beijing-focused policy group, for eventual publication. A significant number of CCP members appearing on the list were found to work in Western universities and consulates, but also in strategic sectors such as defense, banking and the pharmaceutical industry. AstraZeneca and Pfizer, two companies involved in the development of the Covid-19 vaccine, were also concerned. The *Daily Mail* mentioned the figure of 600 members of the CCP working in 19 subsidiaries of British banking giants HSBC and Standard Chartered. Industrial giants Airbus, Boeing, Thales and Rolls-Royce were also concerned.

According to an investigation by CrowdStrike (2019), a firm that specializes in the protection of companies against cyberat-tacks, the development of the C919 aircraft may have been aided by cyber-espionage carried out by Chinese companies linked to the Ministry of State Security against several Western aerospace companies during the period between 2010 and 2015:

> The actual process by which the CCP and its SOEs [state-owned enterprises] provide China's intelligence services with key technology gaps for collection is relatively opaque, but what is known from CrowdStrike Intelligence reporting and corroborating US government reporting is that Beijing uses a multi-faceted system of forced technology transfer, joint ventures, physical theft of intellectual property from insiders, and cyber-enabled espionage to acquire the information it needs.

The fact is that the C919 bears an uncanny resemblance to the A320. It turns out that in 2019, Airbus was the target of several computer attacks launched through subcontractors of the manufacturer, according to *Agence France-Presse* (2019). It suspects that these industrial espionage operations have been driven from China. Four major attacks have targeted subcontractors of the European aircraft manufacturer over the past 12 months, two security sources told *AFP*, which was able to draw the contours and objectives of this series of offensives by interviewing more than half a dozen sources close to the case, speaking on condition of anonymity.

When questioned, Chinese Foreign Ministry spokesman Geng Shuang vigorously rejected the claims:

> In recent years, there have been many reports about cyberattacks in the media. In these reports, without any evidence, the parties concerned always pin the label of cyberattack on China and smear China. This practice is neither professional nor responsible, and even has ulterior motives...[China] is a firm defender of network security. (*AFP*, 2019b)

So much for the invisible part. To this we must add the visible part. This is part of China's legal regulatory framework: technology transfers. Didn't Lenin say: "The capitalists will sell us the rope with which we will hang them"? For decades, all foreign companies wishing to establish themselves on Chinese soil had to associate with a Chinese partner who owned at least 51% of the capital of the joint venture thus formed, and were forced to transfer technology, which allowed China to appropriate the latest Western technologies at a lower price and to train thousands of engineers capable of replicating the best of foreign industry. To gain a foothold in China, EDF and Framatome (Areva) had to accept, willy-nilly, huge technology transfers that enabled China to possess all of the latest civil nuclear technologies in just four decades.[6] Today, Chinese engineers have mastered the entire civil nuclear industry that France took several decades to develop. On September 11, 2020, China inaugurated, not without pride, its first 100% Chinese-made, latest-generation EPR nuclear power plant. This at a time when France is experiencing the greatest difficulties in building its first EPR power plant in Flamanville, paralyzed by ten years of repeated technical delays and constantly rising costs (over 9 billion euros), whose commissioning is now not envisaged until 2024. Thanks to EDF, Framatome and Areva, the Chinese groups China General Energy Group (CGNC) and Guangdong Energy Group (GEG) succeeded in bringing a first EPR reactor, Taishan 1, online on the national grid in December 2018, and a second reactor, Taishan 2, in September 2019, in the southern province of Guangdong. This was a world first that would not have been possible without the technology transfers made by Framatome, a 30% shareholder in the joint venture responsible for operating these two 1750 megawatt reactors. At the height of the construction activity for these two reactors, the site employed more than 15,000 Chinese workers and more than 200 French engineers, the latter being responsible for training their Chinese counterparts. While China did not have a single reactor until 1985, in 2019 it had some 46 reactors in operation and is poised to supplant France and the United States with up to 110 reactors by 2030, when it will become the world's leading nuclear power! Beijing has already announced that the national nuclear industry intends to offer its new EPR reactors for export. Several Chinese plants of an older design are under construction in Pakistan. One-third of the capital invested in the future EPR complex at Hinkley Point in the United Kingdom is of Chinese origin (in partnership with EDF). China will also supply nuclear power plants to Algeria, Argentina, Sudan, Kenya, South Africa, Romania and Turkey.

Technology transfers also enabled China to acquire complete mastery of high-speed trains in record time. Thanks to technologies acquired in the early 1980s from the French group Alstom, the German giant Siemens, Japan's Kawasaki and the Canadian firm Bombardier, China has built the world's largest TGV (*trains à grande vitesse*) network in 20 years, and by the end of 2020 had 35,000 kilometers of high-speed track, 20 times the French TGV network launched in the early 1980s, and two-thirds of all high-speed rail networks in the world. "Chinese railway manufacturers now know how to do everything," according to Philippe Ulrich, director for Asia at Saft, a French company founded in 1918 that supplies batteries to several Chinese TGVs. "They are autonomous, more and more independent. They are trying to have their own technology as much as possible" (Balenieri, 2017). All this without ever having bought a single TGV from foreign companies—all of whom, in the end, found themselves totally ousted from the Chinese market without ever having sold anything. A French industrial source, however, disputes this version of events and asserts that each of the Western suppliers obtained large contracts by accepting technology transfers. It is therefore the lure of profit from these contracts that has allowed China to become autonomous, said the source. It used the comparative advantage of its huge market and the considerable funding available to the Ministry of Railways.

On December 31, 2020, after seven years of difficult negotiations, China and the European Union finally reached an agreement on investment protection in which Beijing explicitly commits to no longer requiring technology transfers as a prerequisite for European companies to operate in China, a Chinese concession obtained mainly for geopolitical reasons.[7] This agreement must still be ratified by the European Parliament, a step which is not a foregone conclusion given the European requirement that China must first join the International Labor

Organization (ILO), which prohibits forced labor. Brussels is asking Beijing for guarantees in view of the accusations made against it concerning the forced labor imposed on hundreds of thousands of Uyghurs in the province of Xinjiang (western China).

Roger Faligot, an investigative journalist and expert on intelligence services around the world, particularly the Chinese to which he has devoted several books,[8] believes that China would never have achieved such an economic and technological ascension since the launch of the first economic reforms and the opening up of China from 1978 onwards by Deng Xiaoping without the help of extremely extensive and effective economic, technological, and scientific intelligence networks across the planet. This gigantic octopus of networks, essentially piloted by the Ministry of State Security (*Guojia Anquanbu*, 国家安全部) located at 14 Dongchang'an Street (Chang'an Street East) in Beijing, right next to the Ministry of Public Security (*Gonganbu*, 公安部), and whose boss is Chen Wenqing, reportedly employs tens of thousands of agents, analysts and experts on Chinese soil and probably hundreds of thousands around the world. The structures of this ministry in charge of economic intelligence have grown considerably since the 1980s, supported by a legion of agents with diplomatic status, but also and above all by clandestine agents whose mission is to infiltrate foreign companies and to weave networks of influence in order to recruit foreign personalities ready to cooperate in one way or another. Added to this are the services of the Ministry of Defense, some of which are also in charge of economic intelligence.

By definition, all these agents work in secret. Some, who have diplomatic status, are known to Western counter-espionage services and are closely monitored, but others, the most numerous, are recruited preferably from the Chinese and Asian population and remain anonymous. "One of the first objectives, from 1978 onwards, was to copy the Japanese, who had powerful industries," Faligot explained in an interview (2021). "But very quickly, the networks spread to the United States, Europe and even Russia." Few cases of espionage are made public in Europe, where the companies that are victims of espionage prefer to remain silent in order to continue working in China. The situation is different in the United States, where "Chinese agents are being prosecuted by the bucketload," he said.

Often, the method is to create joint ventures with leading Western companies to capture the desired technologies or to participate in major international projects. This is what happened with the European GPS satellite network Galileo. "Initially, the Chinese said, 'Yes, yes, we want to participate with the Italians, the French, the Spanish and others,' and then, once the technologies were collected, they left, all to create their own Beidou satellite GPS system," said Faligot.[9]

Chinese intelligence units differ from their foreign counterparts in that they are always led by a pair: an experienced official in the field of study and a Party official who is the actual leader. "Strategic or even tactical decisions are always taken by both the operational guy, who is competent in his field of activity, and the party representative," explained Faligot. On Chinese soil, intelligence is decentralized in the different provinces and regions. The province of Hubei and its capital Wuhan are home to the automobile service, with several major European manufacturers, including the French company PSA, based in the city of 11 million inhabitants. "China has an amazing ability to clone foreign products. For example, this American spy plane that they recovered and completely dismantled, only to reassemble it and return it to the Americans," said Faligot.[10] China's spy networks around the world also rely on military surveillance satellites. China has launched 96 satellites in the space of five years, compared to 109 for the United States and only 2 for France.

Sometimes Western naivety about Chinese espionage is confounding. In February 2021, the British newspaper *The Times* of London reported on an investigation into some 200 academics for unwittingly helping the Chinese government develop weapons of mass destruction. According to *The Times*, these researchers violated strict export laws designed to prevent intellectual property on sensitive subjects from falling into the hands of hostile states. They are suspected of sharing cutting-edge military research with the Chinese, including aeronautics, missiles and cyberweapons. The personalities in the crosshairs belong to a dozen British universities. This levity could cost them dearly as they face up to ten years in prison. Just days earlier, Chinese academics and students were in the Foreign Office's sights. Still according to *The Times*, thousands of them could be denied entry to the UK over the same national security concerns. Between 2018 and 2019, some 7330 Chinese students were conducting research in the UK, mostly on subjects requiring an Academic Technology Approval Scheme (ATAS) certificate. According to a report published by the Henry Jackson Society think tank (Armstrong, 2020), nearly 900 graduates of Chinese universities with links to the Chinese People's Liberation Army were doing postgraduate studies at about 30 British universities with advanced research activities in the 2019–2020 academic year. In Australia, an investigation was launched in November 2020 into murky links between the country's universities and Chinese students suspected of engaging in espionage for the Chinese military, according to the *South China Morning Post*. Prior to the coronavirus pandemic, some 150,000 Chinese nationals were studying at Australian universities, accounting for about 11% of all students enrolled in the country's universities, according to figures from the Sydney-based Centre for Independent Studies (Power, 2021).

Another sector in which the Chinese octopus is spreading its tentacles without us yet being fully aware of it is that of scientific research. In an extremely detailed investigation, *Le Point* Hong Kong correspondent Jérémy André (2021b) highlighted the cooperation agreements between French universities and high-level research centers and their Chinese counterparts, whose links with the People's Liberation Army are well known. For example, Emmanuel Macron and Chinese President Xi Jinping signed a cooperation agreement in physics between Peking University (Beida) and Thales and École Polytechnique, which took shape in June 2020 with a first project: equipping Peking University with a very high-power laser system. This Franco-Chinese research project is strictly civilian, but the French defense procurement agency (DGA) has had close ties with the laboratory for many years, and its work may eventually have defense applications. "This indirect cooperation with the People's Liberation Army is a huge security flaw and the services know it," said French researcher Antoine Bondaz of the Foundation for Strategic Research (FRS), an independent think tank, and author of a study on the subject published back in 2017. In June 2020, a note from the French Embassy in China entitled "Franco-Chinese scientific and academic cooperation in the face of the new national strategy of 'civil-military integration'" dared to raise the issue and call for a "re-examination" of such cooperation agreements.

A well-known Chinese network that, at first glance, has nothing to do with espionage is the Confucius Institutes— nonprofit cultural institutions that had mushroomed over the years. In 2018 there were 548 of these institutions in 154 countries. They were inspired by the Alliance Française, the British Council and the Goethe Institutes. As instruments of *soft power*, they helped spread Chinese language, culture, history and philosophy, taught by Chinese teachers recruited and paid by the Chinese Ministry of Education.

Critics, however, believe these institutions to be centers of Chinese propaganda that sometimes pursue less avowed goals. In the opinion of French journalist Roger Faligot, they served to establish partnerships with leading universities and conduct talent spotting. The director of the Confucius Institute in Brussels, Song Xinning, was denied a visa by Belgium and banned from all 26 Schengen countries for eight years on October 30, 2019, for "undermining national security" by allegedly working with Chinese intelligence in Belgium, an allegation that Song denied.

Most of the Confucius Institutes in the United States, where they were accused of espionage, have had to close their doors in recent years. In August 2020, the US State Department classified them as "foreign missions" working to advance "Beijing's global propaganda and malign influence campaign on U.S. campuses and K-12 classrooms" (Pompeo, 2020). The designation meant they were placed under close surveillance, just like an embassy or consulate. US educational institutions were also required to disclose their financial ties to the institutes. "When it comes to the Confucius Institutes, we have ongoing concerns about activities of the CCP, including through these institutes, given that they might affect academic freedom in the United States," US State Department (2021b) spokesman Ned Price said in February 2021. Once numbering over 100, as of April 2022 there were only 18 Confucius institutes still operating in the United States, although of those, four were scheduled to close, according to the National Association of Scholars (2022). The nonprofit warned, however, that many universities had replaced Confucius Institutes with similar programs and maintained close relationships with Chinese institutions that had been affiliated with the institutes. "These rebranding efforts match those of the Chinese government, which has reorganized

Confucius Institutes under a new organization, the Chinese International Education Foundation," it noted.

Cyberwarfare and disinformation: China leads the way

China, which has more than 800 million internet users, has emerged in recent years as a master of cyberwarfare with industrial espionage in its sights. In February 2012, then US president Barack Obama received a 74-page report from Mandiant, an American company specializing in computer security. This report, the result of six years of investigation, revealed that hundreds of Chinese hackers were working on the internet under the guidance of People's Liberation Army (PLA) unit 61398. The unit's headquarters, according to the report, was a 12-story Shanghai building that housed a cyber army under the close supervision and direction of the high command. The report dubbed the group *Advanced Persistent Threat 1*. It alleged the unit had looted information from 141 American companies in 20 different sectors since 2010. China was also mobilizing significant resources, under the leadership of the PLA's Third Department, to set up specialized domestic cyberspace security forces. In 2015, Beijing created the equivalent of the US Cyber Command: the Strategic Support Force, to consolidate the PLA's resources in the field of cyber, space and electronic warfare. In fact, China is itself facing cyberspace warfare led by the USA.

The US military inaugurated in 2010 its Cyber Command, which employs 6000 experts and whose headquarters is located at Fort Meade in Maryland. According to the *Global Times*, the Chinese Communist Party's English-language daily, China was the main target of thousands of cyberattacks coming from IP addresses in the United States. Chinese experts quoted by the newspaper predicted that the Americans were preparing to wage a large-scale cyberwar and stated that China is ready to launch a strong counterattack. "Aside from implanting viruses, the US has long been hacking information from the terminals of Chinese customers, and has been utilizing apps to tap, steal information and analyze the information they obtained," stated the *Global Times*, quoting a Beijing-based military expert who also specializes in cybersecurity (Sun et al., 2019).

The United States did sign a cyberspace non-aggression pact with China in 2015. But this one fizzled out, according to many observers (Vincent, 2021). In early March 2021, Microsoft Threat Intelligence Center (2021) sounded the alarm that at least several tens of thousands of its Microsoft Exchange business email accounts around the world had been compromised by hackers originating in China. Microsoft said the China-based Hafnium group was using "sophisticated tactics and techniques" to infiltrate businesses hosting Microsoft Exchange on their own on-site servers and was operating through virtual private servers rented in the United States. These hackers managed to exploit four software vulnerabilities to steal the contents of their victims' mailboxes and planted tools that allowed them to remotely control the infected systems. Microsoft fixed the flaws as soon as they were identified and urged customers to make the necessary updates, but the damage was done. Microsoft Exchange is the most widely used business email software in the world (Vergara, 2021). The White House considered the hack serious enough to create a special task force. "This is an active threat still developing and we urge network operators to take it very seriously," a White House official was quoted as saying by Reuters (Mason, 2021). As usual, a spokesperson for the Chinese Ministry of Foreign Affairs rejected these accusations and gave assurances that his country "firmly opposes and fights cyberattacks and cyber theft in all its forms."

In March 2021, Meta announced that it had deleted the accounts of a group of about 100 Chinese hackers who were using Facebook to spy on members of the Uyghur community abroad (Godwin, 2021). According to the social network's cybersecurity teams, the hackers used fake accounts to pose as journalists, students, or human rights activists to gain the trust of their targets and entice them to the malicious websites. Using this technique, the hacker group known as 'Earth Empusa' or 'Evil Eye' in the IT security industry targeted mostly Uyghur activists, journalists and dissidents. The victims largely originated from Xinjiang but resided abroad, in countries including Turkey, Kazakhstan, the United States, Syria, Australia and Canada. "This activity had the hallmarks of a well-resourced and persistent operation while obfuscating who's behind it," Meta's cybersecurity team said (Dvilyanski et al., 2021). An investigative report by the French Institute for Strategic Research at the Military School (Irsem), a research center attached to the Ministry of the Armed Forces, whose author, Paul Charon, is a specialist in China and intelligence, pointed out in March 2021 the disturbing similarities between Chinese propaganda about the origin of Covid-19 and the operation launched in 1985 by the Soviet Union about the supposed creation of AIDS by the US military. "The pandemic, which started in China, has pushed the government to renew its methods, by propagating 'false content'...and using false accounts on Western social networks," explained the daily *Libération*, citing the report. These last techniques had been used in Hong Kong in 2019, noted Charon, but they were supplemented by "methods of secret disinformation, employed by the Soviets" to discredit their American adversary and accuse it of being responsible for the global pandemic (Alonso, 2021).

In November 2018, at the meeting of the Internet Governance Forum (IGF) at UNESCO's headquarters, French President Emmanuel Macron launched the Paris Call for Trust and Security in Cyberspace. This statement calling for the development of common principles for securing cyberspace has so far attracted 564 supporters, including 67 governments, 358 private firms and 139 international organizations and civil society organizations. China and the United States did not join it.

Notes

1 The United States has a similar law, the CLOUD Act, passed in 2018.

2 It should be noted that Western populations are also subject to constant cyber-surveillance today. The latest electronic surveillance tools allow us to know almost everything about the daily habits of those using PCs and smartphones, thanks to access gained to their mailboxes, applications used and internet browsers. In 2013, the revelations about the surveillance capabilities of the NSA, the American security agency, caused a sensation and exposed the extent of the surveillance of people's private lives.

3 *La Guerre hors limites* [War without limits] by Qiao Liang and Wang Xiangsui, Paris, Rivage, 2003, is also a good book to read on this subject.

4 Note that on March 11, 2021, at a virtual summit of the informal "Quad" forum of the United States, Japan, Australia and India, US President Joe Biden, Japanese Prime Minister Yoshihide Suga, Australian Prime Minister Scott Morrison and Indian Prime Minister Narendra Modi agreed to coordinate their efforts to move away from their countries' dependence on rare earths produced in China.

5 Founded on June 5, 2020, the Inter-Parliamentary Alliance on China, which brings together MPs and senators from 15 European Union countries and the European Parliament, aims to strengthen policy coordination against human rights violations in China.

6 It should be noted that France did the same thing with Westinghouse to develop the French nuclear program under a US license for 20 years, and then independently.

7 China was keenly interested in this agreement with the European Union as it hoped to find a valuable political counterweight to the United States, with whom it has had abysmal relations since 2018.

8   Among his books in French: *Les services secrets chinois: De Mao à Xi Jinping*, Nouveau Monde, 2015; *Kang Sheng, le maître espion de Mao* [Kang Sheng, Mao's master spy] (with Rémi Kauffer), Tempus, 2014; and in English: *Chinese Spies: From Chairman Mao to Xi Jinping* (C. Hust & Co., 2019).

9   With the launch of a thirtieth satellite on June 23, 2020, China finalized its Beidou navigation system, which allows it to cover the entire world and free itself from the American GPS system.

10   On April 1, 2001, an American EP-3 aircraft, equipped with observation and listening systems, collided with a Chinese F-8 fighter plane, whose pilot was then lost in the South China Sea. The US plane was forced to make an emergency landing at the Chinese military base of Lingshui, on the southern island of Hainan. The 24 crew members were released 11 days later, after the President of the United States said he was "very sorry" about the incident. The plane was returned to the United States on July 3.

Chapter 4

Democracy in China: A long road ahead

Democracy in China is not for tomorrow and probably not for the day after tomorrow either. On the contrary, its current leaders loudly proclaim the superiority of their authoritarian political model over the declining liberalism and democracy of the West. Where is the truth? A comparative analysis.

> Freedom knows no borders. It only takes one voice calling for freedom in one country to give courage to those on the other side of the world.
> —Kofi Annan (1938–2018), former Secretary General of the United Nations and Nobel Peace Prize winner

When the Chinese regime displays amnesia and rewrites history

The Chinese Communist Party has never drawn up an official balance sheet for the sinister Cultural Revolution and its unspeakable torments which, for ten years (1966–1976), affected hundreds of millions of Chinese people. A tragedy that remains engraved in our memories and that the journalist Yang Jisheng recounts in detail in a book entitled *Reversing Heaven and Earth: The Tragedy of the Cultural Revolution,* published by Éditions du Seuil in September 2020. The original Chinese edition of this book is banned in mainland China. The authorities prefer to keep a very partial and summary judgment of this terrible disaster. Officially, the launching of the Cultural Revolution is attributed to "a group of counter-revolutionaries," thus exonerating its mentor, Mao Zedong. In 1981, the Chinese Communist Party declared that the Cultural Revolution was "responsible for the most serious setback and the heaviest losses suffered by the Party, the country and the people since the founding of the People's Republic of China." It has remained silent ever since, preferring to sweep this terrible episode in the history of contemporary communist China under the carpet. After his death in 1976, the CCP declared that Mao had been "70% right and 30% wrong." Yang's book is a timely attempt to re-establish the truth about those dark hours that cost the lives of millions of Chinese and during which tens of millions of others were persecuted by the Red Guards, young fanatics whom Mao Zedong used to organize mass hysteria in the hope of regaining power that was slipping away. But what he unleashed would soon spiral out of control. "The official history of the Cultural Revolution preserves Mao Zedong's thinking and the CCP, and thereby totally legitimizes the bureaucracy, its hold on political power and its interests," Yang writes in his foreword. "The official history of the Cultural Revolution focuses on the persecution of cadres. In reality, the number of persecuted ordinary people is a hundred times higher."

Just as the British writer George Orwell explained that "I write because there is some lie that I want to expose, some fact to which I want to draw attention," Yang devoted several years of his life to writing this body of knowledge to "expose the lies, to set the truth straight," he says. "From 1966 onwards, for ten years, almost all Chinese people were, in different ways and degrees, involved in the Great Cultural Revolution; all of them have a part of this history engraved in their flesh and bones. Their life, their destiny and their soul have been strongly marked by it. Its political, economic and social impact on China was even more profound," Yang writes. Recruited in January 1968 by the official news agency New China (*Xinhua*), the journalist Yang Jisheng is also the author of another book, entitled in English *Tombstone: The Great Chinese Famine, 1958–1962*, a meticulous investigation of this other disastrous adventure of Maoism that caused several tens of millions of deaths:

36 million deaths from hunger, what does that represent? It is equivalent to 450 times the number of deaths on August 9, 1945, under the atomic bomb in Nagasaki...The Great Famine was far more deadly than the Second World War... Tens of millions of men disappeared, just like that, without a sound, without a sigh, in indifference or daze...It is an unprecedented tragedy in the history of mankind that under normal climatic conditions, in the absence of war and epidemics, tens of millions of people died of hunger and that there was cannibalism on a large scale. (Yang, 2012)

The author's father himself died of hunger during this period, which has also been largely ignored by the Party. And for Yang, the Party plays a determining role: "The Party controls very tightly all politics, economy, culture, thought, the very life of society. The coercive force of the dictatorship extends to every remote village, to every member of every household, to the head and guts of every person."

In a joint interview published on January 25, 2021, Anne Cheng, a leading sinologist and holder of the Chair of Intellectual History of China at the Collège de France, and Nicolas Idier, a historian and sinologist attached to the Centre de Recherche de l'Extrême-Orient, Paris-Sorbonne, revisited the rewriting of history that the Beijing authorities have been doing for several years, to better understand its genesis.

Interviewer: Every official speech, starting with President Xi Jinping, evokes Chinese civilization that has been uninterrupted for 5,000 years. Is this historically accurate?

Anne Cheng: It is a formula that was imposed quite recently in the 2000s. Until now, dating in China has been based on the Historical Memoirs of Sima Qian (145–89), the great historian of the Han period, which starts the Chinese chronology at 841 BC, i.e. the beginning of the Western Zhou dynasty. That is a total of three millennia. In 1996, the Chinese government launched a vast project to determine a reliable chronology of the first three dynasties of antiquity (Xia, Shang and Zhou). In reality, the stake at the heart of this overkill of millennia was to 'pull on the rope as much as possible', to make Chinese civilization go back as far in antiquity as the Egyptian and Mesopotamian civilizations...

If we understand history as the period for which the first vestiges of writing were found—on turtle shells and on the bones of sheep and cattle—it is indeed inaccurate. The so-called oracular inscriptions, which are the ancestors of modern Chinese writing, date at best from the Shang Dynasty, some 3,000 to 3,500 years ago. We are therefore far from the official discourse of 5,000 years of continuous history...

Since the 1950s, Chinese archaeology has been a scientific discipline at the service of a political agenda: there is a close relationship between archaeology and nationalism.

Interviewer: Is China still a civilization?

Anne Cheng: I ask this somewhat provocative question, because the official Chinese discourse takes pleasure in evoking the greatness of Chinese civilization, while trying to make people forget all the violence of the Maoist regime. Whether it be the events of the Cultural Revolution or those of Tiananmen Square (1989): or the 'anti-rightist' campaign (1950–1960), which saw thousands of people perish in the camps. The paradox that I denounce is that China boasts of its history while conscientiously erasing it. It cultivates amnesia and, at best, an extremely selective memory. (Arnaud, 2021)

Cheng doesn't equivocate about what she sees as China's future: "China, in my opinion, is a kind of ocean liner…which, if it continues along its current course, is heading straight for the iceberg. It will take time, but I think that all the countries that claim to be so many great civilizations and are no longer great civilizations cannot hold on for long." (Arnaud, 2021)

In a separate interview, she said: "I think it would do China a lot of good to stop being this 'Middle Kingdom'" (Weill, 2021).

"Uncle Xi," an extravagant cult of personality

Kept at a good distance from any free will, the Chinese population has been subjected since Xi Jinping came to power at the end of 2012 to a permanent and invasive hype about its new *Líder Máximo*. The president's speeches broadcast on state television, compulsory studies of "Xi Jinping Thought" for children and regime cadres, huge billboards with the portrait of the great comrade on street corners: the tools of propaganda have been unleashed to mark the minds of the people. Not since the reign of Mao Zedong has a personality cult taken on such a dimension in China. Millions of plates bearing his effigy, poems glorifying him, books with his speeches, essays sold in more than 5 million copies, videos: Xi Jinping, who has accumulated more power than his predecessors since Mao Zedong, is a great sun illuminating the masses with its benevolence to direct them on the road to progress. Not only has he taken almost all the power over the economy, national security, foreign policy and the internet, but the communist leader, officially nicknamed Xi Dada (Uncle Xi), is the center of an extravagant personality cult. A phenomenon that disappeared after the Cultural Revolution (1966–1976) but has regained its full force in today's China. "Xi is directing a building-god campaign, and he is the god," Zhang Lifan, a Chinese historian and opposition figure, one of the last intellectuals in the country who dares to openly question the country's leadership, told the American magazine *Time*

(Beech, 2016). The country's propaganda organs are patiently forging the image of a providential leader, while at the same time shooting down "hostile foreign forces" abroad that are attacking China. Xi uses the same strategies as Mao to unite the masses behind him and polish his own image, while injecting a healthy dose of Marxist-Leninist ideology into society. Chinese people are invited to compete in the expression of their fervor. The country's poets are asked to contribute. "My eyes are giving birth to this poem/My fingers are burning on my cell phone," wrote one internet user whose poem in praise of the great leader immediately became a huge hit on the web. Many Chinese are convinced that Xi Jinping, the all-knowing and providential leader and redeemer of humanity, is the man who will lead the nation to the top of the world. "He is a powerful leader, just like Chairman Mao was," stated *Time*, quoting the words of Wang Cheng, who manages to sell some 180 Xi Jinping plates every month. For Zhong Feiteng, a professor at the Institute of Asia-Pacific Studies of the Chinese Academy of Social Sciences, "Xi Jinping's vision for China is very confident, very engaged with the world. He is also personally a very confident man." Qiao Mu, who headed the international communications department of the Beijing Foreign Studies Department before being sidelined for his outspokenness, takes a different view: "Xi Jinping is like an emperor who rose from red nobility. People dare not criticize him. But Xi is not a god. He cannot know everything. He cannot do everything" (Beech, 2016).

At their annual session in the Great Hall of the People in Tiananmen Square in Beijing from March 4 to 11, 2021, the members of the National People's Congress (NPC) and the Chinese People's Political Consultative Conference (CPPCC) rained flattery on the Chinese president, something that was not seen during the reigns of his predecessors Hu Jintao or Jiang Zemin. This new tradition of pledging allegiance to the party's general secretary, which dates back to the 19th

Congress in 2017, is somewhat similar to the praise of Mao by some CCP dignitaries. During these bursts of sycophancy, Xi was repeatedly referred to as a "pilot" (*linghang,* 领航), "Party leader" (*dang de lingxiu,* 党的领袖) and even "helmsman" (*duoshou,* 舵手)! (Payette, 2021). In this new reality, those who still dare to speak out to criticize the powerful leader are severely chastised, and those in the public eye are quickly removed from view. Within the party, there is no unanimity, but Xi Jinping has so far managed to skillfully extinguish any organized protest. Few foreign officials dare to directly attack the image of the man who is undoubtedly the reincarnation of the Messiah, the inventor of penicillin, winner of the Chopin Prize of the Warsaw Academy of Music, champion of the Monte Carlo Grand Prix, and holder of the world record for the 200 and 400 meters ahead of Usain Bolt,[1] but who, let's face it, has probably become the most powerful man on the planet today. Joe Biden had the courage to do so, calling Xi "a thug," "a guy who doesn't have a democratic—with a small 'd'—bone in his body," during a February 2020 debate for the Democratic Party presidential nomination. In February 2021, after three weeks as President of the United States, he repeated his words, except for "thug." Biden reaffirmed his view of Xi at a March 2021 press conference, his first press conference since taking office:

> He's one of the guys, like [Russian President Vladimir] Putin, who thinks that autocracy is the wave of the future, (and) democracy can't function in an ever-complex world. He doesn't have a democratic—with a small 'd'—bone in his body, but he's a smart, smart guy. (Renshaw et al., 2021)

The study of Xi Jinping Thought has been a requirement for party cadres, journalists, diplomats and high-ranking officials since 2013. Now enshrined in the Chinese Constitution, it is desirable for all Chinese. But Xi Jinping is no longer just General Secretary of the Party, Chairman of the Central Military Commission, and President for life of the People's Republic of China: since January 2020, he has also been the "people's leader," an appellation that only Mao Zedong had enjoyed until now and which says a lot about Xi's political weight. It means that Xi Jinping is now above all other political leaders, becoming the supreme guide of the entire nation. Although the term had been used once in 2018 by the *People's Daily*, the Politburo chose to use the term, "renmin lingxiu or 人民领袖" in Chinese, at the end of 2020, a particularly turbulent year for the country and its top representative with the coronavirus pandemic and very high tensions with China's Western partners (Leblanc, 2020).

For Xi Jinping's 67th birthday in 2020, He Yiting, vice president of the Central Party School, had published a tribute on the school's website comparing the general secretary of the Party to Karl Marx!

Xi Jinping's new era of socialism with Chinese characteristics is the Marxism of the 21st century…China's development transcends national geographical boundaries and acquires global historical significance, meaning that China is qualified to be the ideological and theoretical pinnacle that guides the innovative development of world Marxism. (Lemaître, 2020)

Quite a program! It is difficult for a foreign observer to get to the bottom of the debates in the party leadership, but there is little doubt that Xi Jinping is firmly entrenched at the helm of the party and the country, and that while Xi Jinping certainly has many enemies, there is little organized opposition to the new helmsman within the party and the country's governing bodies.

Tomorrow's democracy?

Those who predict the imminent fall of the Chinese Communist Party, which celebrated its 100th anniversary on July 1, 2021, have three main lines of thought about how that will happen, according to French sinologist Jean-Pierre Cabestan. A long-time professor at Hong Kong Baptist University and research director at the French National Center for Scientific Research (CNRS), Cabestan believes that the desire of the Chinese for material security will outweigh factors leading to regime change:

> There are three currents of thought on this question of the fall of the regime. The first commonly accepted thesis is that the economic development of China, the expansion of a middle class and the improvement of the level of education will sooner or later lead to a liberalization of the political regime pushed by people who are more demanding of their leaders. A second view is that the regime's authoritarianism and lack of freedoms will be a brake on economic development and particularly on innovation. China should therefore relax its one-party system and move to a form of semi-democracy. A final trend considers that corruption is such that the regime is doomed to failure and that it hinders all economic development. There is a deficit of democratic culture in China, which works in favor of the Communist Party. The Chinese mentality remains very legitimist. People do not look for another regime. The propaganda that says *without a strong Communist Party, the country would go into chaos and insecurity* is widespread and well received.
>
> The Chinese are more worried about their security (the security of people but also of property) than other issues like freedom. Society is also traditionally very distant from politics: having opinions about the nature of the regime is dangerous. So, the Chinese leave this privilege to the

party cadres...More than a tradition, staying out of politics is also the result of the repressive nature of the regime... Of course, there are so-called eroding forces. First, China is undergoing dramatic urbanization with a much greater potential for protest in urban areas than if society had remained fragmented in the countryside. The second force is entrepreneurs, who are sources of autonomous economic and financial power, even if today they are rather silent because they are dependent on the government. The third force is the youth. Youth today is extremely depoliticized, it is conquered by the opium of consumption, but we must be wary because youth can suddenly wake up. Moreover, they do not identify with the party, there is a generation gap for people born after 1989: they live on another planet! And finally, there is a pro-democratic current which is marginal today, but which does not cease to act and to claim the installation of a constitutional mode and a pluralist democracy despite the regular condemnations of the government...Economic development, stability and nationalism are therefore the three forces that fuel the regime's legitimacy; if one of them is crumbling, the other two remain powerful and can in some way compensate for it. (Schildt, 2018)

In his book, *Demain la Chine: démocratie ou dictature?*, which translates as Tomorrow's China: democracy or dictatorship?, Cabestan (2018) is clear that dictatorial trends will continue to predominate:

The Chinese CP is not in mortal danger: drawing lessons from the collapse of the Soviet Union after 1989, it has generally managed to adapt to the new economic and social environment it has created without weakening its monopolistic hold on politics...The Chinese CP has tight control over the army and security forces and no credible political force threatens its future. In other words, the CP's authoritarian, developmental and nationalist project is likely to keep it in power for a long time to come... (pp. 26–27)

Furthermore, he sees no democratic light on the horizon with Xi Jinping in power:

The Chinese CP has never wanted to share political power with other political forces or to relinquish control of the economy altogether...One can argue that the Chinese CP is the largest secret society in the world, a secret society that operates by its own standards and is outside, and often above, the law... (p. 41)

The various decisions, laws and security regulations taken since 2012 attest to this desire to better prevent the emergence of any form of opposition to the CP, in short to nip any political dissent in the bud... (p. 57)

The CP exercises a total hold on the state and is hegemonic on society, maintaining a level of surveillance and repression never known before and that the modern means at its disposal make otherwise effective. All these differences make any transition to democracy in the current Chinese regime particularly difficult... (p. 94)

The dominant political culture in China remains largely undemocratic, shaped by a mixture of traditional Confucian values and Leninist principles inculcated in society by more than 70 years of one-party rule and Communist propaganda... (p. 97)

[The Chinese CP is] engaged in a frontal and relentless struggle against what it calls 'Western democracy' or 'bourgeois democracy' and the universality of human rights, promoting for its part 'socialist democracy and legality' increasingly 'in the colors of China' but always under its absolute leadership... (p. 98)

[However,] in general, the Chinese support their political regime and recognize the legitimacy of the institutions it has established: the Party, the government, the National People's Congress and the People's Liberation Army. (p. 99)

For the Chinese, economic development and social stability far outweigh democracy, professional success outweighs the extension of individual freedoms, and economic and social rights outweigh political rights. "For the foreseeable future, the fear of chaos continues to be a major driver of public support for the current regime and how it views democracy," Cabestan says (p. 109). It must be recognized that in China today, "it is clear that consumption, welfare, and the security of people and property come before democracy" (p. 115), especially since "Chinese society, including its middle classes, remains steeped in Confucian ideology, reverential to authority, respectful of hierarchy, and unfamiliar with the political institutions and practices of truly democratic countries" (p. 115).

In the future, there is little chance for democracy in China, according to Cabestan:

It is more likely that the People's Republic will metamorphose into a regime that is superficially communist, but still largely authoritarian, elitist, paternalistic, fundamentally nationalistic and increasingly imperial, with its economic and diplomatic power convincing it to promote its own model of development around the world... (p. 212)

CP elites believe that they will be able to postpone any political reform forever, perpetuating for a thousand years the one-party regime established in 1949... (p. 265)

That begs the question: what should the West do about this situation? For Cabestan:

The eventual democratization of this country does not depend on us but above all on the Chinese themselves, and more particularly on endogenous forces which, barring international conflict, will continue to confront each other on the economic, social, cultural, legal and political fields with the outside world. Our openness to Chinese society and our availability can help. But let's not have any illusions about the ability of foreign powers, including the United States, to shape China's future...One would have to be blind not to see that the Chinese CP is at war with us, our values and our ideals... (p. 273)

So many reasons to stay the course [concerning China], remain sure of our values, maintain our fight for democracy and inform readers about the political reality of China today, a strong China led by an authoritarian, arrogant and popular political system that will remain in power for a long time to come, but which in the long run is doomed. (p. 285)

Constant indoctrination: Big Brother is watching you

The indoctrination of minds in China begins almost from the cradle. On February 3, 2021, the Party Central Committee issued new guidelines that stipulate the need to strengthen ideological education among the Young Pioneers, a youth organization affiliated with the Party. According to the guidelines, all children in primary and the first two years of secondary school are to be given at least one class a week focusing on Young

Pioneers' activities, while teachers are to be given educational materials focusing on Xi Jinping Thought. Young Pioneers members are to be taught the need to "keep Xi Jinping's teachings firmly in mind" and to do "what Xi Jinping has instructed," the guidelines say. They call for teaching children that "a new life today is the result of correct Party leadership" and "the superiority of our socialist system." Strengthening "political awareness and understanding of values" among children is strategically important to ensure the transmission of "Red genes from generation to generation," the *People's Daily*, the Party's organ, said in a front-page February 2021 article reporting on the guidelines. The Young Pioneers is an organization founded in 1949 that brings together almost all the country's children between the ages of 6 and 14. According to the guidelines, this organization plays "an irreplaceable role" in guiding the younger generation and ensuring that they observe the Party's instructions in accordance with the new guidelines. The number of members of this organization is not precisely known, but figures from 2007 put the number of members at around 130 million (*Bloomberg*, 2021).

An illustration, if one were needed, of the craving of the 800 million Chinese internet users for any space of freedom, an American social audio app called Clubhouse that launched in May 2020 and which remained accessible in China until it was blocked in February 2021 gained at least 2 million Chinese users in the space of a few weeks. They exchanged feverish discussions on sensitive and even taboo political subjects in China, such as the Tiananmen Square massacre of June 4, 1989, Taiwan's independence, the situation in Hong Kong and the repression of the Uyghurs in Xinjiang, which is absolutely impossible on Chinese social media apps (*BBC*, 2021). "For that brief moment, people in China proved that they are as creative and well spoken as people who enjoy the freedom to express themselves," wrote Li Yuan (2021), a *New York Times* reporter in the newspaper's columns. "They lined up, sometimes for hours, to wait for their turns to speak…They held many honest, sincere conversations, sometimes with tears and sometimes with laughter." Li said the conversations helped pierce the caricatures state-run media has foisted upon different groups. "People who had been demonized got a chance to speak out and be humanized." Likewise, the app gave mainland Chinese "a chance to prove that they aren't brainwashed drones," she added. Clarence Lo, a 25-year-old writer, lamented after the app was shut down that it was probably the only such opportunity for mainland Chinese internet users. "We enjoyed it with full knowledge that the excitement would be fleeting," he told the newspaper.

Taiwan: A democratic island in an authoritarian ocean

Taiwan, also known as the Republic of China and formerly known as Formosa, has become a truly democratic bastion since the 1980s: with a multiparty system, freedom of the press, a parliament and president elected by direct universal suffrage, and an independent judiciary—all the attributes of a living democracy. Taiwan's democratic development is a striking rejection of the view held by some that democracy is not for the Chinese nation. Taiwan's population of 23 million, 93% of whom are ethnic Chinese, is overwhelmingly opposed to reunification with the Chinese mainland. A former Japanese colony between 1895 and 1945, Taiwan represents the last link in the reunification of the Chinese nation under the leadership of the Chinese Communist Party after the "peaceful liberation" of Tibet in 1950 and the return of Hong Kong in 1997 and Macau in 1999 to Chinese sovereignty. According to a March 2019 poll conducted for the Taiwan government's Mainland Affairs Council, eight out of ten islanders oppose such reunification. Although diplomatically isolated (as of early 2020, only 15 countries had diplomatic relations with the island), Taiwan has its own government, military and all the political attributes of an independent state. Under the Taiwan Relations Act, adopted on April 10, 1979, the United States undertook to provide the island with military aid to ensure its defense. It states that "the United States shall make available to Taiwan such defense articles and defense services in such quantity as may be necessary to enable Taiwan to maintain a sufficient self-defense capacity..." Although Washington has recognized China since January 1, 1979, and adheres to the "One China" policy, it has an unofficial embassy, the "American Institute," in Taipei through which most bilateral relations are conducted. This office, which employs more than 450 people, represents American interests in trade, agriculture, consular services and cultural exchanges.

According to Beijing's rhetoric, "since ancient times, Taiwan has always been part of China." Really? Not so, according to sinologist Stéphane Corcuff (2021), a Taiwan specialist:

If you trace China's history back to the invention of sinograms, China's history is thirty-three centuries long—and more depending on the degree of nationalist fervor. The integration of Taiwan into its empire by the Manchu occupier thus waited for the thirtieth century of Chinese history. This is not, strictly speaking, the 'ancient times' of Chinese history.

It is true, in fact, that Taiwan was only integrated into imperial China by the Manchus, in February 1684. So that is the answer to Beijing's propaganda. In January 2020, Tsai Ing-wen, a bête noire of Beijing as she is deeply hostile to a reunification of the island with the communist mainland, was re-elected to a second four-year term as president. She easily beat her rival from the Kuomintang, Han Kuo-yu, who was more open to the idea of compromise with Beijing. While the United States has adopted a policy of rapprochement with Taiwan since 2020, the Beijing regime has increased its military intimidation operations against the island. The Chinese communist authorities have claimed for years to favor a peaceful compromise in the search for reunification, but in January 2019, President Xi Jinping made it clear that Beijing did not rule out the use of force to achieve this. A more strident message came from Chinese Defense Ministry spokesman Wu Qian in January 2021. "We say it seriously to the Taiwan independence forces: those who play with fire will burn themselves, and Taiwan independence means war," he said at a press conference in Beijing. "The People's Liberation Army will take all necessary measures to nip in the bud any attempt at independence [in Taiwan] and will firmly defend the sovereignty and national integrity," he added in a clear warning to the United States. Beijing has not been so explicit in years. For now, Taiwan's president has refrained from making any formal declaration of independence, but she explains that her country does not need to do so since it is "already an independent state." This formula allows Taiwan to maintain ambiguity and avoid a brutal Chinese reaction.

The Economist Intelligence Unit (2021), the research and analysis division of the Economist Group, the sister company to the *Economist* newspaper, ranked Taiwan as the leading democracy in Asia in 2020, ahead of Japan and South Korea, in its annual rankings. Moreover, it was upgraded from a "flawed democracy" to a "full democracy," besting the United States which stayed in the *flawed democracy* category. "Taiwan went to the polls in January 2020, and the national elections demonstrated the resilience of its democracy at a time when electoral processes, parliamentary oversight and civil liberties have been backsliding globally," the report said. "Overall, the country seems to have concluded that a well-functioning democracy represents the best means of safeguarding its future." The rankings took into account the electoral process and pluralism, the functioning of government, political participation, political culture and civil liberties. Taiwan has been ranked among the "free" countries for more than two decades by the US NGO Freedom House in its annual "Freedom in the World" survey.

On another front, Taiwan has been a model for the world in its exemplary management of the coronavirus pandemic throughout 2020. Between April 12 and December 22, 2020, the island had no recorded cases of infection. In fact, Taiwan's statistics are unique in the world: 843 cases (of which 746 were imported) and only seven deaths. All this without having imposed any lockdowns. Taiwan had taken precautions and prepared, having learned from the SARS crisis in 2003, H1N1 in 2009 and the Middle East Respiratory Syndrome (MERS) coronavirus in 2015. The government did not need to force compliance as it had developed the trust of citizens through its efforts that encouraged citizen participation in policy development, what it calls *digital democracy*. "This level of government transparency is rare in even the most liberal forms of representative democracy. This model of 'digital democracy' allows citizens to reach consensus on issues in the best conditions and to better monitor their elected officials. It also strengthens trust between civil society and government, which proved to be very beneficial for Taiwan during the Covid-19 pandemic," said the bimonthly *The Diplomat* (Marmino et al., 2021).

But as a result of intense pressure from the Beijing regime, Taiwan was never allowed to join the World Health Organization (WHO).

Taiwan has become an ultra-hot topic on the international stage. While the Trump and Biden administrations have moved closer to Taiwan and have adopted a series of measures to authorize contacts between American and Taiwanese officials, the Chinese government is doing its utmost to discourage such contacts between foreign countries and the island's administration, carrying out intense lobbying to isolate the island on the international scene.

Omnipresent Chinese propaganda

Chinese media outlets are all subject to strict censorship by the Party. The same applies to the various sources of information and discussion forums on the internet. China has a huge propaganda machine for its population, as well as for the outside world. Journalists in the state media, which make up almost the entire media landscape of the country, have been required since the fall of 2019 to take an exam to assess their loyalty to power and the Party, and to test their knowledge of Xi Jinping Thought. Throughout their careers, journalists must focus on reporting "positive news" about their country. In addition to a variety of obscure magazines in various languages, Beijing maintains an elaborate system of radio broadcasts and television channels broadcasting abroad. Its China Global Television Network (CGTN) broadcasts to 165 countries in five languages and is a subsidiary of China Central Television (CCTV), which is under the direct control of the Chinese Communist Party. CGTN gained a foothold in London, where it opened an office in January 2018 to broadcast "objective" news on European affairs and politics "with a Chinese perspective." The London bureau, with about 100 journalists, broadcast 1 hour of programming per day since the beginning of 2020, compared to the 13 daily hours broadcast from Beijing, 7 from its Washington bureau and 4 from Nairobi. China Radio International (CRI) has the largest foreign service among Asian media. It operates more than 50 shortwave transmitters. CRI's programs can be received on medium wave in most major cities on the East Coast of the United States. The New China Agency (*Xinhua*) news agency, founded in 1931 by the CCP, employs more than 10,000 people worldwide and has offices in 140 countries. It is attached to the State Council and broadcasts news that strictly represents the official party line.

Inside China, the press is under complete control. The broadcasting of foreign media is tightly censored. Thus,

Google, Instagram, Facebook, Twitter and Snapchat have been blocked for years by the Chinese "Great Firewall." So too are the websites of *The New York Times, BBC, Guardian, Washington Post, Reuters, AFP, El Pais, Hindu, Spiegel, Economist, Le Monde, Libération, Radio France Internationale* and many others. Being an accredited Western journalist in China is a constant struggle. One difficulty is that foreign correspondents, especially those who speak Chinese, are subject to extremely close surveillance. Their every move is spied upon, their movements followed, their telephone conversations eavesdropped upon. Their mail is opened and their internet activities and mailboxes spied upon. The danger is that these journalists cause serious trouble for their Chinese sources, as well as their friends. Most Western journalists in China experience, at some point in their assignment, the nagging anxiety of having caused an informant or a friend to be sent to prison. On the other hand, work visas are becoming shorter and shorter. When I was a correspondent in Beijing in the 1980s, the visa was usually for one year. When the authorities were not happy with a story, the journalist was invited to "drink tea" with an official of the Ministry of Foreign Affairs. The journalist was then reprimanded, often severely. But more often than not, the matter ended there. Nowadays, the visa conditions have been tightened considerably. One-month visas have become common practice and, in extreme cases, the visa is for just two weeks! Visas have become a sword of Damocles hanging over journalists. How, in these conditions, can one not be tempted to self-censor, constantly in fear of being forced to leave the country and possibly lose one's job? In 2020, China expelled the most foreign correspondents since the Tiananmen Square massacre in June 1989. China kicked out at least 18 foreign journalists working for the *New York Times, Wall Street Journal* and *Washington Post* in 2020, according to a count by the Foreign Correspondents' Club of China (FCCC) in its annual report (*AFP*, 2021c).

"Wherever the readers are, wherever the viewers are, that is precisely where the propaganda organs must extend their tentacles," Xi Jinping declared in February 2016. In October 2017, Xi announced that all Chinese media must be under the direct authority of the Party. "Party, government, military, civilians and academia; in the east, west, south, north and center, the Party is in charge of everything," he stated during a lengthy speech delivered at the 19th CPC Congress. The state administration of the press, radio, cinema and television are now controlled by the CCP. New directives place "information production and culture" under the "unified leadership of the Party," in this case the Central Propaganda Department of the CCP. CCTV's "main responsibilities are to propagate the Party's theories, political line and policies; to plan and manage major propaganda reports" and, abroad, to "tell China's story well" (Pedroletti, 2021). It is this direct link between CGTN and the CCP that led to the revocation of the channel's license to operate in Britain in February 2021 by the nation's media regulator, Ofcom, in what constitutes a serious slap in the face to Chinese soft-power ambitions. The revocation comes a year after the US State Department designated CGTN and other official Chinese media as "foreign missions." Chased out of the United Kingdom, CGTN immediately turned to France and asked the Conseil Supérieur de l'Audiovisuel (CSA) for permission to broadcast to all of Europe from Chinese soil. Authorization was given on March 3. I was told by a member of the CSA whom I know well that this authorization was "purely technical and automatic" insofar as CGTN transmits from a European satellite. "If the CSA had wanted to prevent it, it could not have done so. On the other hand, the channel will now be placed under the control of the CSA and will therefore have to respect the law on freedom of communication and the CSA will be vigilant," said this source. The fact remains that CGTN turned to France and not to Germany, Poland or Estonia, and I conclude that France has indeed dropped its pants. To conclude on this subject, let us note that France could have demanded reciprocity from China by giving the France24 TV channel the right to broadcast to Chinese soil. Obviously, it did not do so.

Labor camps: A stubborn reality

Hartmut Idzko, journalist and Asia correspondent for the German public broadcaster ARD for many years, made the 2014 documentary film entitled *Laogaï, le goulag chinois* [Laogai, the Chinese gulag] about the system of forced labor in China and the importance of labor camps in the country's economy and for producing goods for export:

I knew, of course, that in the 1950s, during the time of Mao, there had been many labor camps in China. But it wasn't until I visited the Laogai Museum in Washington, DC, that I learned that these camps still existed, and in large numbers. It was a shock! Today, there are nearly a thousand camps, one in almost every Chinese city. At present, it is estimated that four million people are interned there. Often, they are opponents of the regime and not ordinary prisoners. The Chinese government can lock people up for four years without trial. Just recently, more than 180 civil rights activists were detained. Such arrests are the order of the day in China. Back home, at best, it's mentioned in a newspaper blurb...

[Interviewer] How do the Chinese camps differ from the labor camps in the Soviet Union or Germany during the Nazi era?

The big difference is the administration of the camps, which is dependent on the labor power of the inmates, which was not the case in the gulags or concentration camps. The camp staff did not receive a salary from the state, they lived off what the prisoners produced. This explains why there is no targeted extermination in the Chinese camps as there was under the Nazis. The guards have an interest in keeping the prisoners alive so that they can exploit them. The camps are under the control of the regional administration. It would therefore be illusory to try to put an end to this system from Beijing.

[Interviewer] In the past, forced laborers were used in China for infrastructure construction and agriculture. What role do they now play in the Chinese economy?

The exact figures are not public, of course. But we can consider that the labor camps contribute massively to the country's economy. It is a market worth billions. Often, they are modern factories that Europeans come to visit and where they can place orders directly. But behind the building, they do not see the prison where the goods are produced: Christmas lights, packaging for the pharmaceutical industry, clothes, stuffed animals, or machine parts...Almost every cheap Chinese product that ends up in our stores has been made in a labor camp. Without the 'laogais', China would not be able to produce at such low prices.

The black book of the Chinese labor and concentration camps has yet to be written.[2]

A new conception of human rights, successful entryism at the UN

While we wait for better days for democracy in China, the regime's propaganda has adopted a new conception of human rights. Here is an excerpt from a segment entitled 'China, the great offensive,' broadcast on the program *Complément d'enquête*

[Complementary investigation] (2021) on France2 television on February 25, 2021:

In October 2020, here is one of these 'Wolf Warriors'[3] of Chinese diplomacy at work at the United Nations. Because despite the repression against the Uyghurs or the situation in Hong Kong, despite the protests of NGOs, China is still a member of the UN Human Rights Council. It was re-elected on October 13, 2020—a heresy, according to this former ambassador interviewed by *Complément d'enquête*. What was the Chinese diplomat seeking to pass that day? Nothing less than a resolution that would change the very notion of human rights. Jean-Maurice Ripert, French ambassador to China until summer 2019, deciphers what this draft resolution said. "That when we talk about human rights, we must look first and foremost at the level of development and preserve the freedom of choice of the political and social regime. As if the Chinese had freedom of choice in China... This is called relativism: it is the denial of the universal value of human rights. Human rights are good for some people, but not for others." Walter Stevens, head of the EU delegation in Geneva, confirms that "Indeed, little by little, China is trying to introduce certain concepts that change the concept of human rights, which is universally shared." This time it failed...Faced with the resistance of diplomats, the resolution will in the end not be presented. For the Chinese regime, it is a small defeat. But Beijing is not in a hurry: the country has a long-term vision. "What does China say? 'Deal with me, and we will build a different world.' It's the principle of the bicycle wheel: one center, 193 spokes (that's the number of member states of the United Nations). 'You can do anything, as long as it is with me.' In Chinese, notes Jean-Maurice Ripert, the word 'Zhōngguó' does not mean 'the Middle Kingdom'...it means 'the center of the world', you must keep that in mind."

In early March 2021, the Chinese Embassy in France posted a statement by Ambassador Lu Shaye, who said:

Others among you would say that democracy is universal suffrage on the principle of 'one man, one vote' and a multiparty system, and that freedom is above all freedom of expression. Universal suffrage and multipartyism are indeed democracy, but only the form of democracy, not the substance of democracy, nor a criterion for judging what is democratic and what is not. At its core, democracy is the right and ability of the people to lead a happy life and to participate in the government of the state. Even in Western countries, universal suffrage and multiparty democracy have different forms.

This is the Chinese conception of democracy. As a comment, I would add that in China there is no multiparty system, no universal suffrage, no plurality of debate, no independent justice and no free press.

It should be added that China has accumulated considerable power of nuisance within the UN over the years. It is one of the five permanent members of the Security Council, along with the United States, Russia, France and the United Kingdom, and as such, it has blocked every draft resolution tabled by the Western camp to condemn the military coup in Burma (Myanmar), with the help of Russia. China plays both sides of the fence: in addition to its veto in the Security Council, the non-democratic and supposedly obsolete group that represents the "1945 world order," it is the heavyweight and therefore the main influencer of the ineffable Group of 77, which, contrary to its name, has 134 members out of 193 in the UN General Assembly, the entity that only the ignorant and the naive still believe is democratic because it functions in theory according to the principle: one state, one vote... Thanks to a very effective entryism with emerging countries that are favorable to it, Beijing has managed to take control of a long series of institutions linked to the UN. In peace missions, China is now taking a leading position. Today, more than 2500 Chinese soldiers are serving as Blue Helmets in Lebanon, Mali, the Democratic Republic of Congo, or South Sudan. China is also increasingly successful in blocking Western attempts to pass resolutions denouncing the human rights situation on its territory in UN bodies, in particular the Human Rights Council in Geneva, of which it is a full member. In October 2020, China succeeded in having its membership in the Human Rights Council renewed for a new three-year term despite the revelations about the situation of Uyghurs in Xinjiang and the abundant reports about Beijing's oppression of Hong Kongers. The next day, Chinese Foreign Minister spokesman Zhao Lijian triumphantly stated:

> This is the fifth time China has been elected to the Human Rights Council since its inception [in 2006]. This demonstrates the international community's full recognition of China's human rights development and progress, and China's participation in global human rights governance.

Finally, in just a few years, China has seized control of the FAO (Food and Agriculture Organization of the United Nations), ITU (International Telecommunication Union), ICAO (International Civil Aviation Organization), UNIDO (United Nations Industrial Development Organization) and, indirectly, the WHO (World Health Organization).

In this atmosphere of overexcited nationalism, certain news items can unleash passions. For example, Chloe Zhao was accused of being a "traitor" by some Chinese people after she became the first Asian woman to win a Golden Globe in February 2021 for directing *Nomadland*. Her film, which also won the nod for best drama, follows a woman who journeys through the American West after losing her husband and job, and who meets up with other van-dwelling modern-day nomads. China's media heaped praise on "the Chinese director" as a source of national "pride." But then comments Zhao supposedly made to an American magazine in 2013, in which she criticized her birth country as a "place where there are lies everywhere," began to circulate on Chinese social media and sparked a furor. The comment could not be found on the website of the magazine, nor could another one in which Zhao called the United States her home. The uproar didn't stop *Nomadland* from taking the Oscar for best picture, but China censored the broadcast of the award ceremony and mentions of Zhao and the film on social media. The film has never been released in China (Zhang, 2021).

Then there was the fever that suddenly gripped Chinese social networks in March 2021 over comments by the Swedish clothing retailer H&M that it was "deeply concerned" about reports of forced labor in the cotton fields of Xinjiang and that it did not source cotton from the region. Although H&M's statement had been made the previous year, it was now creating an avalanche of vengeful comments on social networks. "Spreading rumors to boycott Xinjiang cotton while also wanting to make money in China? This is wishful thinking!" the Chinese Communist Youth League said in a message posted on the Weibo platform. "We're not going to swallow this," it added. H&M, as well as several other brands in the crosshairs of Chinese internet users, are members of the Better Cotton Initiative, a group that promotes sustainable cotton production and which, in October 2020, announced that it had given up sourcing from Xinjiang. Chinese actor Huang Xuan announced on his Weibo page that he had ended his contract with H&M, stressing that he was opposed to "slander and rumor." He was later followed by actors Wang

Yibo and Victoria Song. Some people on Weibo called for H&M to leave China and for Chinese people to boycott its products (*Reuters*, 2021b). China is H&M's fourth-largest market. Some hotels in China posted signs at their entrances announcing that people wearing H&M clothes would not be allowed inside. In the following days, the fury spread to American sportswear giant Nike (as well as its subsidiaries New Balance, Under Armour, Tommy Hilfiger and Converse), which had also previously expressed concern about the treatment of Uyghurs in Xinjiang, and then to the German firm Adidas, which also announced that it would no longer use cotton from Xinjiang, and then to the British luxury goods firm Burberry and finally to the German sportswear firm Puma. The famous Chinese actress Zhou Dongyu, who was Burberry's ambassador to China, abruptly announced that she had terminated her contract with the British brand until it "clearly and publicly states its position on Xinjiang cotton." Actress Liu Yifei, who played Mulan in the Disney film, announced that she was ending all partnerships with Adidas, to the applause of her fans. In total, at least 27 Chinese actors, actresses, and singers publicly terminated their ties with these Western brands in the space of only two days. Hong Kong MP Regina Ip announced that she would no longer buy Burberry products. "Burberry was one of my favorite brands. But I will stop buying it. I am siding with my country by boycotting companies that spread lies about Xinjiang," she said. China's state-run CCTV also joined in, saying that H&M "was wrong to become a hero of the right" and that the company should now "pay a heavy price for its wrong actions." The *People's Daily*, the mouthpiece of the Chinese Communist Party, was not to be outdone, and published a banner on its pages entitled 'I support Xinjiang cotton.' As of March 24, 2021, at least four Chinese online shopping platforms—Alibaba, Pinduoduo, JD.com and Tmall—had removed H&M products. The Japanese group Uniqlo subsequently got caught up in the turmoil for having declared it no longer sourced cotton from Xinjiang, while the Hong Kong pop star Eason Chan cut his ties with Adidas. His post on Chinese platform Weibo instantly received support from almost 800,000 users. "I know you won't let us down. I'm from Xinjiang," said one. On March 29, 2021, the Office of the United Nations High Commissioner for Human Rights (2021) threw another spanner in the works when it said several of its experts had received information that more than 150 Chinese and foreign companies that supplied "well-known global brands" might be involved in human trafficking, forced labor and other human rights violations in Xinjiang. It did not name the companies or the brands. "According to sources, Uyghur workers have reportedly been subjected to exploitative working and abusive living conditions that may constitute arbitrary detention, human trafficking, forced labor and enslavement by the use of forced labor," the OHCHR statement said.

In addition to the nationalist fury it has provoked in China, this controversy, which is still far from over, highlights another question: do businesses have a duty to uphold the universal values of human rights and individual freedoms? In other words, is there morality in business? "As far as our trade relations are concerned, China is an unavoidable economic partner on a global scale, but our relations must not be at the expense of our principles, our values and the model of society that we defend, nor must they be free of reciprocity," said Franck Riester, France's junior minister in charge of Foreign Trade and Economic Attractiveness, in March 2021, during a hearing with lawmakers.

Notes

1   These are five descriptions of Xi Jinping by a Chinese friend, for which the author of this book takes full responsibility.

2   The sinologist Jean-Luc Domenach has published a reference book on the prison world of China under the title *L'archipel oublié* [The forgotten archipelago], Fayard, 1992. He also wrote the preface to an excellent book on the same subject by Chinese dissident Harry Wu, *Laogai. Le goulag chinois*, Dagarno, 1999.

3   The term commonly refers to a new breed of Chinese diplomats who, following party directives, have taken a deliberately aggressive stance to tell the world about China's so-called successes, especially those associated with Beijing's handling of the coronavirus pandemic. The term, taken from a 2015 Chinese action-adventure film, *Wolf Warrior*, directed by Wu Jing and shot for African audiences, touts the merits of Chinese army special forces confronting a group of mercenaries hired by a drug lord. The actions of these diplomats have in fact often deeply irritated their Western interlocutors.

Chapter 5

China's conquest of the planet

Whether it is its titanic New Silk Roads program, its presence in Africa, its aggressive diplomacy towards its Western partners or its predominant influence with emerging countries, China has become a global player in the world geopolitical game. Where will its global ambitions end? Will China be able to assume its new international responsibilities, which are immense? A bull in a china shop.

> The first field of operation is the one that allows the predator to get as close as possible to its prey and to bring back the fruits of its plunder.
> —François Heisbourg, special adviser to the Foundation for Strategic Research (2020)

The New Silk Roads: An instrument of domination?

One of the most far-reaching international projects in recent world history by Xi Jinping's China, but also arguably the most criticized, is the so-called New Silk Roads—Belt and Road Initiative (BRI), or One Belt One Road (OBOR, Yidai Yilu 一带一路) —a massive program to connect China to the vast majority of the world's economies through land, air and sea trade routes. When, in September 2013, he had used a visit to Kazakhstan to proclaim to the world the launch of this pharaonic project, the Chinese president at the same time showed his true colors: "We will create a community of common destiny for humanity and initiate the reform of the global governance system." Nothing less. "But I want to be clear, the New Silk Roads is an open cooperation platform. It is not designed to serve any political agenda," he took pains to add. So is it really China's intention to create a new global hegemonic order? That remains to be seen. The fact remains that this project and its implementation on the ground smack of neo-colonialism.

Olivier Guillard, an Asia specialist and researcher at CERIAS at the Université du Québec à Montréal, believes China's actions can be considered neo-colonialism:

> By definition, neo-colonialism is the action of the former colonial power in a country that has become independent. But in a narrower sense, it could well apply to China's pharaonic undertaking, at least to part of the New Silk Roads in South Asia. The way in which the financing of infrastructure via loans outside market rules allows Beijing to monopolize the economic assets of a state is instructive. (Guillard, 2021)

Sinologist Jean-Pierre Cabestan (2019) regards the New Silk Roads as an instrument to gain hegemony:

> What is the BRI, in reality? Has China, having regained its power, returned to the benevolent policy it once had towards its traditional environment? Or has Xi Jinping's China, amidst an increasingly open strategic rivalry with the United States and the West in general, decided instead to create a new empire, a buffer zone of nations dependent upon its financial manna and therefore neutralized, an empire designed to weaken the domination of the powers that, strategically and ideologically, are fighting it? The term 'empire' is obviously too strong. China does not intend to replace the United States, especially militarily. On the contrary, it wants to destroy the American Empire. And to do this, it needs to establish a new hegemony, becoming the only one capable of counterbalancing and weakening the American hegemony and the systems of alliances that flow from it.

Not so, says David Dodwell (2021), managing director of the Hong Kong-APEC Trade Policy Study Group think tank:

> So the seeds of Belt and Road Initiative were sown, not aimed at global hegemony or covert extension of political influence, but out of a defensive recognition of China's own strategic vulnerability, and its critical (and growing) reliance on food, oil and minerals coming from poor, and often unstable countries across Asia, Africa and South America.

The New Silk Roads program has primarily taken the form of colossal Chinese investments, estimated at several trillion dollars, into the infrastructure of the countries through which these roads pass. But this almost limitless Chinese ambition is arousing both enthusiasm and concern. If China's economic and political interests in this gigantic program are clear, it is not guaranteed that its partner countries will benefit from it. The term "New Silk Roads" refers to the Silk Roads, an ancient network of trade routes linking the present-day city of Xi'an in China to Antioch in present-day Turkey. Opened in the second century BC, these trade routes were named after the most precious material transported by merchants linking Asia and Europe: silk. However, these routes were gradually abandoned from the fifteenth century onwards, supplanted by the India route. If the silk routes developed under the Han dynasty (漢朝, 206 BC to AD 220) mainly linked China to Europe, Xi Jinping's stated ambition is even broader since he intends to develop trade routes with not only Europe, but also Africa, the Middle East and the rest of Asia. Today, there are two major routes: the maritime route through the Straits of Malacca, Palk, Bab-el-Mandeb and the Suez Canal, and the land route through China's Xinjiang Province, Kazakhstan, Russia and Europe. But the New Silk Roads are actually much more numerous, so much so that it is difficult to map them accurately and keep them up to date. The primary objective of this ambitious program, which many observers compare to the Marshall Plan but on a much larger scale, is to facilitate and secure the transport of Chinese products to the main consumer countries and to ensure China's supply of resources, particularly oil and natural gas.[1]

A little background: the term "Silk Road" refers to a handful of routes that once linked China to the Roman Empire. Only China possessed the secrets of silk manufacturing, which developed sometime in the middle of the third millennium BC. Legend has it that the art of unwinding the cocoons of silkworms (*Bombyx mori*) was discovered by an empress, the wife of the Yellow Emperor (Huang Di, 黄帝), a mythical ruler who reigned from 2697 to 2598 BC), considered the father of Chinese civilization. Centuries later, those same silk threads wove a vast commercial network linking China to Rome as the soft, resistant and shimmering material was very popular in Europe. The Silk Road originated from the ancient imperial capitals Luoyang and Xi'an, crossed the Yellow River at Lanzhou in western China, and then entered the Gansu corridor, continuing along the edge of the desert and high mountain ranges. The trade flowed along this route thanks to merchants from Central Asia. In addition to silk, they transported horses, cattle, hides and furs, as well as luxury goods such as ivory and jade. The Silk Road in antiquity therefore refers primarily to the ancient trade route that connected Central Asia to China. The period of greatest prosperity of the Silk Route was under the Tang dynasty (唐朝) which ruled from AD 618 to 907. In the eleventh century, the Mongols, then the masters of Asia, gave new impetus to the Silk Road, which had fallen into disuse after the expansion of the Arab world and Islam from the seventh century and the civil wars that ravaged China. Venetian merchant and explorer Marco Polo provided detailed testimony about the Silk Road in his book *The Travels of Marco Polo*, published in 1298. While the Chinese continued to trade silk for furs with the Russians north of the original Silk Road, trade and traffic along the route declined considerably from the end of the fourteenth century.

The New Silk Roads are far more ambitious. Some 138 Asian, African and European countries, or almost two-thirds of the world's countries, have since signed agreements under this program. These countries represent nearly 55% of the world's GDP, 70% of the world's population and, most importantly, 75% of the world's energy reserves. The estimated cost of the first programs is around $900 billion, but China's loans to the signatory countries could reach a whopping $8 trillion. The New Silk Roads may signal a revolution in global trade. China has equipped itself with an extraordinary vehicle for soft power, but above all with a formidable tool for political and economic domination. However, this comes at the cost of considerable and irreversible damage to the environment. It is precisely with these two subjects that the problem lies!

The New Silk Roads program has been heavily skewed towards fossil fuel projects in the energy sector, as an article in *The Conversation* points out:

In a study by the World Resources Institute (WRI),[2] researchers estimate that between 2014 and 2017, in the energy sector alone, 91% of the credits granted jointly by the six largest Chinese banks and 61% of the loans of the China Development Bank (CDB) and the China Exim Bank within the framework of the BRI, financed fossil fuels.

According to a study by the Institute for Energy Economics and Financial Analysis (IEEFA),[3] more than a quarter of the coal-fired power plants built outside China in 2018 may have been financed by Chinese institutions...

Yet the infrastructure financed today will determine the development trajectories for decades to come. The countries concerned risk being trapped by economic choices that lead to potentially irreversible environmental degradation.

If the development trajectories of the New Silk Roads countries follow this course to 2050, maintaining a trajectory compatible with the 2°C objective contained in the Paris Agreement would require a 68% reduction in annual CO_2 emissions compared to current projections. (Bertuzzi et al., 2020)

De facto, an impossible goal to meet. Faced with widespread criticism, China reacted. Guidelines to promote a *green* initiative were published in May 2017. A coalition of actors (nations, UN agencies, academic institutions, and companies)—the BRI International Green Development Coalition—was launched in April 2019 to direct financing towards greener investments. Green investment principles were signed by 27 financial institutions including the China Development Bank and China Exim Bank, the two main state-owned banks providing financing under the initiative.

To avoid *greenwashing*, these principles, guidelines and coalition of actors will have to be monitored and implemented. Certain measures would make it possible to improve the environmental impact of the financing granted: among other things, strengthening environmental and social standards in the appraisal and monitoring of projects, systematizing economic, social and environmental impact assessments of projects, or setting a volume of projects with climate-biodiversity co-benefits.

A recent study by the China Development Bank and the United Nations Development Programme (UNDP) shows that the issue of harmonizing environmental and social standards for financing and investment is a growing concern for Chinese actors. However, the CO_2 emission projections of the BIS's main partner countries raise questions about the BRI's growth model and measurement tools. The redirection of financial flows to sustainable projects is becoming urgent and is the subject of much discussion, both in international and national forums, and within the private sector (Bertuzzi et al., 2020).

In late November 2020, Chinese President Xi Jinping highlighted the continuation of the New Silk Roads at the Asia-Pacific Economic Cooperation (APEC) forum, but Beijing for the first time signaled that its lending policy to BRI partners would now have to conform to stricter standards, suggesting that the project would enter a slowdown phase. "China will strengthen the harmonization of its policies, regulations and standards with its (BRI) partners and deepen cooperation with them on infrastructure, industry, trade, technological innovation, public health and people-to-people exchanges," Xi said in a speech to his counterparts from the 21 APEC member economies. These seemingly innocuous words may in fact reflect the beginning of a turnaround: China, after years of unlimited funding of countless BRI projects, is reaching a moment of truth due to the inability of many countries to repay their debts as well as a Chinese debt that is now reaching alarming heights. There are no official figures for total Chinese loans to BRI countries, but according to the US financial data and analysis provider Refinitiv, in the first quarter of 2020 these loans plus Chinese investments into 1590 projects surpassed $1.9 trillion, out of a total of $4 trillion disbursed by Beijing to finance various projects around the world. The World Bank, for its part, estimates that China invested about $500 billion in BRI projects with 50 developing countries between 2013 and 2018, including about $300 billion in guaranteed loans. Xi Jinping did not say more on the subject, but analysts say his cautious remarks do seem to signal a shift in Chinese policy towards the New Silk Roads. China's public debt has climbed in recent years to 165% of GDP in the first quarter of 2020, compared to a debt of 150% of GDP in the same period last year, according to figures from the Institute of International Finance (IIF). China's total debt, including household, government and non-financial corporate debt, reached nearly 290% of GDP in the first quarter of 2020, up from 255% a year earlier, according to the IFF, an amount considered dangerous by foreign observers.

Alicia Garcia-Herrero, chief economist for Asia-Pacific at Natixis, believes China will have to trim the sails of the New Silk Roads:

> China will need to be more selective in the projects it can finance, especially in emerging economies. [Belt and Road Initiative] countries in the midst of major infrastructure projects, and also indebted due to them, may no longer find the resources available to continue with these projects. (Zhou, C., 2020)

Meanwhile, the debt trap has become a major fact of life for South Asian countries. In recent years, Bangladesh has relied heavily on Chinese loans to finance a host of infrastructure projects ranging from power to rail. According to the German media outlet Deutsche Welle (DW), Bangladesh has received more than $20 billion in loans and investments from China to complete its projects. The World Bank recently lamented the fact that the country's external debt has more than doubled in the space of a single decade, rising from $25 billion in 2009 to $57 billion in 2019.

Turning to Pakistan, a close ally of China: the regional press was looking—not without reason—in late December 2020 at the theme: "Is Pakistan 'drowning in debt' and losing political and strategic autonomy to China?" The country's public debt jumped from 64.8% of GDP in 2018 to 77.5% in 2019 and was approaching 80% in 2020, according to IMF (n.d.) data. Foreign debt soared from $60.1 billion in 2013 to $115.7 billion in 2020 (World Bank, n.d.). The volume of Chinese loans to Pakistan is said to exceed $22 billion. The precarious situation—especially in times of economic sluggishness and the Covid-19 pandemic—

led the *Eurasian Times* (2020) to warn: "A country like Pakistan with a tradition of larger expenditure than earnings, limited infrastructure and economy, high inflation, big corruption, and victim of increasing circular debt, is a big prospect for debt-trap." Not without reason.

Sri Lanka went looking for external financing after the end of the island's civil war in the spring of 2009 to carry out a slew of infrastructure projects, each more grandiose—and above all challenging—than the last, such as the Hambantota port, the Colombo-Katunayake highway and the Mattala airport. Beijing was generally receptive. For Beijing, investing in Sri Lanka was a strategic move because the island is just off the coast of India, which is often considered a rival. Unable to repay its debts to China, Sri Lanka was forced to sign an emphyteutic lease in 2017 ceding control of the Hambantota port for 99 years.[4]

As of June 2021, the island had a public external debt of over $50 billion, a colossal sum for an economy with a GDP of only $84 billion in 2019. One-tenth of the debt was owed to Chinese creditors. Sri Lanka was able to amass the debt despite the country having received 16 IMF bailouts over the past half-century. Only Pakistan has a worse record, turning to the IMF 20 times, more than any other nation in the world (Guillard, 2021b).

The BRI often causes sadness and anger in the emerging countries it passes through because of the damage it causes to the environment and to local traditions and ways of life. This is the case in Kyrgyzstan, a former Soviet republic in Central Asia, where the Chinese presence is not well received by the inhabitants, who are historically suspicious of their Chinese neighbors, as *Le Monde* journalist Brice Pedroletti (2021b) recounted:

A logistics zone built in At-Bachy, in the Kyrgyz steppe, capable of accommodating 100 trucks per day for an investment of $30 million, was initially revised upwards within the BRI framework to $280 million for a surface area 66 times larger than the initial project, i.e. 200 hectares and 10,000 jobs, with the construction of parking lots, a school and a hospital. Frustration is palpable among the local population who live from small businesses and especially from livestock. When they saw on television that the 'Chinese' base had obtained a 49-year lease, their fears turned to anger. "We won't be here in forty-nine years. Manas [the hero of the great Kyrgyz epic] defended his land [against the Chinese] to pass it on to us, his descendants," said a 61-year-old shopkeeper. "There are not enough skilled workers here. So where would they come from, these thousands of employees? From China, for half of them! And the Kyrgyz would only have had menial jobs, security. The area is upstream from the villages to the west, where the wind and the river come from: it would have polluted us. Our resources are far too limited," said Janusaliev Mederbek. "Nobody ever asked us what we thought. This is soft expansion. China wants to take our land, that's all," he said. The project was eventually abandoned.

This raises the question of the purpose of the BRI. For Yuan Jiang (2021), a Chinese scholar specializing in China and Russia at the University of Queensland, Australia, it is clearly to spread its influence: "Undeniably, China has been attempting to peddle its influence through the BRI. Every country seeks to promote its influence abroad, and China, soon to be the world's largest economy, has more tools to do so than most."

It is in Africa that the Chinese presence is most visible and most pervasive. Over the years, China has become the top commercial partner of African countries, having almost driven out the former French and British colonists, making the continent a new land of conquest and a new sphere of influence. It distributes huge loans and is constantly increasing its financial assistance for the development of African countries. Chinese-African trade has expanded from $12 billion in 2002 to a peak of $203 billion in 2015, according to UN data compiled by the China-Africa Research Initiative (n.d.) at Johns Hopkins University's School of Advanced International Studies. It came in at $176 billion in 2020. China surpassed the United States as Africa's top trading partner in 2008.

China has built ports, airports, railroads, pipelines and thousands of miles of roads. Without China, Africa's infrastructure would have remained much less developed. This is undeniable. But because of this Chinese "generosity," public debt in sub-Saharan Africa represented 45% of GDP at the end of 2017, an increase of 40% in three years, with China by far the largest creditor. According to the World Bank, in 2018 there were about 1 million Chinese workers on African soil, employed in various tasks such as retail, agriculture and construction.

The rapprochement between China and Africa has its origins in the Bandung Conference, held from 18 to 24 April 1955 in the eponymous city in Indonesia.[5] The conference brought together 29 African and Asian countries, which proclaimed their willingness to assist each other and to stand together. The conference marked the entry of the decolonized countries of the Third World into the international arena, outside the two blocs of the West and the Soviet Union, and gave rise to the non-aligned movement. Sixty years later, the spirit of this conference has hardly changed. "China and Africa have always formed a community of destiny. Our past, our common struggles have led us to forge a deep friendship," Xi Jinping declared in December 2017. Between 2005 and 2017, China lent $137 billion to African countries. Zimbabwe's debt rose from 48% of GDP in 2013 to 82% in 2017. During the same period, it doubled for Mozambique to reach 102% of its GDP. According to the World Bank, 27 African countries have had a "a worrying increase" in their debt. "There are African countries that are very indebted from this point of view and for which we can feel a certain amount of concern. Can we continue to lend to them like this?" questions Thierry Pairault, a researcher at the CNRS and a specialist in China in Africa.[6]

According to Xi Jinping, the China-Africa relationship is "a win-win collaboration." So, is it? It is true that when China lends money, it isn't terribly concerned about the political situation in the country concerned. Moreover, it offers a very practical "all-in-one" solution: it brings not only money but also its construction companies, its technical expertise and, in some cases, its own workforce. Antoine Bondaz, a researcher specializing in Chinese foreign and security policy at the Foundation for Strategic Research (FRS), head of the Taiwan Security and Diplomacy program and a lecturer at Sciences Po Paris, notes that countries borrowing from China have chosen to do so, admittedly, due to China's policy of "turning a blind eye" to the solvency and transparency criteria imposed by European countries, the United States, Japan, or the IMF and World Bank:

Basically, the objective sought by Beijing is to increase the interdependence of many countries, not only on the Eurasian continent, but also in Africa, also in Latin America, with China. I would not say that it is a vector of domination. What is certain is that it is a vector of influence. China is well aware today that its weight is above all an economic weight and that it is a considerable lever that can be translated into political influence. And that is why today the Silk Roads is not only railroads, it is also a digital silk road, also a silk road in terms of norms and international standards. It is a silk road that translates into many areas and especially the economic field. This is one of the areas. It is an area of influence of China, but we cannot blame it for doing so. Countries have a choice. After that, once they have signed up and become dependent, it's another thing. Many countries in the region have the option of making China a preferred partner or not. That there is a predatory nature potentially, yes. Obviously, but it is not a predation that is imposed. It is up to these different states to make political and strategic choices. That China is trying to use it as a political lever is obvious. These countries are not forced to accept this influence. As for the debt trap, countries are not obliged to contract a debt with China. Some do so because the criteria imposed by China in terms of transparency or solvency are quite different from those imposed by European states, the United States, Japan, or through international organizations such as the IMF and the World Bank. No one is forcing them to do so. (Bondaz, 2021)

Chinese authorities have rejected allegations that they set a debt trap for African nations and threw the blame on Western nations:

...it seems that some Western skeptics have chosen to ignore the win-win nature of China-Africa cooperation in natural resources such as oil. In their descriptions, China sees the world's second largest continent as nothing more than a land of abundant resources ripe for pillaging.

Such accusations have cast aside the most basic facts that Beijing has always treated its African partners with respect and equality, and that China's investment flowing into Africa has always sought to bring benefits to both sides.

Historically speaking, China has never been a colonizer. And it never intends to be one.

China's Africa policy differs greatly from that of the Western colonizers who started to divide and rule the continent for dominance and resources since the Age of Discovery. (Li, J., 2019)

For the US ambassador to the United Nations, Linda Thomas-Greenfield, an African American, the case is clear. A former ambassador to Liberia and assistant secretary of state for African affairs from 2013 to 2017, Linda Thomas-Greenfield knows what she's talking about because, as a diplomat for 35 years, she has closely monitored China's investment strategy in Africa:

> ...it has not worked for Africans, and it has not worked in the same way that the Chinese would have expected it to work. I have seen over the 35 years of my career an increased amount of activity by the Chinese. But where they have failed, and we constantly see reports that indicate this, is that Africans still prefer, if at all possible, to work with the United States. And we need to take advantage of that sentiment and be more proactive in our engagements on the African continent. (Senate Hearing 117-45, 2021)

Whether or not African nations do in fact have a choice, the fact remains that on the other side of the coin of this "fraternal aid," China has been engaged for years in a large-scale exploitation of Africa's natural resources that some observers do not hesitate to describe as systematic looting. Among them is Julien Wagner, author of *Chine-Afrique, le grand pillage* [China-Africa, the great pillage]. In an interview broadcast in September 2017, this China-Africa expert said he believes that the presence of the Chinese has slowed efforts to reduce corruption:

> The level of corruption, both on the Chinese side and the African side, is very high. Let us be clear, this was also the case with the Europeans. But since the end of the 1990s, the legal constraints that they have imposed on themselves have made it possible to greatly reduce the level of corruption...
> Easy credits have turned into a debt trap for some states, which have become insolvent vis-à-vis Beijing. This is the

case of Angola, whose oil is only used to pay the 20 billion dollars that the country owes to China.

It is important to know that most of the time, loans are not repaid in money. They are repaid in gold, oil, gas or copper. Chinese companies are repaid by exploiting, for example, zinc over 20 years...

When the Chinese arrived in Africa, their intention was not to make money. They came with the idea of getting their hands on the resources. The strategic interest was stronger. As some inconveniences and unpaid loans occurred, they didn't stop lending, but they started overcharging to offset the risks...

They're not going to let go. They are going to continue to take market share from the West and make this continent their playground. Africans can use this as a lever for development, but today we can see that this is not the win-win partnership promised by the Chinese. (*Rédaction Afrique*, 2017)

Indeed, when China lends money, it sometimes makes borrowers, Africans and others, sign covenants that stipulate that in the event of non-repayment of the loan, a sort of barter deal takes its place. Instead of repaying in money, the debtor must repay in raw materials or even in infrastructure.

Africa has been the favorite region for private investors to buy arable land, accounting for 41% of deals, according to a report by ActionAid International (2014), which cites Land Matrix, an independent organization that has a rich database of land transactions recorded around the world. China has also been one of the main buyers of arable land. It ranked tenth, with 1.34 million hectares, way behind the United States which topped the list at 7.09 million hectares. For comparison, those Chinese land holdings were nearly equivalent in size to the Balkan nation of Montenegro, while the US holdings were slightly larger than Ireland. It should be noted that China has very little arable land, being primarily a country of deserts, mountains and high plateaus. It is certainly an immense country, but one lacking in resources.

The debt trap is sprung

The reality is that Chinese loans inflated the debt-servicing costs of many African countries to the point where the International Monetary Fund (IMF) felt compelled in 2018 to draw the attention of African leaders to this issue. That warning came before the Covid-19 pandemic, which caused the debt burden to become even more onerous for many nations.

As mentioned above, many African countries agreed to repay their Chinese loans in commodities or secured their loans with them. These resource-backed loans are not new, and they can be a useful means for countries that could not otherwise access credit. However, a report by the NGO Natural Resources Governance Institute (NRGI), a New York-based NGO, notes that: "After the commodity price crash, the heavy reliance on this mode of financing in many resource-rich countries has also brought about crippling levels of debt" (Mihalyi et al., 2020). When commodity prices were higher, these deals may have been made at advantageous terms for the borrowing nations. But when commodity prices crashed — somewhat ironically because of China's zero-Covid policy that saw strict lockdowns disrupt production and hence demand for commodities from Africa — the terms of those deals became onerous. Borrowers had to export considerably larger volumes to meet monetary amounts for repayment. In 2020, Zambia could no longer handle its debt burden, estimated at 120% of GDP, and became the first African country during the pandemic to default on its foreign debt, which topped $17 billion at the end of 2021, of which a third was owed to China, according to Zambian government data (Savage et al., 2022). Thierry Vircoulon (2021), who specializes in African issues at the French international relations think tank IFRI, has said that China's status as a major lender means "resolution of the problem must now pass through Beijing."

Zambia pursued the traditional method of seeking an IMF financing agreement, which is contingent on demonstrating sustainable public finances, to help win debt restructuring. It reached a deal with the IMF for a $1.3 billion program in September 2022. Talks on restructuring $8.4 billion of the country's debt got underway in 2022, with China becoming a co-chair. Vircoulon noted in his 2021 article that China had been reluctant to join other creditors in multilateral debt restructuring as it would imply "on the one hand, submitting to the management of its bilateral debt under multilateral rules, and on the other hand, becoming transparent about its debts, the conditions of which are generally opaque." In October 2022, US Treasury Secretary Janet Yellen accused China of obstructing the talks: "the barrier to making greater progress is one important creditor country, namely China," she said (*AFP*, 2022).

China may not be the only impediment, however. Zambia chose to seek multilateral debt restructuring through a new G20 nations (including China) pandemic-era initiative called the Common Framework, which requires private creditors to accept the same terms as state lenders. "The prominence of private lenders is what is going to complicate any attempt to resolve debt," Grieve Chelwa, the director of research at the Institute on Race, Power and Political Economy at The New School in New York, told *Peoples Dispatch* (Singh, 2022).

In September 2022, over 100 economists and development experts, including Jeffrey Sachs, called on private creditors such as the world's largest asset manager, BlackRock, to agree to a significant cancellation of Zambia's debt. The activist group Debt Justice put BlackRock as the largest owner of Zambia's bonds, holding $220 million out of $3 billion.

Zambia's debt-restructuring talks were ongoing as of the end of 2022.

As of that date, Chad was the only nation to have restructured its debt via the Common Framework. Ethiopia also requested relief in early 2021, but a civil war that broke out later that year complicated its progress. Chad's case demonstrates how private creditors have been able to delay and dilute debt relief under the Common Framework mechanism. Swiss commodities trader Glencore, which held about one-third of Chad's foreign debt of $3 billion, held up an initial deal reached by bilateral creditors in 2021, until November 2022. And the deal didn't reduce Chad's debt. It only pushed back payments due in 2024 to avoid a crunch (Ramadane, 2022; Bretton Woods Project, 2022). The deal came in from immediate criticism from World Bank President David Malpass, who expressed concern about Chad's debt sustainability despite the deal: "The agreement reached by the creditors provides no immediate debt reduction. As a result, the debt service burden of Chad remains heavy and is crowding out priority expenditures on food, health, education and climate" (Shalal, 2022). The Chad deal also shows a major pitfall of resource-backed loans. The country had an oil-backed loan with Glencore. It applied for relief at the beginning of 2020, when oil was trading between $60 and $70 per barrel, just before oil prices crashed at the beginning of the pandemic. It reached a deal when oil prices rebounded following Russia's war in Ukraine, at over roughly $80 per barrel. The volatility of oil prices and the prospect they could move lower means Chad could soon find itself facing unsustainable debt payments once again.

In 2022, Sri Lanka was hit by its most severe economic and political crisis since independence in 1948. Depleted foreign currency reserves meant Sri Lanka could not bring in essential imports. The island nation produced most of its own food but relied on imports for fertilizer and 100% of its fuel. The drop in agricultural productivity and lack of fuel caused a severe deterioration in living conditions, with medicines also becoming scarce and prices on everything rising. Sri Lankans had to stand in line for days at gas stations and even began using wood as fuel instead of gas. Fed-up citizens quietly began to take to the streets in March.

In April, there were no longer enough foreign currency reserves for Sri Lanka to pay its foreign debt and the country defaulted for the first time in its history. Protesters began to set up tents in central Colombo as part of anti-government protests. The protesters did not appear to belong to any particular political group, and some brought along their families, at times giving the protests a festival-like atmosphere. By July, the protests succeeded in forcing President Gotabaya Rajapaksa to resign and flee the country, a turn of events that would have been hard to imagine at the start of 2022. After all, Rajapaksa had won the presidential election in November 2019 with a record number of votes. His prime minister was his brother Mahinda Rajapaksa, regarded by many as a hero for having ended the nearly 30-year civil war with the Liberation Tigers of Tamil Eelam in 2009 while enhancing Sri Lanka's economic growth.

How did Sri Lanka end up in such a predicament? Other than commodity exports, Sri Lanka's main sources of foreign exchange were tourism and remittances from Sri Lankan workers abroad. However, tourism revenues fell sharply due to the Covid-19 pandemic, just as tourists were returning to Sri Lanka after the Easter terror attacks of April 2019. Russia's invasion of Ukraine also had an impact, as both Russians and Ukrainians made up a large percentage of tourists to Sri Lanka. Remittances from Sri Lankans working abroad also declined.

No doubt these blows played a role. Sri Lanka, however, was not the only country to suffer a drop in tourist income and remittances. So, why did these events precipitate a crisis in Sri Lanka? A high debt load is part of the answer.

Already in 2017, Sri Lanka was no longer able to repay the construction costs of the Hambantota port in the south of the country and was forced to hand over the lease to operate the port to a China-Sri Lanka joint venture for 99 years. Many saw this as a classic example of Chinese debt-trap diplomacy. It was a canary in the coal mine regarding Sri Lanka's debt problems, if not just the rising debt owed to China.

Sri Lanka's borrowing from China, which includes financing from the Asian Infrastructure Investment Bank and the Export-Import Bank of China, only comes to about 10% of the total of the country's international debt, which is about the same level as Japan. Even including loans from state-owned enterprises and other government-backed financing, China's share of Sri Lankan debt still only comes to around 20%. The biggest financial burden on the Sri Lankan government is not borrowing from China but the need to repay bonds it placed on international markets, which account for slightly more than half of the country's external debt. But the question is whether Sri Lanka's international bond-issuing binge is related to borrowing from China. Sri Lanka began to raise money via bond placements on international financial markets to cover 30% of the cost of international projects it needed to finance. Initially, the government only issued $500 million to $1 billion of bonds every few years. But as funds can be raised more quickly and on looser terms on international markets than by borrowing from multilateral institutions or through bilateral negotiations, the Sri Lankan government increased the amount and frequency of its international bond issuance. The disadvantages to this approach are higher debt-servicing costs and the need to repay loans in lump sums every five to ten years. While the most dubious Chinese infrastructure projects date from the 2000s or early 2010s, both Chinese lending to Sri Lanka and Sri Lanka's borrowing on international markets rose considerably during the second half of the 2010s. As a result, for the 2019–2021 period, Sri Lanka's external debt-repayment obligations amounted to about $4 billion, about half being attributable to bond repayments.

The repayment schedule for external debt was fixed, and the government knew in advance that repayment would be burdensome. One option raised in early 2021 was to take out a loan from the International Monetary Fund. However, the central bank governor at the time rejected this option, possibly due to the strict conditionality associated with IMF loans. Implementing the IMF's requirements would likely have placed a huge burden on the public. The government instead prioritized maintaining Sri Lanka's creditworthiness in international markets by continuing timely repayment of bonds and other debts. But Sri Lanka's declining foreign currency reserves eventually eroded confidence in the country. As of mid-2020, Sri Lanka had reserves sufficient to pay for four to five months of imports. But by the end of 2021 the situation became critical when reserves dropped to the equivalent of only one month of import payments. The government managed to make it into 2022 through currency swaps with India and Bangladesh. But banks and companies soon refused to open letters of credit necessary for facilitating imports. This is what ultimately triggered the economic meltdown in early 2022.

The Sri Lankan government also knew that repaying foreign loans required the accumulation of foreign currency. Sri Lanka's main sources of foreign currency came from its exports, tourism, and remittances from Sri Lankan workers abroad. Exports had been on a slowly declining trajectory as a percentage of GDP, however, and the overall balance of trade was barely positive thanks to a generally low level of imports plus tourism and remittances. Sri Lanka, therefore, had only a small buffer in the event of contingencies affecting tourist income and remittances. The government should have been more active in promoting new industries, enhancing the value added on existing export industries, and expanding and diversifying exports.

If the direct cause of Sri Lanka's economic crisis was a series of unfortunate and troubling events rather than predatory lending by China, it is nonetheless clear that Sri Lanka had found itself in a debt trap. China played an important role in leading Sri Lanka into that tragedy, even if it played a supporting rather than the leading role. Ultimately, the development and commercial projects that Sri Lanka borrowed to finance did not help the country develop exports sufficiently to repay the debts it contracted, even if some poor policy choices by the government complicated matters as well.

China's predatory propensity is not limited to Africa or the BIS countries. Europe is also clearly a target, according to Heisbourg (2020):

> [If on] the eve of the new millennium, China did not have the means to behave as a predatory power on a planetary scale and therefore even less so against Europe…Europeans must expect that predation will be all the more ferocious as it will include its share of hatred and revenge…China's capacity to predate on Europe will depend on Beijing's success or failure to impose its rules of the game, particularly in the South China Sea, through which half of the maritime trade of European countries passes.

An overwhelming presence in Southeast Asia

Due solely to its colossal economic power, China has a strong presence in Southeast Asia, where it is exerting increasing political influence. At $8.25 billion in 2017, China was in fourth place in terms of foreign direct investment in Asia, behind the European Union, Japan and the United States. But when Hong Kong is included, China leaps to second place at $12.8 billion, just behind the United States. China's outsized role is particularly visible in Cambodia, a poor country that has fallen entirely into Beijing's orbit and where the Chinese presence is overwhelming.

Beijing renewed its relations with Phnom Penh after the restoration of the monarchy in 1993. Ties have strengthened since Hun Sen's coup in 1997. China is Cambodia's largest supplier (37% in 2018), its largest creditor (40% of external debt), and the largest investor. With 2 million entries in 2018, the Chinese also form the largest contingent of tourists. Cambodia has joined the New Silk Roads program. Among the projects are the highway between Sihanoukville and Phnom Penh (and 2,230 km of expressways), the new Siem Reap airport and the reconstruction of the Sihanoukville container port. Cambodia is attracting Chinese looking to invest in rental real estate, which provides a return three times higher than in Shanghai. Infrastructure construction and real estate investment is boosting the construction sector and justifying industrial projects. Among the most ambitious is the China Baowu Steel Group, which will move two blast furnaces (3 million tons) from Xinjiang to the north of Cambodia to meet the Kingdom's demand. (Chaponnière, 2019)

Chinese merchants arrived by the hundreds of thousands to take control of the workings of the local economy in cities like Sihanoukville. It was a small, peaceful fishing port in the south of the country until 2017, when the Chinese arrived in droves, taking advantage of an easing in the immigration rules. The population is now reaching 90,000, of which 80,000 are Chinese, and Mandarin can be heard spoken everywhere.

Mandarin is ubiquitous. It is often written in larger letters than Khmer on facades and posters. Near construction sites, the local language is sometimes even absent. And very often, the equipment, the containers transformed into temporary premises and the raw materials for construction arrive directly from China. (Béraud, 2019)

Almost 90% of businesses are in Chinese hands: hotels, casinos (there are 88 in the city compared to five in 2015), restaurants, massage parlors and brothels, according to Chuon Narin, the police chief for Preah Sihanouk Province. The influx of the Chinese has been accompanied by new scourges denounced by the indigenous population: illicit gambling, prostitution, drug trafficking and money laundering. In Sihanoukville, the Chinese can engage in illegal practices that are severely punished in China. "On the Chinese mainland, the authorities have a greater capacity to maintain order. But the Chinese groups that come to Sihanoukville are not all investors. They come to take advantage of the inability of the local authorities to enforce law and order. This has become a problem," according to Neak Chandarith, head of international studies at the University of Phnom Penh (Huang, K., 2019).

Cambodian Prime Minister Hun Sen has imposed a "Great Firewall," similar to China's, on internet users in his country, thanks to which all online traffic has been monitored and controlled since February 2021. A measure immediately decried by human rights organizations. "Prime Minister Hun Sen struck a dangerous blow against internet freedom and e-commerce in Cambodia by expanding the government's control over the country's internet," said Phil Robertson, deputy Asia director of Human Rights Watch. "Cambodia's National Internet Gateway is the missing tool in the government's toolbox for online repression" (*Reuters*, 2021c).

Myanmar, formerly known as Burma, is another Southeast Asian country over which China has exercised a kind of tutelary domination for decades, if not centuries. This has provoked a certain degree of anti-Chinese sentiment, even open hostility, among Myanmar's population, which was exacerbated after the army's coup d'état on February 1, 2021. In the days following the coup and the arrest of Burmese leader Aung San Suu Kyi, thousands of demonstrators spontaneously gathered in front of the Chinese Embassy and called for a boycott of Chinese goods and services. There were also rumors that Chinese soldiers had joined with Myanmar's army to help quell the rebellion and that Chinese technicians were working to set up a "Great Firewall" in Myanmar like the one in China to control and censor Burmese social networks and thus better muzzle the protest. Official Chinese media ignored the coup, merely mentioning "a major cabinet reshuffle." Some Chinese-funded projects, such as the Myitsone Dam, have catalyzed popular discontent with China. This hydroelectric dam project on the Irrawaddy River in northern Myanmar has been suspended since 2011. Originally due to have been completed in 2017, it would have been one of the world's 20 largest hydroelectric dams. The local population had protested the environmental damage of this project.

Questions have also been raised about the role and support given by Chinese authorities to the military junta that overthrew the immensely popular civilian government of Burmese icon Aung San Suu Kyi on February 1, 2021. The Burmese people quickly turned their anger against the Chinese presence in Myanmar. On March 15, 32 factories owned by Chinese investors in the industrial suburbs of Yangon, Burma's economic capital, were set on fire and two Chinese workers injured in the ensuing scuffles. Burmese protesters armed with iron bars hurled incendiary projectiles at the factories, causing losses estimated by Beijing at $37.8 million, while vehicles and stores belonging to Chinese residents were vandalized (Wang et al., 2021). History will no doubt shed light on China's role in these tragic events. "Burmese protesters are explicitly saying that they want China as an economic partner, but not to be dictated to by China," said Sophie Boisseau du Rocher, a researcher specializing in Southeast Asia. "Everywhere in Southeast Asia, we are seeing a growing discontent with Chinese entryism. What is happening in Burma has a systemic and regional dimension. In a way, we are all Burmese today. Because if the Chinese model of governance wins in Burma, it will win elsewhere in the world," she added (Defranoux, 2021).

China's expansionism is generating increasing concern in Europe as well. This is the case in Estonia, a former Soviet republic and one of the smallest countries in the European Union with a population of 1.3 million. In its annual report published on February 18, 2021, the Estonian Foreign Intelligence Service highlighted Beijing's attempts to silence any criticism of it and to dominate the high-tech sectors in Estonia as well as in other democracies. "Implementing China's foreign policy doctrine, or creating a 'community of common destiny,' will lead to a silenced world dominated by Beijing. Faced with growing confrontation with the West, China's main goal is to create a divide between the United States and Europe," the report said. According to the document, the Chinese leadership "has a clear objective of making the world dependent on Chinese technology," with 5G as a tool and the Chinese giant Huawei as an instrument (Allen-Ebrahimian, 2021). In February 2021, the General Intelligence and Security Service of the Netherlands also expressed concern about Chinese threats to the country's interests. Chinese cyber-espionage poses "an imminent threat" to the Dutch economy in areas such as banking, energy and infrastructure. In Finland, the director of the Security and Intelligence Service, Antti Pelttari, pointed out in mid-February 2021 that "authoritarian countries are trying to get hold of Finland's critical infrastructure," referring to both China and Russia. Pelttari opined that Huawei should not be allowed to deploy its 5G network equipment in Finland (Allen-Ebrahimian, 2021b).

While not exactly a surprise, let's add that the United States increased the proportion of its spy budget devoted to China by nearly a fifth in 2021. This decision reflects rising concern about Beijing, which the Trump administration considered a major economic, security and counterintelligence threat. While the specific amounts remain confidential, officials say that spending on China has been boosted across various line items in the annual intelligence budget, which weighs in at about $85 billion, to gather secret information, analyze its current activities and anticipate its future directions. "When the evidence is so clear, and increasingly clear, that China and China alone can compete with us in all spaces, when we've looked at all of the different threat streams...the resources needed to be shifted," the Director of National Intelligence, John Ratcliffe, said in a statement on the 2021 budget. He added that the shift in resources involves "money and manpower" and suggested that some counterterrorism analysts would focus more on China. In a December 2020 op-ed in the *Wall Street Journal*, Ratcliffe further wrote that "the People's Republic of China poses the greatest threat to America today, and the greatest threat to democracy and freedom world-wide since World War II."

Threats and intimidation

Since Australia dared to ask for an international investigation into the origin of Covid-19, nothing has gone well between Beijing and Canberra, descending to the point of exchanging public insults. A particularly telling episode was the posting by Chinese foreign ministry spokesman Zhao Lijian of a photo montage on his Twitter account in November 2020. In it, a man dressed as an Australian soldier held a bloody knife to the throat of an Afghan child. The image caused outrage in Australia. The publication of this tweet—note that Twitter is banned in China—came a few days after the publication in Australia of a report on alleged war crimes committed by Australian soldiers in Afghanistan between 2005 and 2016. The investigation found that 39 unarmed prisoners, both Afghan combatants and civilians, had been killed by 19 Australian soldiers. However, it did not find evidence to corroborate rumors that Australian soldiers had murdered two Afghan teenagers with knives. Australian Prime Minister Scott Morrison said China should be "ashamed," and called on Beijing to apologize for and immediately delete the "outrageous post." He said his government was also calling on Twitter to remove what he called "a false image and a terrible slur." Not only did Beijing refuse, but also the official Chinese press was full of virulent comments directed at Australia. "What the Australian government should do now is to look deeply into these facts and bring those responsible to justice, express a formal apology to the Afghan people and solemnly promise never to commit this abominable crime again," wrote the *People's Daily*.

This dispute came against a backdrop of deep political and trade tensions between the two countries. They have continued to sharpen since Australia barred Chinese telecom group Huawei from its 5G networks and became the first country to call for an international investigation into the origin of Covid-19. In response, Chinese authorities have adopted a long series of trade retaliations against Australia, including the imposition of high tariffs that, after beef, barley, timber, cotton, seafood and coal, have targeted Australian wines.

In November 2020, Morrison rejected these "acts of intimidation" coming from Beijing and declared that he would not give in to Chinese pressure, as his country had no intention of sacrificing its democracy for the sake of trade. "[If] having a free media, having parliamentarians elected and able to speak their minds is a cause for concern, as well as speaking up on human rights in concert with other countries like Canada, New Zealand, the UK and others in international forums, if this is the cause for tension in that relationship, then it would seem that the tension is that Australia is just being Australia," he said on TV.

In mid-November, Beijing had sent a list of 14 grievances to Australian authorities. China criticized what it called government subsidies for "anti-Chinese" research projects, Canberra's condemnation of China's policies towards the

Uyghurs and Hong Kong, and the Australian authorities' veto of a dozen Chinese investment projects in Australia. "If you make China the enemy, China will be the enemy," an unidentified Chinese official was quoted as saying by the *Sydney Morning Herald* (Kearsley et al., 2020). For Australia, a country of 23.5 million facing the Chinese giant and its 1.4 billion inhabitants, the game seems very unequal. It highlights a certain political courage of the Australian government because this political-trade dispute is not without economic consequences, as China was at this point by far its top trading partner, with more than 40% of Australian exports going to China. The current crisis between the two countries looks set to last. In fact, the feud dates to 2019, when Australian authorities publicly denounced the increasing Chinese interference in Australia's domestic affairs, including through donations to political parties as part of a plan to influence Australian politics. In 2015, Australian intelligence agencies were shocked to discover that the country's political parties were being actively funded by generous donors who were agents of the Chinese Communist Party. China had also been slowly penetrating Australian universities and research centers to siphon off cutting-edge technologies. Seduction, flattery, money, threats and even coercion: the Australian press revealed that thousands of Chinese agents had insinuated themselves into the country's public life, with Beijing's number-one goal being to undermine the alliance between Australia and the United States. In August 2019, Australian MP Andrew Hastie, chairman of the Parliamentary Intelligence and Security Committee, publicly compared the rise of China today with that of Nazi Germany before World War II. In 2019, the Australian parliament passed a series of laws to combat espionage and foreign interference.

After Australia, whose turn will it be? Is the Sino-Australian crisis only bilateral or does it also set an example for the rest of the world? For Scott Morrison, China's attitude towards

Australia should be a challenge to "the whole world." He is not alone in thinking that. The *Financial Times* said in an editorial (2020) that the spat was much more than a bilateral affair. "It demonstrates how a more assertive China is now seeking to intimidate nations that are a long way from its shores...[and] sets a worrying precedent since China is making demands that would impinge upon the country's domestic system—affecting basic liberties such as freedom of speech," wrote the London daily. It said democratic nations should monitor the situation closely and be ready to support one another to push back against Chinese pressure. "Without such co-ordination, Beijing will be encouraged in its efforts to divide and rule, inflicting real political and economic damage on democratic countries that defy its will," it added.

Australia's allies stepped up to the plate. On November 30, Australia received the support of its neighbor, New Zealand, through its prime minister, Jacinda Ardern. Her government, she said, had sent a diplomatic note to China on the subject: "New Zealand has registered directly with Chinese authorities our concern over the use of that image...It was an unfactual post, and of course that would concern us" (Menon, 2020). On March 9, 2021, Japan's ambassador to Australia, Yamagami Shingo, stressed that Australia was not alone in facing an increasingly aggressive China. "I can assure you all that Australia is not walking alone because this is something Japan has experienced about ten years ago," he said at a conference organized by *The Australian Financial Review*. "Each and every day Japan is struggling because of...China, and the rise of China, the dramatic increase of defense spending and increasingly assertive, even aggressive behavior, both in the South China Sea and East China Sea...[It is a] cause of great concern to us" (Smith, M., 2021). Very undiplomatic words. Indeed, the growing threat of China in the region has greatly strengthened the alliance between Japan and the United States, as evidenced by the multiple contacts made by the Biden administration since his arrival at the White House and the Japanese government.

The conflict of the century with the United States

The rivalry between China and the United States has been running at fever pitch since 2018, first under the Trump administration but then escalating following the arrival of Joe Biden in the White House in January, 2021. Washington appears to have finally realized that China's unstated ambition is to replace the United States as the world's leading power and put an end to America's global leadership. The confrontation is being played out in the economic, commercial, political and geostrategic arenas. But the new American president is determined to stand up to China and regain the advantage where his country has lost it. Since his inauguration, Biden has surrounded himself with a solid team of experts on China, illustrating his desire to make China his top priority and to better counter Beijing's ambitions. The president's picks in virtually every department of the administration show a mix of Asia experts as well as former Obama administration advisers. "It's not a secret that the relationship between the United States and China is arguably the most important relationship that we have in the world going forward," Antony Blinken said during his first news conference as Secretary of State on January 27, 2021.

Among Biden's first decisions concerning China was the creation of a China task force in the Defense Department to assess strategies to meet the challenges posed by China. "It will require a whole-of-government effort, bipartisan cooperation in Congress and strong relations and partnerships," Biden said. "That's how we'll meet the China challenge and ensure the American people win the competition of the future." Defense Secretary Lloyd Austin has already pledged a "laser focus" on ensuring that the United States will maintain a competitive advantage over China and be able to stem Beijing's efforts to become a dominant global power. Ely Ratner, a China expert who previously served as national security adviser to Joe Biden when Biden was Obama's vice president, led the task force. Ratner had spoken out in the summer of 2020 to call for the US to adopt an array of strategies on China, including one to block Beijing's high-tech authoritarianism and its dominance in the South China Sea:

> Rather than a replay of the Cold War, a new kind of competition is emerging—one that eludes neat concepts such as containment and engagement that defined America's previous approach to great-power politics...That means preparing for a more differentiated competition with Beijing, one in which rivalry plays out issue by issue and countries balance an array of relationships with both capitals. (Fontaine et al., 2020)

Also in the Pentagon is Deputy Secretary of Defense Kathleen Hicks, for whom China represents the primary challenge: "that is the centerpiece that I work on every day" (*Fireside Chat with Kathleen Hicks*, 2022). Meanwhile, the Deputy Secretary of Defense is Michael Chase, who distinguished himself by his research on the modernization of the Chinese military apparatus when he was part of the Rand think tank. Finally, there is Chief of Staff Kelly Magsamen, former Deputy Assistant Secretary for Security Affairs in the Asia-Pacific Region. At the State Department, in addition to Antony Blinken, there is Mira Rapp-Hooper, who published a paper on how Washington can best regain military and economic primacy to better contain China. Melanie Hart, Joe Biden's choice for China policy coordinator, co-authored a report in October for the Center for American Progress think tank in which she explained the need for the United States to adopt a comprehensive strategy to counter Chinese state subsidies to Chinese telecom giant Huawei. In the security arena, the National Security Council (NSC) will be led by China experts who have all spoken out about the Chinese challenge. For example, Kurt Campbell, the architect of Obama's "pivot to Asia" strategy, became the top official for the Indo-Pacific region on the council that advises the president. The appointment of many experts who had previously served in the Obama administration should not be interpreted as a continuation of that policy under the Biden administration, especially considering Biden's warning of "extreme competition" ahead with China, according to Cornell University law professor Sarah Kreps. "All of the signs coming out of the administration are that even if many of the individuals are the same as a decade ago, the policies will not be," she was quoted as saying by the *South China Morning Post*. "The specifics are still unclear but the change in tone from the Obama administration is unambiguous" (Zheng, S., 2021).

On the economic front, new Treasury Secretary Janet Yellen has already warned that the United States is preparing to "use every tool" available against Chinese practices deemed "abusive." Finally, the new US ambassador to the United Nations, Linda Thomas-Greenfield, a career diplomat and expert on China's presence in Africa, has emphasized that she will oppose China's "heavy-handed agenda" on the UN stage. Her deputy, Jeffrey Prescott, was deputy national security adviser to Joe Biden when the latter was vice president and is a recognized expert on Chinese affairs who founded the Yale Center Beijing. As the final piece of the puzzle, the number-two person at the Treasury, Wally Adeyemo, told lawmakers ahead of his confirmation that the US intends to hold China accountable for its compliance with international rules to ensure fair competition for US companies wherever they are. "China is our top strategic competitor," he said. He called for the US to work with its allies to "demonstrate to the Chinese that they are isolated when they violate the rules." By comparison, French President Emmanuel Macron has, to my knowledge, no China expert in his entourage to advise him.

On February 19, 2021, the US president set the tone for future US-China relations in a foreign policy speech. The European Union and the United States "must prepare together for a long-term strategic competition with China," Biden told the annual Munich Security Conference via video link from the White House. "Competition with China is going to be stiff," he warned. "We have to push back against the Chinese government's economic abuses and coercion that undercut the foundations of the international economic system," he said. "We must stand up for the democratic values that make it possible for us to accomplish any of this, pushing back against those who would monopolize and normalize repression" (Biden, 2021c).

Beijing's claims in the South China Sea

Another hot-button issue that looks like a predatory move is China's claim to more than 80% of the South China Sea, in particular the Spratly and Paracel Islands. Beijing delineates its claims by its controversial "nine-dash line," a U-shaped line extending from the southern Chinese coast to the south of Malaysia, a huge area of some 3,500,000 square kilometers. China's claims were invalidated in 2016 by the Permanent Court of Arbitration (PCA) in The Hague at the request of the Philippines. Beijing has not given up. China proclaims its sovereignty over these islands and reefs based on historical considerations which are often fictitious. Beijing considers that the Spratly Islands and the Paracels have been Chinese territory for almost two millennia. China points to ancient manuscripts that speak of these islands as being Chinese, as well as pottery and coins found on them, as evidence. For Beijing, historical sources (the authenticity of which may be questioned) indicate that around 110 BC, the Han dynasty (206 BC – AD 220) installed an administration on the island of Hainan, to the south of the Chinese mainland, whose territory included the archipelagos of Nansha (Spratlys) and Xisha (Paracels). For experts, the existence of Han dynasty coins is not a convincing argument of Chinese control, but rather an indication of commercial relations between China and Southeast Asia. Some of these islands are also claimed by Vietnam, Taiwan, the Philippines, Malaysia and Brunei. This area has become a global hotspot due mainly to its militarization by China. These other countries with claims on islands are competing for its fishery wealth and the probable presence of large undersea oil and natural gas deposits. In total, 10% of the world's fishing is carried out in the South China Sea. This area is also a strategic crossroads for trade routes of paramount importance as it is the shortest route between the North Pacific and the Indian Ocean. Some 70% of the world's container traffic and 50% of oil and liquefied natural gas passes through the South China Sea.

China has significantly increased its presence in this area in recent years with the construction of artificial islands and military infrastructure on several islets and islands, including runways that allow for the landing of combat aircraft, the deployment of missiles and the placement of long-range radars. As a result of the strategy of conquest that it has pursued since 1987, China now controls the entire Paracel Islands and much of the Spratlys.

In 2018, it installed electronic warfare equipment on two of its fortified outposts in the Spratlys (Fiery Cross and Mischief reefs). These powerful stations are capable of jamming communications and radar systems. In the same Spratly Islands, surface-to-air and air-to-air missiles were deployed in April 2018 on the Fiery Cross, Subi and Mischief reefs east of Vietnam, west of the Philippines, and far south of mainland China. Vietnam regularly protests the intrusion of Chinese vessels into its Exclusive Economic Zone (EEZ),[7] to no avail. The Philippines and Indonesia do the same. But none of them has the military capacity to match China's overwhelming forces, and that gap will likely grow in the years ahead.

In July 2020, Secretary of State Mike Pompeo unveiled a hardening of US policy towards Chinese territorial claims in the South China Sea. "We are making clear: Beijing's claims to offshore resources across most of the South China Sea are completely unlawful, as is its campaign of bullying to control them," he said in a statement. Pompeo evoked the 2016 ruling by the Permanent Court of Arbitration in The Hague which rejected Beijing's claims in the region. It was a considerable change in position by the United States, which had hitherto declined to take a position on the territorial disputes in the region and only affirmed "freedom of navigation" rights. His successor, Antony Blinken, went one step further in January 2021, declaring that the United States would offer its military support to Southeast Asian countries concerned by Chinese claims in the South China Sea. In a telephone conversation with Philippine Foreign Minister Teodoro Locsin, "Secretary Blinken pledged to stand with Southeast Asian claimants in the face of [Chinese] pressure," a State Department spokesman said. Blinken "stressed the importance of the Mutual Defense Treaty for the security of both nations, and its clear application to armed attacks against the Philippine armed forces, public vessels, or aircraft in the Pacific, which includes the South China Sea," the spokesman added. He "also underscored that the United States rejects China's maritime claims in the South China Sea to the extent they exceed the maritime zones that China is permitted to claim under international law as reflected in the 1982 Law of the Sea Convention" (US Department of State, 2021c).

Pompeo's hardening of policy followed Chinese military maneuvers around the Paracels in early July 2020 that abruptly raised tensions in the area. In addition to Pompeo's statement, Washington responded by sending to the area two aircraft carriers, the *Ronald Reagan* and the *Nimitz*, accompanied by their armadas, a deployment level not seen since 2014. Meanwhile, France, Germany and the United Kingdom created surprise in September 2020 by simultaneously sending to the UN notes in which they said that they consider China's claims in the South China Sea "unjustified" and contrary to international law. This was the first time that the three largest European powers—part of the G7—expressed a common view and confirmed their unified position on the South China Sea issue. Moreover, this position was carefully weighed, discussed and prepared by these three countries. It demonstrates their concern about the disputes in the South China Sea, as well as the need to clarify the European views on this issue. In the European diplomatic notes, it is said that "the fact that a continental state considers itself an archipelagic state in order to draw a straight baseline is unjustified" (*APN News*, 2020). Japan, in turn, declared Chinese claims in the South China Sea "groundless" because they do not respect the terms of the United Nations Convention on the Law of the Sea (Zhou, L., 2021). China expert Antoine Bondaz (2021) provides some precision about the issue:

Most of these countries rely on the verdict of the Permanent Court of Arbitration in The Hague, which had ruled in 2016 and stated, not that China's claims are null and void, but that Chinese claims, especially those it calls 'historical,' are not valid from the point of view of international law. That is, international law does not recognize 'historical' claims as being, in purely legal terms, a sufficient argument. This is not to say that China does not have the right to have claims in the South China Sea, but it is to say that China's argument based upon 'historical' claims legitimizing China's sovereignty over an entire area (which is what China does, it claims not just islets but a whole area, the so-called 'nine-dash line'), that, in purely legal terms, is something that is not acceptable.

China is steadily increasing its presence in the area. In March 2021, the Philippine Coast Guard discovered some 220 Chinese fishing boats and coastguard vessels sailing in formation in a disputed area of Whitsun Reef, located within the Philippines' Exclusive Economic Zone but claimed by China. As soon as this flotilla was discovered, the Philippines protested to Beijing. The Chinese Embassy tried a few days later to calm tempers by explaining that these boats were not taking part in a military exercise but had found refuge in the area because of bad weather. But once the weather improved, the boats did not leave. The affair festered to the point where Philippine President Rodrigo Duterte, who is ardently pro-Chinese, had to take matters into his own hands. His aides publicly criticized China, saying that the Chinese incursion into its waters was likely to damage bilateral relations. Although Beijing insisted that the vessels were only fishing boats, it was clear the flotilla was surrounded by military vessels. The Philippine leader's personal lawyer, Salvador Panelo, explained that the prolonged presence of these boats represented a "stain" on relations between Manila and Beijing and risked degenerating into "unwanted hostilities that both countries would rather not pursue." Panelo added: "We can negotiate on matters of mutual concern and benefit, but make no mistake about it—our sovereignty is nonnegotiable" (*Reuters*, 2021d).

The statement marks a 180-degree turn in the Philippines' position towards China, which in recent years had been accommodating to Beijing while Manila was slowly distancing itself from the United States. In order not to offend Beijing, President Duterte had gone so far as to ignore the decision of the Permanent Court of Arbitration in The Hague rendered in 2016 at the request of the Philippines, which invalidated Chinese claims in the South China Sea and ruled in favor of Manila, stating on numerous occasions that confronting China could lead to war. This incident seems to have been a gross strategic error on the part of China, as the crisis with Manila pushed the Philippines out of its zone of influence and into the arms of the Americans. Washington quickly seized the opportunity. "The United States stands with our ally, the Philippines, in the face of the PRC's maritime militia amassing at Whitsun Reef," Secretary of State Antony Blinken tweeted. "We will always stand by our allies and stand up for the rules-based international order." Mao once said that "Reactionaries will only have lifted a stone to let it fall on their feet." Beijing discovered it could do so as well. The damage in relations with the Philippines was made worse by the discovery in April 2021 that the Chinese navy has apparently built several hard structures on reefs called the Union Banks, of which Whitsun Reef is a part, in further proof of Beijing's intention to continue militarizing the South China Sea.

To assert "freedom of navigation," several Western countries regularly send warships to the South China Sea. This is the case for the United States, Australia, France and the United Kingdom. The French amphibious attack ship and helicopter carrier *Tonnerre* and the light stealth frigate *Surcouf* left their home port of Toulon in February 2021 and sailed through the Indo-Pacific region and the South China Sea before taking part in a combined naval exercise with vessels from the American and Japanese fleets. Asked about the purpose of this mission, the commander of the *Tonnerre*, Captain Arnaud Tranchant, explained that the French fleet wanted to "work to strengthen" France's partnership with the four "Quad" countries: the United States, Japan, Australia and India. This incursion by the French navy into the South China Sea followed the French nuclear attack submarine *Emeraude* and its logistical support vessel *Seine*, which cruised in the same area from February 8, arousing the wrath of Beijing (Wang, A., 2021).

The French mission followed the presence in the South China Sea since February 2021 of two US aircraft carriers, the USS *Theodore Roosevelt* and the USS *Nimitz*, accompanied by their flotillas, in what was the largest US deployment in the area for seven months. Britain's brand-new aircraft carrier HMS *Queen Elizabeth* took to the South China Sea in its first operational mission at the end of July 2021.

In reality, there is little China can do about the passage of foreign naval vessels in international waters. Any actions would risk triggering an armed incident that could degenerate in this strategic region that has become a particularly "hot" area of the world. In February 2021, the United States warned China against using force in the South China Sea, reaffirming at the same time that Chinese claims in the area were "illegal." The State Department expressed "concern" about new legislation passed in January 2021 by the National People's Congress (NPC) that authorizes Chinese coastguard vessels to use their weapons against foreign vessels that "illegally" enter its waters. "We are specifically concerned by language in the law that expressly ties the potential use of force, including armed force by the China Coast Guard, to the enforcement of China's claims in ongoing territorial and maritime disputes in the East and South China Seas," said State Department spokesman Ned Price. "Language in that law, including text allowing the coast guard to destroy other countries' economic structures and to use force in defending China's maritime claims in disputed areas, strongly implies this law could be used to intimidate the PRC's maritime neighbors," he added (US Department of State, 2021d).

China has also been steadily increasing its military spending in recent years. In March 2021, Chinese Premier Li Keqiang announced a military budget of $260 billion (1355 billion yuan) for 2021, a 6.8% increase from 2020. Although this is a far cry from the US military budget ($934 billion for 2021, more than all the military budgets of all other countries combined), it is the second largest in the world.[8] In a speech at the opening of the annual plenary session of the National People's Congress, China's parliament, Li said that the increased budget would allow the People's Liberation Army (PLA) to "strengthen its combat readiness capabilities." Days later, Xi noted that China was facing "an unstable and uncertain security situation." He added: "The entire military must coordinate the relationship between capacity building and combat readiness, be prepared to respond to a variety of complex and difficult situations at any time, resolutely safeguard national sovereignty, security and development interests, and provide strong support for the comprehensive construction of a modern socialist state" (Wong, 2021). This budget is, by comparison, 16 times larger than Taiwan's budget of $13.2 billion, which was up 4% year-on-year. Moreover, China's official military budget is considered by experts in the field to be much lower than the real budget since it does not include the cost of research on new weapons.

Mask and vaccine diplomacy

China exported some 220 billion surgical masks in 2020, according to figures from the Chinese Ministry of Commerce. This spectacular figure corresponds to 40 masks per person living outside China. As the world's leading manufacturer of masks, Beijing did not hesitate to use them diplomatically, with highly publicized donations abroad. On January 21, 2021, Hua Chunying, a spokeswoman for the Chinese Foreign Ministry, said that China had "provided the United States with more than 42 billion masks, or nearly 127 per person, more than 900 million gloves, 780 million protective suits, 50.66 million goggles and 15,905 fans since March 2020." She went on to say: "We have done our best to provide support and assistance to the American people." What she did not note is that the masks and other personal protective equipment were not "provided" to the United States, but "sold," and some turned out to be defective.

China also exported 2.3 billion protective suits and 1 billion screening kits against the Covid-19 virus, "making an important contribution to the global fight against the epidemic," vice minister for commerce Qian Keming told the press (*AFP*, 2021d). But let's face it: Beijing donated only a small part of these masks and personal protective equipment (several million pieces in total), while the vast majority were sold, and no doubt at a handsome profit. Moreover, China has engaged in a very aggressive political and diplomatic offensive of vaccine donations to many countries, such as Zimbabwe, Hungary, Morocco, Algeria and others, in the hope of currying favorable public opinion throughout the world. As of February 15, 2021, China had shipped a total of 46 million doses of its domestically developed vaccines (Sinovac and Sinopharm), which outnumbered the 40.5 million doses administered to Chinese nationals! As of that date, only 3% of Chinese had received one dose of vaccine, compared to more than 15% in the United States, 22% in the United Kingdom and even 70% in Israel. One can say that this clearly shows that the Chinese authorities valued developing their soft power through vaccine diplomacy over the health of their own citizens, but it should be kept in mind that the coronavirus was not circulating extensively in the country at this time. It is true that very early on, Chinese President Xi Jinping had promised to make Chinese vaccines a global public good. In response to this Chinese campaign, the United States, India, Australia and Japan promised in March 2021 to deliver 1 billion doses of vaccines to poor populations in the Indo-Pacific region by the end of 2022 (McCarthy, 2021). These vaccines will all be produced in India, helping shore up New Delhi in its multifaceted rivalry with Beijing.

A long March towards the truth about the origin of Covid-19

The exact origin of the coronavirus that causes Covid-19 remains unknown despite mounting pressure from around the world for China to finally shed light on its emergence and be held accountable for the pandemic that has killed 2,653,641 people (including a member of my closest family) as of March 14, 2021, and upended the lives of billions in the most serious health crisis the planet has seen in over a century.

There is a serious lead suggesting that it may well have originated from bats in a mine in Yunnan (southwest China) in 2012, thus well before the outbreak of the respiratory illness that became known as Covid-19 in Wuhan at the end of 2019. There were immediate suspicions that the coronavirus responsible for Covid-19 had hopped over to humans from wild animals after videos emerged of sick pangolins and other creatures at a Wuhan wet market in December. Some wild bats, which are a known vector in spreading viruses, were also visible. But could this have masked the fact that a "zoonotic jump" took place earlier?

In any case, the authorities in Beijing did not like the hypothesis that the virus had jumped over from animals at the Wuhan wet market, which was indeed at the center of the outbreak. So, the Chinese propaganda machine whirled into action, accusing the US military of being responsible for the contamination in Wuhan during the World Military Games organized in the city in October 2019. Official Chinese media even broadcast a video on social networks referring to "200 mysterious biosafety laboratories set up by the American army all around the world" that were likely to have let the new coronavirus escape. Then it moved on to the equally improbable thesis of frozen food imported from abroad. The truth is, of course, to be sought elsewhere. One lead is becoming more and more credible, but it is one which the Chinese authorities are trying to stifle: the contamination in 2012 of workers at a mine in Yunnan. The virus then circulated quietly until an eminent Chinese researcher brought the virus back to the secure laboratory of the Institute of Virology in Wuhan. And this is where the key question arises: was there an accident and did the virus escape from the laboratory? This is one of the key questions raised by a group of 26 international scientists in a March 2021 open letter. They denounced the lack of access given to investigators from the World Health Organization (WHO) and recommended that the possibility of an accidental leak not be ruled out. According to the signatories of the letter, it should be possible to examine different scenarios about the outbreak's origin, in particular the one where an employee of the Wuhan laboratory could have been accidentally infected during the transport of sick animals, while taking coronavirus samples from them or while handling waste from this type of sampling.

A well-documented article published by the newspaper *Le Monde* explains a sequence of events that lends credence to the mine theory: on April 25, 2012, a 42-year-old man was admitted to the hospital in Kunming, the capital of Yunnan Province, some 1500 kilometers southwest of Wuhan. He had a persistent cough for two weeks, suffered from a high fever and, above all, experienced worsening respiratory distress. The next day, three other patients, aged between 32 and 63, were admitted to the same institution with similar symptoms. The next day, a 45-year-old man was admitted to the hospital. A sixth patient, aged 30, joined them a week later. All of them shared more or less the same symptoms of severe pneumonia. Their chest scans showed both lungs with so-called 'ground glass' opacities, which are now recognized as a relatively common characteristic of Covid-19, although not specific to it. Three of them showed signs of thrombosis, an obstruction of the vessels which is again quite typical of Covid-19 complications. All of them worked in a disused mine in Tongguan, Mojiang Township, populated by several colonies of rhinolophs—better known as horseshoe bats. The six men spent up to two weeks cleaning the mine's galleries of the flying mammals' guano. Three of them died in the hospital, after 12, 48 and 109 days of hospitalization respectively. The two youngest escaped after a stay of less than a week, while another, 46 years old, left the hospital after a four-month stay.

Beijing is keeping a tight lid on the matter, and the mine in question is now hermetically sealed, carefully kept away from prying eyes. The Chinese government's culture of silence and concealment is once again being displayed, but this time on a global issue. Foreign news crews have been ruthlessly chased away by angry villagers, while cameras have been set up at the mine entrance, and roadblocks are blocking all passage on the mine's access roads.

The mission of a team of experts from the World Health Organization to Wuhan in February 2021 to try to determine the origin of the virus ended in a complete fiasco. Not only had the Chinese authorities negotiated the terms of the investigation with the UN organization to the detriment of the independence of the expertise. Not only had the experts, who were certainly reputable, all been co-opted by Beijing. But also, according to an investigation by the *New York Times*, their work had to make do with work already carried out under the aegis of Beijing. Nevertheless, a lab link has gained credibility. At the very beginning of the outbreak, any mention of the laboratory trail was categorized as pure conspiracy theory, or associated with anti-China attacks by Trump and his administration. However, this hypothesis did not actually come from the Trump camp, as Jérémy André, *Le Point*'s Hong Kong correspondent, points out (André, 2021c). Jamie Metzl, a researcher at the Atlantic Council, an American think tank, who had worked for Joe Biden's Senate office and was a former adviser during the Clinton administration, was the first in Washington to argue that a research accident could have led to the pandemic. This figure close to the Democratic establishment first outlined back in April 2020 the many arguments and evidence leading him to conclude that there is "an 85 percent chance that the pandemic began with an accidental leak" (Metzl, 2022). This is an opinion that carries weight as it comes from a specialist in public health and genetic- engineering research with a strong familiarity with

China—someone who is less suspected of wanting to politicize the issue than Donald Trump or Mike Pompeo. On March 11, 2021, Chinese Premier Li Keqiang pledged that China would continue to cooperate with research into the origin of the virus. "We will continue to work with the WHO to take this work further," he said. Hundreds of scientists around the world have joined efforts to hold China to its word. Beijing's credibility, once again, has been undermined.

Notes

1   On this subject, see Alexandre Debaune's academic work entitled *Les Nouvelles Routes de la Soie: un cadeau empoisonné pour l'Asie Centrale?* [The new silk roads: a poisoned chalice for Central Asia?] https://misterprepa.net/les-nouvelles-routes-de-la-soie-un-cadeau-empoisonne-pour-lasie-centrale/

2   World Resources Institute, or WRI, is an American think tank founded in 1982.

3   Institute for Energy Economics and Financial Analysis (IEEFA) is an American think tank.

4   According to some sources, it was Sri Lanka that was behind the lease proposal, not China.

5   As an example of the "brotherly" ties between China and Indonesia, in 2021 Chinese companies were putting the finishing touches to the construction of a high-speed railroad line from Bandung to Jakarta, financed of course by Chinese loans under the New Silk Roads program, which led to the construction of the longest tunnel in the country.

6   On this subject, watch the video *Pourquoi la Chine investit l'Afrique* [Why China is investing in Asia] by Asia Balluffier and Antoine Schirer of *Le Monde,* available at https://www.lemonde.fr/international/video/2019/02/22/pourquoi-la-chine-investit-l-afrique_5427046_3210.html

7   Maritime domain over which a coastal state exercises a sovereign right.

8   China currently has three active aircraft carriers (compared with 11 for the United States) and will soon have a fourth, which will be nuclear-powered and for which construction began in early 2021. Moreover, it is useful to keep in mind that the United States has about 800 military bases in more than 70 countries, compared to only one for China, in Djibouti.

Conclusion

When the sun rises in the east and sets in the west, Europe stutters.

When the sun rises on the East, it sets on the West. This aphorism has long been used by those who seek to convey the ineluctable nature of China's ultimate victory on the world stage. Nothing is less certain. At the end of this investigative work, I have come to the conviction that the China of 'President-for-Life' Xi Jinping is on a collision course with the rest of the world. Beijing is earning the distrust, if not the enmity, of many of its Western partners, not to mention public opinion. Since the Chinese dictator came to power in 2012, China and its wolf warriors have managed the feat of falling out with much of the world. Deeply angry with the United States,[1] and angry for a long time, Beijing no longer gets along either with the United Kingdom, Canada, Australia, India, Sweden or, to a lesser degree, with Japan, South Korea and New Zealand, and perhaps soon also with France and Germany, the latter of which has long been a supporter of dialogue with China. All this at a time when many of its neighbors in Southeast Asia live in fear of the growing influence of China in the region. The European Union, for its part, has explained through the voices of its leaders that it has now lost its "naivety" with regard to China, which it now classifies as a "systemic rival." Even Turkey, which had long ago fallen into China's orbit, has recently begun to hold China accountable for its treatment of the Uyghurs, who it should be remembered speak a Turkic language, thus becoming the first Muslim country to break its silence on this tragedy. Even Singapore's prime minister, Lee Hsien Loong, who could hardly be accused of being anti-Chinese, said the political direction taken by the Beijing regime has created tensions with countries large and small. "There is significant uncertainty [and] anxiety over which way China is going and whether this will be good for them," he told BBC World News' *Talking Business Asia* program. "I do not think that is in China's interest," he added (Vaswani, 2021). On March 12, 2021, US President Joe Biden, Japanese Prime Minister Yoshihide Suga, Australian Prime Minister Scott Morrison and Indian Prime Minister Narendra Modi agreed to work together to combat China's "aggression" and "intimidation" against some of their countries at a virtual summit of the "Quad," the informal forum that brings together their four nations. They denounced the Chinese for their "coercion of Australia, their harassment around the Senkaku Islands [uninhabited islets administered by Japan but also claimed by China under the name of Diaoyu in the East China Sea], [and] their aggression on the border with India,"[2] White House National Security Adviser Jake Sullivan said at the end of the summit (Delaney et al., 2021).

In another example of China's deepening isolation, China has plummeted in the annual soft-power rankings in recent years. It dropped from fifth to eighth place worldwide between 2020 and 2021, according to the 2021 Global Soft Power Index, behind Germany, Japan, the United Kingdom, Canada, Switzerland, the United States and France. The decline is testimony to a permanently tarnished image on the international scene, a collateral consequence of the repression in Xinjiang and Hong Kong, as well as the constant intimidation of Taiwan (BrandFinance, 2021).

Renowned Chinese sculptor and director Ai Weiwei, who now lives in Portugal, is very pessimistic about the future of Western democracy vis-à-vis China:

That is the new reality. Because of globalization, big corporations are deeply involved with China and there is not a border, ideology or any kind of argument. Just profits.

The Chinese side is China's strategically winning. The wave of 30 or 40 years of democratization is coming to an end. If you look at what's happening in US or in Brazil and so many other states, there is a huge backlash with regard to democracy and the liberal state. Many of these countries are in domestic crises, opening a great advantage to authoritarian states. Leaders like Bolsonaro, Vladimir Putin or the Chinese Xi Jinping are strongmen who skillfully managed to get what they want. I think they will last for a long time yet and it seems there is no way to stop them...We are living a very fragile moment. I don't think the pandemic will alarm people enough for them to devise a clear strategy to deal with what human society is facing in the future. In many ways, we are dealing with realities that are unprecedented for human society. Technology, powerful states like China and the West's incapability to deal with that authoritarian state, plus the huge climate problems. All of this puts our human future in question. (Chade, 2021)

Legitimate points, even if, since he spoke in 2021, efforts by Western nations to regain strategic autonomy in terms of semiconductors and raw earths have gathered pace. Yet I do not share his pessimism, even if it is true that we have entered a phase of acute ideological warfare between authoritarian regimes, foremost among them China, and Western societies. Authoritarian regimes have been advancing, self-confident and comforted by ardent nationalism, while democracies have been plunged into an unprecedented moral crisis, dazed by a loss of reference points, a rejection of elites and an endless questioning of the destiny of the world. Disinformation, conspiracy theories and fake news are causing havoc, plunging millions of gullible and naive people into obscurantism, while communitarianism and populism are corrupting our societies all over the world.

China is taking advantage of this deep moral crisis and these fault lines to advance its position. Yang Jiechi, then the Chinese Communist Party's main official for foreign affairs, made it clear that China is now posing as an alternative system to liberal democracy during the first face-to-face meeting between high-ranking Chinese and US officials after Joe Biden came to power, held in March 2021 in Alaska. Beijing no longer intends to leave Washington with a monopoly on the world model and is challenging the legitimacy of the United States as a global ideal. The United States, said Yang Jiechi, "does not represent international public opinion, nor does the Western world." In the background of the raging China-US confrontation, two models of society are facing off. Despite several lights flashing on the dashboard of democracy, I remain firmly convinced that debate and intellectual ferment will help it prevail over one-track thinking, the disappearance of free will, and censorship.

We have arrived at a moment of truth. And yet, almost all the sinologists and enlightened Chinese that I know, as well as many experienced journalists who write on China, have gone silent. Far be it from me to speak for them, but I certainly understand the desire to keep one's head down in the hope of being allowed further access to the country. But let's open our eyes. Isn't keeping silent when you know something a bit like being an accomplice?

Recently, a friend of mine, whose identity I will not reveal, wrote me the following:

The China of a part of my ancestors that I discovered has absolutely nothing to do with what can be said here. I do not want to don ideological glasses and pontificate. Nor do I wish to feed an incredible hatred against a people composed of humans just like others and with an ancient culture that is different from the West, this hatred can lead to uncontrolled derivations. My model is neither the Chinese regime, nor the

United States and especially not the propaganda wars. My other ancestry obliges me to be wary of any unanimity and not to follow extreme right-wing or fundamentalist sources.

Touched by his sincerity as well as his naivety, I answered that although I have been enamored with China for 40 years and with all the extraordinary advances the country has made since 1978, I am torn and upset today. No, there is no hatred directed against China and especially not against its people. But there are, on the other hand, serious questions about appalling and shocking practices, as well as serious questions about political and environmental policies that have serious consequences for the planet, our common good. In the West we have a free press, contrary to China where it is censored, muzzled and under the orders of the government. Thanks to this free and pluralist press, which is one of the bulwarks for the functioning of our democracies, Beijing can no longer durably hide its secrets from the rest of the world. There is today a collective awareness in the world about these atrocities and these issues. This awareness, I am firmly convinced, will spread in the coming years, and the Chinese regime, if it wants to save face, will have no choice but to provide more convincing answers than what we have heard so far. But I confess I am not sure that it has the capacity and, more importantly, the will to do so. The world today is an open world like never before. Barriers are falling and, with them, masks too. The twenty-first century will no longer be America's century, and probably not China's. China may become the world's leading economic power by 2028, but it will not be the world leader. It can't be. To become the world leader, it would need a political system that would be a credible alternative to the model offered by America, a powerful soft power that will not be undermined by the counterproductive arrogance of wolf-warrior diplomacy. It will also need a military with a global reach capable of intervening simultaneously in the four corners of the planet. All these criteria have not yet been met, obviously. This century will be the century of information and knowledge. Human beings are thirsty for knowledge and truth. In the end, truth will triumph over lies, and light over darkness. Nothing and no one will stop the power of the written word and the image. I am convinced that the Xi Jinping regime will lose this information war. It is only a matter of time. Xi Jinping has bet on the irreversible and inexorable decline of the West to impose his rule on the world. This bet will be lost. On the contrary, Xi Jinping's China will now find the West in its path. Indeed, the United States, despite its internal problems, has just entered a phase of economic, political and technological renaissance that will last for years, while Europe is not far from following suit. Moreover, both individuals and states are learning from this crisis to repair mistakes, to find affinities they did not know they had, and to renew ties that had frayed.

In 2017, at the 19th Congress of the Chinese Communist Party, Xi Jinping quoted the following motto to remind those who might have forgotten it: "In the north, south, east, west, center, the Party rules everything," a vivid expression evoking a return to totalitarianism. But already Xi Jinping and his regime are falling into the trap they set for themselves: dishonor and discredit. On March 7, 2021, then foreign minister Wang Yi proclaimed that the Chinese Communist Party would last another thousand years. The truth is that we are probably witnessing the beginning of the demise of a system that has run its course, with China already being the last great communist country in the world. The resounding failure of the Sino-American talks in Alaska in March 2021 illustrated that the gap between the two great world powers is wider than ever, and this does not bode well for the future. Two radically different conceptions of the world are now confronting each other in broad daylight: that of an open society and that of a hermetically sealed society. Today, the problem we are facing goes far beyond the rivalry between China and the United States for world supremacy. It is a head-on clash between two models of society. One embraces the universal values that are widely accepted by humankind, while the other categorically rejects them. Democracy versus totalitarianism. Even Joe Biden speaks in these terms: "Look, I predict to you, your children or grandchildren are going to be doing their doctoral thesis on the issue of who succeeded: autocracy or democracy? Because that is what is at stake, not just with China...We've got to prove democracy works," he said at his first presidential press conference in March 2021.

At the end of this book, the big question is whether we are heading towards a large-scale confrontation, with China, Russia, Iran and North Korea on one side and the United States and its allies, mainly Japan, South Korea, Australia and the European Union, on the other. This confrontation is currently taking place in a situation that is more volatile than ever, with Russia having invaded Ukraine in February 2022. This aggression is being met with fierce resistance from Ukrainian forces and by massive arms deliveries from the West, both of which Moscow failed to anticipate. Denied a quick victory and hampered by sanctions, Russia has turned to China for military assistance. Meanwhile, China itself is facing increasing Western economic pressure and greater US resolve over Taiwan. China and Russia thus find themselves more than ever allies of circumstance, a dangerous situation that raises the specter of an escalation that could spiral into a Third World War.

To avoid this outcome, it will be necessary for American and Chinese leaders to find common ground. This will be a difficult task given the great antagonisms between the two world superpowers, on the economic and technological levels of course, but also in the field of ideology and, above all, in that of their respective geopolitical ambitions. The United States intends to remain the world's policeman, while China wishes to snatch that place from them. Neither Beijing nor Washington can appear weak, at the risk of discrediting themselves in the eyes of their allies and, in the case of the United States, of public opinion.

One needs to ask if China's move towards an open alignment with Moscow is a tacit recognition by Xi of China's relative weakness. Takashi Suzuki, a professor at Japan's Aichi University and an expert on Chinese politics, told *Nikkei Asia* on February 20, 2023, that Xi Jinping is well aware that China is gradually falling into a disadvantageous position as time goes by, especially with its economy stagnating and the possibility of India overtaking China.

"If Xi is pushed to the wall, he could make misjudgments on issues like Taiwan. As the late Prime Minister Shinzo Abe described in his recent memoirs, Xi is a 'hardened realist' but he could come to adopt extreme and unrealistic policies," the Japanese newspaper pointed out. "It is risky to push China too far, both politically and economically," added the newspaper, which also stressed the validity of Joe Biden's desire to continue dialogue with his Chinese counterpart.

It will therefore take a good deal of wisdom, intelligence, tact and patience for the leaders of these two countries to find the narrow path of mutual trust. There is nothing to say that they will not succeed. But today, considering the current situation, one can only wonder how useful it is for Washington to preach the continuation of this dialogue. One key test will be whether Beijing supports Moscow's war effort. Chinese President Xi Jinping visited Moscow in March 2023. During this visit he and his Russian counterpart Vladimir Putin reaffirmed the unbreakable friendship between China and Russia. However, the Chinese head of state refrained from endorsing the joint Sino-Russian declaration of 4 February 2022, which states the friendship between Russia and China has "no limits." While Xi did not do so, Putin did. It can be interpreted as a signal of China's desire not to appear too close to Russia amid the war in Ukraine. While the visit gave Putin a public relations boost, there was no public announcement by Chinese authorities that they would provide Russia with much-needed military supplies. But it should also be noted that China has never condemned Russian aggression in Ukraine and never called it a "war."

Notes

1   See my book *Le leadership mondial en question: L'affrontement entre la Chine et les États-Unis* [Global leadership in question: The confrontation between China and the United States], l'Aube, 2020, which deals extensively with this issue.

2   At least 20 Indian and four Chinese soldiers died in a confrontation on the disputed border in Ladakh, northern India, on the night of June 15–16, 2021, the first deadly military clash in 45 years between the two Asian giants.

Afterword

Since the first publication of this book in French in August 2021, much has transpired. Some developments have been integrated into the body of the book, while others I have chosen to treat here.

I shall endeavor to trace those most essential to where we stand at the beginning of 2023.

The August 2022 visit to Taiwan by Nancy Pelosi, then the speaker of the US House of Representatives, was a very important test for mainland China, as it represented the presence on the island of the highest-ranking American politician in 25 years. Taiwanese President Tsai Ing-wen received Pelosi, who took the opportunity to not only cross the t's but also dot the i's about the US commitment to Taiwan. Pelosi repeatedly stated that the United States would never allow China to take over Taiwan. Not surprisingly, the authorities in Beijing did not take the visit well. But they not only expressed their anger; they also unleashed military operations on a scale not seen since 1950 in what took the form of an encirclement of Taiwan and, to some extent, a trade and political blockade.

This backfired spectacularly. It highlighted China's growing isolation while Taiwan received messages of solidarity from neighboring nations. The Chinese overreaction also generated an amount of coverage of Taiwan in the Western media unseen in decades. It also helped to justify the policies of military rearmament already launched by China's neighbors and the renewal of their alliances with the United States, and gave them fresh impetus.

Take the example of Japan. The keystone of the country's pacifist post-World War II constitution is that its military is for defensive purposes only. After Fumio Kishida took office as Japan's prime minister in October 2021, he quickly became an advocate of strengthening his country's military capabilities. During his first inspection of Japanese troops the following month, Kishida stressed that the security situation around Japan was changing rapidly and that "the reality is severer than ever" due to North Korea's launching of ever more powerful ballistic missiles and China's military buildup and increasingly assertive activity in the region. "I will consider all options, including possessing so-called enemy base strike capability, to pursue strengthening of defense power that is necessary," Kishida said (*Associated Press*, 2021).

The acquisition of such a "strike capability" against foreign military targets was a radical departure from Japan's defensive posture and was highly divisive. It has since become referred to as a "counterstrike" capability to convey the idea that the capability is considered defensive in nature. That is what it was called in an updated national defense strategy adopted at the end of 2022.

The first update in Japan's national security and defense strategies in a decade made ample reference to Russia's invasion of Ukraine as an indication that the global power balance has shifted and the competition across the political, economic and military spheres is intensifying. But the strategy document put special emphasis on China: "Such trends are especially notable in the Indo-Pacific region, where China has been continuing and amplifying its unilateral changes to the status quo by force and such attempts" (Ministry of Defense of Japan, 2022). North Korea and Russia have also further intensified their activities, it added. The document said that the United States believes the rivalry with China is likely to intensify, with the coming decade being critical: "As the interstate competition between China and the United States in particular is expected to further intensify in various fields, the United States has presented a view that the next ten years will be the decisive decade for its competition with China."

Japan's national security strategy continues to view the alliance with the United States as the cornerstone of an effective defense. But it says that Japan must be able to make an effective contribution and that a deterrence capability is necessary to dissuade "unilateral changes to the status quo by force," such as Russia's invasion of Ukraine or a possible Chinese invasion of Taiwan:

> To protect one's own country from such states, it is necessary to have deterrence capability, thereby making said states realize that unilateral changes to the status quo by force are difficult; it is also necessary to build one's own capability, that is defense capability focusing on opponent capabilities, to discourage opponents from harboring the intention to launch an aggression.

The counterstrike capability is seen as being part of this deterrent, as well as being part of the military alliance with the United States:

> It must operate with US forces and integrate a variety of missions such as cross-domain operations, hybrid operations including information warfare, and missile interception and counterstrike...Japan needs capabilities with which to disrupt and defeat invading forces over long distances, thereby deterring invasion itself.

Kishida has moved quickly to boost military funding, seeking an additional 770 billion yen ($6.8 billion) in spending in the fiscal year that started in April 2022, to fund the purchase of missiles, anti-submarine rockets and other armaments to counter escalating military activities by China, Russia and North Korea. His proposal for fiscal year 2023 is for a massive 26.3% increase to 6.8 trillion yen ($51.4 billion). That would take

Japan's defense spending to just under 1.2% of GDP, blowing past the informal limit of roughly 1% that successive Japanese have followed since World War II. Kishida in November 2022 set a target of military spending reaching 2% of GDP (which is what NATO alliance countries are encouraged to spend) by 2027.

The 2023 military budget includes $1.6 billion to buy cruise missiles. Defense Minister Yasukazu Hamada said in February 2023 that Japan plans to bulk-order Tomahawk cruise missiles from the United States by March 2024 as part of its rapid military buildup (*Reuters*, 2023). These ship- and submarine-launched missiles, which according to their manufacturer, Raytheon, can strike targets accurately from 1000 miles (1600 km) away, would help Japan to acquire a counterstrike capability.

As part of the deepening military cooperation with the United States, Japan in January 2023 authorized the transformation of a US Marine Corps regiment based in Okinawa to become a force capable of rapidly deploying to remote islands and armed with advanced weapons including anti-ship missiles that could be fired at Chinese ships in the event of an invasion of Taiwan (Nakashima et al., 2023).

Kishida has also not hesitated to raise the issue of Taiwan, including when meeting with Xi Jinping in November 2022 in Thailand on the sidelines of the Asia-Pacific Economic Cooperation (APEC) summit meeting. "I reiterated the importance of peace and security in the Taiwan Strait," Kishida told reporters after the summit, but did not indicate the Chinese leader's reaction (Murakami et al., 2022).

This geostrategic shift by Japan undoubtedly represents a fundamental shift in the geostrategic balance in East Asia, the region seen as the center of gravity for global economic growth in the years ahead. It accentuates an increasing isolation of China in this area as alliances between some of China's neighbors deepen around the United States.

Take for example the Philippines, which has begun renewing its military ties with the United States after they reached a nadir in the early 1990s, when a dispute over leasing costs resulted in the United States leaving its massive naval base in Subic Bay, the linchpin in the US ability to project force in the Southeast Asian region. In 2014 the Philippines signed an Enhanced Defense Cooperation Agreement with the United States. This allows the United States to rotate troops into the Philippines for extended stays, and allows the United States to build and operate facilities on Philippine bases for both American and Philippine forces, but not to establish permanent bases. In February 2023, the Philippines agreed to provide US military forces access to another four of its military facilities. During a visit to Manila to conclude the arrangement, US Defense Secretary Lloyd Austin called it "part of our efforts to modernize our alliance. And these efforts are especially important as the People's Republic of China continues to advance its illegitimate claims in the West Philippine Sea."

Meanwhile, Australia has also deepened its military alliances. In September 2021 it announced it would partner with the United States and United Kingdom in a tripartite alliance called AUKUS. The Australian defense ministry said the alliance is "based on our enduring ideals and a shared commitment of our three countries to a stable, secure and prosperous Indo-Pacific region." The most concrete element in the announcement was that the partnership would help Australia to acquire conventionally armed nuclear-powered submarines while still adhering to its nuclear non-proliferation obligations. Nuclear submarines, which are capable of staying submerged and thus hidden for a longer time, would pose an additional challenge to Chinese forces. Australia has been aligned with the United States and United Kingdom, as well as Canada and New Zealand, in a signals intelligence grouping called Five Eyes since World War II. It then joined in 1951 with the United States and New Zealand in ANZUS, a non-binding collective security agreement. A Defense Trade Cooperation Treaty came into force in 2013. Similar to the one the United States has with Britain, the treaty makes it much easier to gain access to advanced weapons. US troops have been rotating into Darwin every year since 2012 to train with their Australian counterparts.

The United States has also stepped up its military support for Taiwan, with lawmakers in December approving up to $2 billion a year between 2023 and 2027 for the acquisition of military equipment, and US agencies required to fast-track Taiwan's weapons requests and purchases. Finally, Congress legislated to allow the participation of Taiwanese armed forces in the US joint military exercises in the Pacific (RIMPAC) in 2024. The legislation stresses that the US decision to establish diplomatic relations with China in 1979 was based on the idea that Taiwan's future would be settled by peaceful means. As such, any attempt to impose its future on the island by any other means, "including boycotts, embargoes, is a matter of grave concern to the United States." It added that since the election of Tsai Ing-wen as president in 2016, Taiwan has been subjected to intimidation campaigns by the authorities in Beijing aimed at weakening it "diplomatically, economically and militarily."

The law also stipulates the need to strengthen Taiwan's "diplomatic, economic and territorial status" if necessary.

Tensions between China and the United States were ratcheted up in early 2023 by the disastrous odyssey of a Chinese spy balloon over US territory which ended in a complete fiasco for China. The immediate consequence was a return to arm-wrestling between Washington and Beijing, with the non-negligible risk of an uncontrolled escalation between the two superpowers of the planet.

On the orders of US President Joe Biden, on February 4 an American F-22 Raptor fighter plane shot down the balloon, which was cruising at an altitude of 18 kilometers and had just passed off the country's east coast. A search and recovery mission was launched to determine the surveillance capabilities of the Chinese aircraft, initially presented by the Beijing authorities as a simple meteorological observation balloon which had ventured into American airspace by mistake. Yet it quickly became clear that the balloon did so with the aim of spying on sensitive American military facilities, in particular in the state of Montana, where there are numerous silos housing Minuteman III intercontinental nuclear missiles, as well as air bases housing strategic bombers, which are also nuclear capable. After initially minimizing the incident and expressing "regret," the Chinese authorities hardened their tone when the balloon was destroyed and demanded the return of the recovered debris to China, which Biden categorically ruled out.

Washington did not directly respond to the Chinese government's assertion that by shooting the balloon out of the skies the United States had "seriously affected and damaged" relations between the two countries. Biden appeared to be walking a fine line between trying to keep tensions from escalating with the Chinese and not appearing soft amid mounting clamor among lawmakers and commentators. "It's not a question of trusting China, it's a question of deciding where we should work together and where we have opposition," the US president said when questioned by reporters two days after the balloon was shot down. National Security Adviser Jake Sullivan said on February 6 at a debate in Washington that "the United States is not looking for a new Cold War" with China. While defending its position of firmness, the United States even reiterated its desire to maintain open "lines of communication" with its great strategic rival. "Even in this time of heightened tension, in the context of the discovery of the high-altitude surveillance balloon, we wanted to be able to pick up the phone to speak to one another," State Department spokesman Ned Price said on February 6. Price said that the United States had

had contacts with the Chinese authorities since the destruction of the balloon, while specifying that no "discussion" had taken place on the rescheduling of the visit of the Secretary of State Antony Blinken to China.

The postponement of this trip, which many had hoped would renew dialogue between the two countries following a period of increased tensions over trade and Taiwan, was the first consequence of the balloon incident. Blinken had been due to leave Washington for Beijing soon after this balloon became visible to the naked eye by the inhabitants of Montana. But as Chinese claims that the aircraft was a meteorological observation balloon lost credibility when it maneuvered over sensitive military sites, the secretary of state postponed the visit.

Several US intelligence officials quoted by the *Washington Post* in the days after the balloon was downed said that it was part of a vast surveillance program run by the Chinese People's Liberation Army for several years, mainly from the southern Chinese island of Hainan. This program aims to collect military intelligence in countries such as India, Japan, Vietnam, Taiwan and the Philippines, a strategic area for Chinese interests. But the program also operates in many other countries on five continents, according to these officials. "What the Chinese have done is based on incredibly old technology but combined with modern communications and elaborate observation capabilities," said one of the experts. "This is a massive effort," he added.

When an American Sidewinder missile downed the balloon, it also blew China's image to pieces. Faced with the extent of this fiasco for China, a series of questions arises: Why and how could such an operation have been decided in Beijing? What was the aim of the Chinese authorities, who knew very well that balloon flights would eventually be detected and would inevitably cause a cataclysm in the already tense relations between China and the United States?

The extreme opacity that surrounds the decision-making process in the Chinese leadership means one can only postulate about various scenarios. Among them is a failure in the coordination between China's diplomatic and intelligence services. According to this scenario, neither the Communist Party nor the Chinese government had been warned by military intelligence officials, who acted independently. Although the Chinese leadership is obviously very embarrassed by the repercussions of this disastrous affair, this thesis seems unlikely to some experts. Indeed, even though China's leadership has recently shown a certain disorganization and feverishness, how can one seriously imagine that it was not kept informed of such an operation, which goes to the heart of the rivalry between China and the United States?

The *Financial Times* suggests another possible explanation: an act inside China's leadership aimed at destabilizing President Xi Jinping and sabotaging Antony Blinken's visit to Beijing. "An open question is whether Xi Jinping knew about the mission and approved it, and what the assumptions were about its potential impact on [US] relations," said Drew Thompson at the Lee Kuan Yew School of Public Policy in Singapore. "We don't know whether this demonstrates that the People's Liberation Army is not co-ordinating politically sensitive missions with the party leadership, or whether the PLA is throwing a wrench into Xi Jinping's effort to lower the temperature of the US-China relationship," he added (Mitchell et al., 2023).

Another scenario is that of a deliberate operation to challenge, if not provoke, the United States in the context of Russia's invasion of Ukraine and strong signs of China's willingness to move closer to Moscow. If this thesis were to be confirmed, it would have very serious consequences for Washington-Beijing relations. Xi Jingping's March 2023 visit to Moscow was inconclusive in this regard. Moscow did not receive any public commitments from the Chinese about supplying Russia with much-needed military equipment. That would have been a direct affront to the West. Washington is, of course, watching closely whether China supplies weapons, particularly ammunition, covertly. A number of comments by Chinese diplomats in early 2023 lend weight to the thesis that China is shifting towards Moscow's camp, however. On February 6, China's ambassador to France, Lu Shaye, justified Russia's invasion of Ukraine by saying its security interests were threatened by the United States when the war began. A Chinese foreign ministry spokeswoman, speaking in the clearest of terms since the war began on February 24, 2022, laid the blame for the conflict on the United States. China's top diplomat, Wang Yi, visited Moscow just before the first anniversary of the start of the Ukraine war as part of a European tour, where he was received by President Vladimir Putin. While no firm developments were announced, Wang told Putin: "With the Russian side, we are ready to strengthen our strategic partnership and our in-depth cooperation," according to a Russian translation of his statement. For his part, Putin was clear about the importance of pulling China into an alliance. "The cooperation between China and Russia on the world stage is very important to stabilize the international situation," he said at the meeting with Wang Yi (*AFP*, 2023b).

Besides the concerns that China could provide Russia with critically needed supplies to continue its offensive in Ukraine, the shift away from a neutral position on Ukraine raises questions about whether Xi is ready for a major military confrontation with the United States. The backdrop to the balloon adventure is Beijing's often stated desire to "conquer" Taiwan, which Beijing considers a mere province, by force if necessary. Xi Jinping has repeated this statement with greater urgency in recent months.

The Speaker of the US House of Representatives, Kevin McCarthy, met with Taiwanese President Tsai Ing-wen in California in April 2023, despite repeated threats of retaliation from China. "We are not isolated," Tsai Ing-wen said. The

Taiwanese leader welcomed the presence of a large US congressional delegation during her visit. She said this was proof of Washington's "unwavering" support for Taiwan. Pro-Beijing and pro-Taiwan demonstrators faced off in front of the Ronald Reagan Presidential Library as Tsai, who was officially in "transit" through the United States on her way home from a tour of Latin American countries, arrived for the meeting. Beijing was extremely annoyed, with its foreign minister stating that "China is firmly opposed" to the meeting between the third-ranking US official and the Taiwanese leader, who comes from a pro-independence party. Beijing also stated that it was ready to "firmly defend its national sovereignty and territorial integrity," without expressly mentioning possible military maneuvers. It ran air and sea drills encircling Taiwan.

The discovery and downing of three other possible spy balloons—origins unknown—in the week following the downing of the original balloon will serve to keep the issue at the top of the agenda, as will any information gleaned from recovered wreckage. So too will the fact that Republicans have seized upon the issue to paint Biden as weak on China. All of this will make it difficult to reschedule Blinken's visit to China, which was supposed to lead to renewed dialogue and change the direction of bilateral relations.

The catastrophic management of the Covid-19 pandemic has demonstrated that the Chinese Communist Party is not omnipotent and that, like other totalitarian regimes, it can be surprisingly brittle. China was the last major country in the world where the authorities still imposed draconian confinement measures on the population to stem the pandemic. By November 2022 the Chinese had had enough of these. Protests spread like wildfire to more than a dozen cities in China, on several occasions taking on openly political colors, and quickly became the largest anti-regime demonstrations since the Tiananmen Square massacre in June 1989 and a challenge to the country's master, Xi Jinping. Starting in Zhengzhou, capital of the central province of Henan, anger against the zero-Covid policy boiled over among some of the 200,000 workers at the Taiwanese mega-factory Foxconn, which assembles Apple's iPhone. A few days later, the protests spread to Urumqi in Xinjiang, then to Beijing, Guangzhou, Nanjing, Chengdu, Chongqing and Shanghai. In China's economic capital, a crowd that gathered on November 27 shouted "Xi Jinping resign! CCP resign!" Shouting such slogans in public in China is rare and can lead to heavy prison sentences. It demonstrated the degree of frustration and anger among the Chinese population, who are faced with living conditions that have become unbearable for many. The protests also spread to the capital's two largest campuses: Beida, Peking University and the prestigious Tsinghua University, a first since 1989. Hundreds of students gathered to lambast the authorities' management of the Covid-19 pandemic, denouncing the strict lockdowns as contrary to fundamental public freedoms. The Nanjing University of Communications was also the scene of demonstrations, as were other campuses across the country.

At the demonstrations in Shanghai and elsewhere, some people came with white flowers to express their solidarity with those who died in a November 24 fire in their building in Urumqi, a city of 4 million people. At least ten people died in the fire in the capital city of the Xinjiang region, which is home to some 10 million Uyghurs, the Turkic-speaking Muslim minority that has been the victim of a relentless crackdown since 2015. The victims were trapped in their apartments when the flames spread from the 15th to the 17th floor of their building. The door was locked from the outside by guards who were enforcing strict containment orders, according to residents' accounts. According to one official version, fire trucks coming to rescue the building's residents could not park nearby because of the private cars crowding the parking spaces. The local authorities even stated that "the capacity of these people to save themselves was too low," an explanation that further amplified the anger on Chinese social networks, with expressions of discontent quickly censored as is always the case in China. This censorship has also become a source of anger. Many of the demonstrators in these cities carried white sheets of paper, with no messages, because it was the only way to express their hostility to the censorship. A few days earlier, hundreds of demonstrators had gathered in the streets of Urumqi, a city that is very closely monitored because of the presence of Uyghurs. Many of the demonstrators carried Chinese flags while demanding an end to the confinement. One woman held up sheets of paper with the number 10 in Uyghur and Chinese, referring to the number of deaths in the city. Several people in the crowd did the same, according to the *Washington Post*. "After a while, everyone started doing the same thing," said Meng, a photographer who told the newspaper and gave it his pictures of the demonstration. "Nobody said anything, but we all know what it means. Delete what you want. You won't be able to censor what is not said," he said. At Nanjing Communications University, posters ridiculing the country's zero-Covid policy were quickly torn down. But then a student stood for several hours in front of the remains of one of the posters, holding up a sheet of white paper. Several hundred students then joined him, the newspaper reported. Some of them placed white flowers on the ground to honor the memory of the Urumqi fire victims and began to sing "Rest in Peace." Others sang the Chinese national anthem, one part of which goes: "Stand up! People who don't want to be slaves anymore!" Then they sang the Internationale, before shouting "Long live the people," the *Washington Post* reported. In Beijing, students hung blue masks stained with red ink on the banisters of the Film Academy, according to *Radio France Internationale*. At Harbin University in the northern province of Heilongjiang, messages in red letters were taped behind dormitory windows: "Give me liberty or give me death—silent tribute to the victims of Urumqi." The slogan was not chosen at random: it was chanted by the hundreds of thousands of demonstrators who gathered in Tiananmen Square in May and June 1989 to demand more democracy in China. On June 4, on the orders of then leader Deng Xiaoping, the People's Liberation Army fired live ammunition into the crowd, killing up to 2000 people according to the most credible estimates of foreign observers on the ground.

On the evening of November 27, 2022, between 300 and 400 people gathered for several hours on the banks of the Liangmahe River, which runs through central Beijing. According to *AFP* journalists who witnessed the scene, some shouted: "We are all people from Xinjiang! Go, Chinese people!" Other universities also saw similar protests, including those in Xi'an and Wuhan, the city where the first cases of Covid-19 were detected in late 2019. In this city, students at the University of Technology placed candles on the ground forming the numbers 11.24 in memory of the Urumqi fire victims. The images of the white sheets brandished by the protesters in Urumqi and then elsewhere in major Chinese cities quickly flooded social networks, including the messaging system WeChat, with the Chinese censors having great difficulty in quickly eliminating them as they were so numerous. These white sheets very quickly became the symbol of protest wherever it was expressed. In the small town of Wuzhen, in Zhejiang Province south of Shanghai, a young woman appears in a video walking through the streets with chains around her wrists, a bandage over her mouth and white paper in her hands. The video was quickly deleted from social networks. The white sheets were already the symbol of the protest in Hong Kong in 2020: the demonstrators were expressing their opposition to the national security law imposed in June by Beijing, which has had the effect of silencing all forms of protest in the former British colony. Initially caught off guard by the huge flow of images and comments on social networks, Beijing's censors eventually got the upper hand, so that little or nothing was visible the next day. "Tens of millions of posts were filtered out" and then those deemed subversive were removed, according to Kerry Allen, a BBC media analyst. It's an ingenious ploy because for the authorities "to fear white sheets [to make them grounds for arrest] would be an admission of weakness," she added. This wind of protest was a real political challenge for the Chinese government. It demonstrated, on the one hand, the unsuspected courage of the demonstrators who deliberately took great risks and, on the other, the impossibility for the authorities to keep a tight lid on these events, despite the considerable means of censorship at their disposal. However, these same authorities have enormous means of repression to silence the protests, in blood if necessary, as was the case in June 1989. Bringing together a few tens of thousands of demonstrators in total, out of a Chinese population of 1.4 billion, these demonstrations may seem insignificant at first glance. But they are just the tip of an iceberg of pent-up anger among Chinese who are afraid to come out into the open, knowing the punishment they would face if they did.

Even though the protests dissipated after the abandonment of the zero-Covid policy (see below), they will go down in the history of contemporary China as proof that the "social stability" that the Party has done everything it can to erect as dogma is more fragile than people think. "I don't know if people can appreciate just how unusual this is in a Chinese context," said John Delury, a sinologist at Yonsei University in Seoul, quoted by the *Financial Times*. "To hear these spontaneous groups chanting 'we want freedom', singing protest anthems and ironically using patriotic songs to protest the lockdowns—it's astonishing." "Xi should learn something from this," said Lance Gore, a China expert at the National University of Singapore, who was born in Maoist China and attended Peking University in the 1980s. "He's not God. He can't control everything. He has to learn that modern government requires negotiation, compromise and give-and-take" (Mitchell et al., 2022).

Venting of pent-up anger over restrictive zero-Covid policies was also triggered by the live broadcast of the World Cup football matches in Qatar by the national television channel CCTV. Censors usually wield firm control over what outside information is presented to the Chinese. But the live feed from the matches also occasionally showed the stands, and the Chinese discovered to their amazement that the thousands of fans were not wearing masks, even though they themselves were still obliged to wear them constantly as soon as they left their homes. The images immediately sparked a wave of indignation across the country. The censors realized they had made a mistake and quickly corrected it, so that the CCTV cameras no longer showed images of fans shouting for joy in the stands without masks, or hugging each other to greet their team's victory. But the damage was done. And the damage is much deeper than it seems. "'Zero-Covid' is only a surface problem. The real problem is there is no constraint on the state's intrusion into private citizens' rights," a student told the *Financial Times*, while asking to remain anonymous to avoid police reprisals.

The main difficulty China had in abandoning its zero-Covid policy was that since early 2020, the chief architect of the management of the pandemic was none other than Xi Jinping himself. At the CCP's 20th Congress in October, he clearly stated that the zero-Covid policy would remain in place because "it saves lives." Since the pandemic began, the guiding motto of the Chinese authorities had been "Life rather than economy" and they willingly accepted the impact of draconian confinement upon the nation's economy. But two other poor choices also meant that the abandonment of the zero-Covid policy was likely to be extremely deadly. The first is the refusal to use Western messenger-RNA vaccines, whose proven effectiveness is far superior to that of the Chinese Sinopharm and Sinovac vaccines.

This refusal was for reasons of national pride, as Beijing and its propaganda could not accept the obvious: the weaknesses of Chinese scientific and medical research compared to that of the West. The second mistake was not taking earlier steps to boost the country's low rate of vaccination, especially among the elderly. Hence the serious risk of a deadly spike in deaths when confinement measures were finally relaxed.

But, facing the growing anger in the country and the enormous strain on the economy, the regime made an about-face and abandoned zero-Covid restrictions over the period from November 2022 to January 2023. Since January 8, Chinese people have once again been allowed to travel anywhere in the world, while foreigners can cross Chinese borders without special restrictions. Except that, alarmed by the explosion of infections that seems to have spiraled out of control in the country, a dozen nations, including France, took measures to screen the arrival of Chinese travelers, fearing that they could spread new mutations of the Omicron variant. As usual, the Chinese government responded by criticizing "discriminatory" measures and threatened unspecified retaliatory measures.

The abandonment of zero-Covid didn't mean that China abandoned its tendency to keep things hidden. As it dropped confinement measures, China also narrowed the definition of what it considered to be a death from Covid-19, which prompted criticism from the World Health Organization (WHO) that the country was underreporting Covid deaths. From December 7 to January 5, China had officially recognized only 23 deaths from Covid-19 in an obvious attempt to not add to the prevailing panic in the country and to the anxiety around the world (*AFP*, 2023c). On December 25, the National Health Commission stopped publishing the number of daily cases, without giving an explanation. This detailed and authoritative information had been published since January 21, 2020. But faced with mounting evidence of crematoriums and hospitals being overrun, on

January 14 Chinese officials finally acknowledged that there had been almost 60,000 Covid-related deaths over the previous month. That figure included not only those who died due to respiratory failure, but also those whose underlying conditions were aggravated by Covid-19. Nevertheless, as the figure was only for deaths in medical institutions, it was certainly an undercount (*AFP*, 2023d).

The true figure could be orders of magnitude higher. The UK-based health-modeling firm Airfinity (2023) has provided a series of forecasts on the Covid-19 pandemic in China. In its February 6 update, it estimated the number of total deaths from December 1, 2022, to January 17, 2023, to be 608,000. This latest episode shows that the Beijing regime still prefers to conceal reality, just as it has done since the fall of 2019 when a first case of Covid-19 was identified in the city of Wuhan, whether it concerns the origins of the virus or its spread throughout the country.

Chinese authorities recognized that the lifting of the zero-Covid policy would cause an increase in infections. As Lei Zhenglong, an official at the National Center for Disease Prevention and Control, explained in *China Daily*, the changes, including no quarantine for people infected or in close contact with someone infected, "will result in a surge of infections and increased demand for medical services, and will lead to a shortage of medical resources in the early phase. The public may be anxious about being infected due to the surge, and [there will be] fear resulting from infection" (Cheng, S. 2022). The United States, the European Union and Taiwan offered to send millions of vaccines to China. But Beijing did not take them up on the offer, again no doubt due to worries about the message this would send. Some treatments nevertheless became available in Beijing in January, albeit in small quantities. Concerns became so great that, in order to try to limit the number of serious cases, the authorities started to distribute a Pfizer treatment, Paxlovid, in some districts of the Chinese capital. This distribution was done in small shipments and under very close surveillance, as the Chinese are ready to do anything to obtain the drug.

Not everyone had access. One Beijing health center received only a few boxes, as a doctor interviewed by *France Info* explained on January 3: "We were able to get this drug here, but it is reserved for people over 65. And still, not everyone can get it like that. We reserve it for those who need it the most and only for those who officially reside in the neighborhood," said the doctor.

Haunted by images of overcrowded hospitals, many Chinese saw the Pfizer treatment as the only solution to avoid a severe form of Covid-19. In the face of overwhelming demand, a parallel market began to develop. Anti-corruption authorities in the capital began keeping a close eye on health centers and announced that each box prescribed was being traced to prevent it ending up on the black market.

Criticism emerged even in the Hong Kong press, which is loyal to Beijing. According to the *South China Morning Post* of December 23: "China is woefully unprepared for the inevitable chaos that has ensued since the restrictions were lifted. The question is: since China has had nearly three years to learn from other countries and prepare for the reopening, how can such a fiasco be explained?"

The abandonment of the zero-Covid policy, forced onto the government by the people, did little to restore their trust. For three years the Chinese had been told their country was at the forefront of fighting against the pandemic—a success story. In fact, it was the opposite: the last major country to be hard hit by a vertiginous rise in infections and mortality. Official propaganda was once again shown to be empty. The epic size of the failure to prepare adequately undermined the legitimacy that the Communist Party had cultivated with its successful management of the economy.

On that front, nothing was settled either. Far from it. On Thursday, January 5, the *Nikkei Asia* described a "chaotic" situation with a breakdown of supply chains in the country's high-tech sector. "Beijing's sudden abandonment of its 'zero Covid' policy was supposed to resuscitate a collapsing economy. But this precipitous 180-degree turn from extreme controls to no controls at all has thrown supply chains into chaos with high levels of contamination producing a severe labor shortage," wrote Cheng Ting-Fang and Cissy Zhou in the Japanese newspaper's columns.

This chaos is causing many foreign investors to consider leaving the country and choosing other locations for their offshore production. The idea that is gaining ground in the West is to reduce dependence on China.

The American giant Apple has already been forced to inform its customers of major delays in deliveries of MacBooks and AirPods. The same goes for South Korean manufacturer Samsung, which assembles some of its smartphones in China.

Koji Arima, CEO of Japanese automotive parts company Denso, told *Nikkei Asia* that its main customer Toyota had already decided to reduce its dependence on Chinese industry for semiconductors and to strengthen its cooperation in this field with Taiwanese producers.

The American computer manufacturer Dell has announced its intention to abandon the use of Chinese microprocessors in favor of other manufacturers. For one of the leaders of these supply chains quoted by the *Nikkei Asia*, "this trend seems irreversible."

Meudon, France, February 23, 2023

References

ActionAid International (2014) *The Great Land Heist* [Online] Available at https://actionaid.org/publications/2014/great-land-heist (Accessed 3 February 2023)

Agence France-Presse (*AFP*) (2019) 'Espionnage: Airbus cible d'une série de cyberattaques via ses sous-traitants', 26 September [Online] Available at https://o.nouvelobs.com/high-tech/20190926.AFP5409/espionnage-airbus-cible-d-une-serie-de-cyberattaques-via-ses-sous-traitants.html (Accessed 24 January 2023)

(2019b) 'China rejects "smear" after Airbus hacking report', 27 September [Online] Available at https://www.rfi.fr/en/contenu/20190927-china-rejects-smear-after-airbus-hacking-report (Accessed 24 January 2023)

(2021) 'Xinjiang a "shining example" of China's human rights progress: minister', 22 February [Online] Available at https://www.france24.com/en/live-news/20210222-xinjiang-a-shining-example-of-china-s-human-rights-progress-minister (Accessed 21 January 2023)

(2021b) 'Ouïghours: l'UE, le Canada et les USA sanctionnent la Chine, Pékin réplique', 22 March.

(2021c) 'Chine: situation "considérablement détériorée" pour les médias étrangers (rapport)', 1 March [Online] Available at https://www.france24.com/fr/info-en-continu/20210301-chine-situation-consid%C3%A9rablement-d%C3%A9t%C3%A9rior%C3%A9e-pour-les-m%C3%A9dias-%C3%A9trangers-selon-un-rapport (Accessed 25 January 2023)

(2021d) 'China exported more than 220 billion masks in 2020: government', 29 January [Online] https://www.rfi.fr/en/business-and-tech/20210129-china-exported-more-than-220-billion-masks-in-2020-government (Accessed 28 January 2023)

(2022) 'Yellen says China a "barrier" in African debt relief', 14 October [Online] Available at https://english.alarabiya. net/News/world/2022/10/15/Yellen-says-China-a-barrier-in-African-debt-relief (Accessed 28 January 2023)

(2023) 'International fusion energy project faces delays, says chief', 6 January [Online] Available at https://phys. org/news/2023-01-international-fusion-energy-delays-chief. html (Accessed 24 January 2023)

(2023b) 'Russia-China ties key to "stabilise international situation": Putin', 22 February [Online] Available at https:// www.channelnewsasia.com/world/russia-china-ties-key-stabilise-international-situation-vladimir-putin-wang-yi-3297026 (Accessed 23 February 2023)

(2023c) 'China insists Covid data "transparent" after WHO criticism', 5 January [Online] Available at https:// www.rfi.fr/en/international-news/20230105-china-insists-covid-data-transparent-after-who-criticism (Accessed 5 February 2023)

(2023d) 'China reports almost 60,000 Covid-related deaths in a month', 14 January [Online] Available at https:// www.rfi.fr/en/international-news/20230114-china-reports-almost-60-000-covid-related-deaths-in-a-month (Accessed 5 February 2023)

Airfinity (2023) 'Airfinity's COVID-19 forecast for China's infections and deaths', 6 February [Online] Available at https:// www.airfinity.com/articles/airfinitys-covid-19-forecast-for-china-infections-and-deaths (Accessed 6 February)

Allen-Ebrahimian, B. (2021) 'Estonia warns of "silenced world dominated by Beijing"', *Axios*, 17 February [Online] Available at https://www.axios.com/estonia-warns-of-silenced-world-dominated-by-beijing-09e54843-6b45-491a-9bfd-e880f6f14795. html?fbclid=IwAR2CEYo8oDoE6RBPUX9W5A8RCyb_ gojlycB6-cJBbzRWyO5zIfnnhAJlxAo (Accessed 28 January 2023)

(2021b) 'Growing number of countries issue warnings on China's espionage', *Axios*, 16 February [Online] Available at https://www.axios.com/2021/02/16/china-espionage-europe (Accessed 4 February 2023)

Alonso, P. (2021) 'La Chine à l'école russe de la désinformation', *Libération*, 9 March [Online] Available at https://www. liberation.fr/international/la-chine-a-lecole-russe-de-la-desinformation-20210309_ZKICU6EJ3BEHDMR55NAJS556VA/ (Accessed 25 January 2023)

Alper, A., Sterling, T. and Nellis, S. (2020) 'Trump administration pressed Dutch hard to cancel China chip-equipment sale: sources', *Reuters*, 6 January [Online] Available at https:// www.reuters.com/article/us-asml-holding-usa-china-insight-idUSKBN1Z50HN (Accessed 23 January 2023)

Amnesty International (2020) 'EU companies selling surveillance tools to China's human rights abusers' [Online] Available at https://www.amnesty.org/en/latest/press-release/2020/09/ eu-surveillance-sales-china-human-rights-abusers/ (Accessed 17 January 2023)

André, J. (2021) 'Comment la Chine pousse ses pions à l'université', *Le Point*, 25 February [Online] Available at https://journal.lepoint.fr/comment-la-chine-pousse-ses-pions-a-l-universite-2415125 (Accessed 21 January 2023)

(2021b) 'Comment Pékin profite de nos chercheurs', *Le Point*, 19 March [Online] Available at https://www.

lepoint.fr/monde/comment-pekin-profite-de-nos-chercheu rs-19-03-2021-2418494_24.php (Accessed 24 January 2023) (2021c) 'Covid: "La thèse du laboratoire de Wuhan n'est pas une théorie du complot"', *Le Point*, 17 February [Online] https://www.lepoint.fr/monde/covid-la-these-du-laboratoire-de-wuhan-n-est-pas-une-theorie-du-complot-17-02-2021-2414409_24.php#xtmc=andre-metzl-coronavirus&xtnp=1&xtcr=1 (Accessed 28 January 2023)

Anglade, C. (2020) 'Pour lutter contre la sécheresse, la Chine ambitionne de faire la pluie et le beau temps', TF1info, 16 December [Online] Available at https://www.tf1info.fr/ environnement-ecologie/pour-lutter-contre-la-secheresse-la-chine-ambitionne-de-faire-la-pluie-et-le-beau-temps-2173009.html (Accessed 22 January 2023)

APN News (2020) 'Mer de Chine: la France, l'Allemagne et le Royaume-Uni dans la bataille diplomatique', 2 October [Online] Available at https://asiepacifique.fr/mer-de-chine-france-allemagne-royaumeuni-bataille-diplomatique/ (Accessed 28 January 2023)

Armstrong, S. (2020) *Brain Drain: The UK, China, and the Question of Intellectual Property Theft*, Henry Jackson Society [Online] Available at https://henryjacksonsociety.org/publications/ chinaiptheft/ (Accessed 24 January 2023)

Arnaud, B. (2021) 'La Chine réécrit-elle son histoire?', *Sciences et Avenir*, 25 January [Online] Available at https://www. sciencesetavenir.fr/archeo-paleo/archeologie/la-chine-reecrit-elle-son-histoire_151199 (Accessed 25 January 2023)

Associated Press (2021) 'Japan PM Kishida vows to step up defense amid China, North Korea threats', 27 November

[Online] Available at https://english.alarabiya.net/News/world/2021/11/27/Japan-PM-Kishida-vows-to-step-up-defense-amid-China-North-Korea-threats

Austin, R. and Buckley, C. (2019) '"Absolutely No Mercy": Leaked Files Expose How China Organized Mass Detentions of Muslims', *The New York Times*, 16 November [Online] https://www.nytimes.com/interactive/2019/11/16/world/asia/china-xinjiang-documents.html

Bachelet, M. (2021) *Bachelet updates Human Rights Council on recent human rights issues in more than 50 countries*, Office of the High Commissioner for Human Rights, 26 February [Online] Available at https://www.ohchr.org/EN/NewsEvents/Pages/DisplayNews.aspx?LangID=E&NewsID=26806 (Accessed 21 January 2023)

Badinter, R. (2015) 'Discours de Monsieur Robert BADINTER lors du rassemblement européen pour le Tibet', *France-Tibet* [Online] Available at http://tibet.fr/%20actions/paris-14-mars-2015-discours-de-monsieur-robert-badinter-ancien-ministre-de-la-justice-lors-du-rassemblement-europeen-pour-le-tibet/ (Accessed 22 January 2023)

Balenieri, R. (2017) 'La Chine a fait un TGV toute seule', *Libération*, 4 July [Online] Available at https://www.liberation.fr/futurs/2017/07/04/la-chine-a-fait-un-tgv-toute-seule_1581577/ (Accessed 24 January 2023)

Bastianelli, N. (2021) Comments delivered at web seminar organized by *Asialyst* and INALCO.

Bastianelli, N. (2021b) Unpublished interview conducted by Pierre-Antoine Donnet, 29 January.

BBC (2020) 'Over half of Chinese adults overweight, study finds', 23 December [Online]. Available at https://www.bbc.com/news/world-asia-china-55428530 (Accessed 21 January 2023).

(2021) 'Clubhouse discussion app knocked offline in China', 8 February [Online] Available at https://www.bbc.com/news/technology-55982137 (Accessed 25 January 2023)

Beech, H. (2016) 'China's chairman builds a cult of personality', *Time Magazine*, 31 March [Online] https://time.com/magazine/south-pacific/4278204/april-11th-2016-vol-187-no-13-asia-europe-middle-east-and-africa-south-pacific/

Beiser, V. (2018) 'Dramatic Photos Show How Sand Mining Threatens a Way of Life in Southeast Asia', *National Geographic*, 15 March [Online] Available at https://www.nationalgeographic.com/science/article/vietnam-mekong-illegal-sand-mining (Accessed 22 January 2023)

Béraud, A. (2019) 'Le Cambodge sous influence chinoise', *Radio Canada*, 24 May [Online] Available at https://ici.radio-canada.ca/nouvelle/1171564/cambodge-chine-influence-economie-politique (Accessed 28 January 2023)

Bertuzzi, M., Tremel, L. and Melonio, T. (2020) 'De "Nouvelles routes de la soie" durables, un défi impossible?', *The Conversation*, 9 February [Online] Available at https://theconversation.com/de-nouvelles-routes-de-la-soie-durables-un-defi-impossible-130672 (Accessed 25 January 2023)

Biden, J. (2021) *Remarks by President Biden in Press Conference*, 25 March, The White House [Online] Available at https://www.whitehouse.gov/briefing-room/speeches-remarks/2021/03/25/remarks-by-president-biden-in-press-conference/ (Accessed 21 January 2023)

(2021b) *Remarks by President Biden at Signing of an Executive Order on Supply Chains*, 24 February, The White House [Online] Available at https://www.whitehouse.gov/briefing-room/speeches-remarks/2021/02/24/remarks-by-president-biden-at-signing-of-an-executive-order-on-supply-chains/ (Accessed 23 January 2023)

(2021c) *Remarks by President Biden at the 2021 Virtual Munich Security Conference*, 19 February, The White House [Online] Available at https://www.whitehouse.gov/briefing-room/speeches-remarks/2021/02/19/remarks-by-president-biden-at-the-2021-virtual-munich-security-conference/ (Accessed 28 January 2023)

Bischoff, P. (2022) 'Surveillance camera statistics: which cities have the most CCTV cameras?', 11 July, *Comparitech* [Online]. Available at https://www.comparitech.com/vpn-privacy/the-worlds-most-surveilled-cities/ (Accessed 17 January 2023)

Bloomberg (2013) 'Beijing air akin to living in smoking lounge', January 31.

(2019) 'Huawei personnel worked with China military on research projects', 27 June [Online] Available at https://www.bloomberg.com/news/articles/2019-06-27/huawei-personnel-worked-with-china-military-on-research-projects (Accessed 23 January 2023)

(2021) 'China Teaches School Children "Do as President Xi Tells You"', 4 February [Online] Available at https://www.bloomberg.com/news/articles/2021-02-04/china-teaches-school-children-do-as-president-xi-tells-you (Accessed 25 January)

Le Bois International (2020) 'Le Laos tente d'endiguer le trafic illégal des bois', 18 March [Online] Available at https://www.leboisinternational.com/premiere-transformation/le-laos-tente-dendiguer-le-trafic-illegal-des-bois-668168.php (Accessed 22 January 2023)

Boittiaux, P. (2018) 'La Chine imbattable sur le marché du ciment', *Statista*, 10 July [Online] Available at https://fr.statista.com/infographie/14616/la-chine-imbattable-sur-le-marche-du-ciment/#:~:text=A%20situation%20corrobor%C3%A9e%20by%20the%20world (Accessed 22 January 2023)

Bondaz, A. (2021) Unpublished interview conducted by Pierre-Antoine Donnet, 22 January.

Borak, M. (2021) 'Taiwan prosecutes semiconductor recruiters accused of illegally poaching talent for Chinese company', *South China Morning Post*, 10 March [Online] https://www.scmp.com/tech/tech-war/article/3124845/taiwan-prosecutes-semiconductor-recruiters-accused-illegally-poaching

BrandFinance (2021) *Global Soft Power Index 2021* [Online] Excerpt available at https://brandfinance.com/press-releases/uk-ranked-3rd-in-world-for-soft-power-prowess (Accessed 21 February 2023)

Bretton Woods Project (2022) 'Chad gets debt rescheduling, not relief, and is left dependent on oil revenues', 8 December [Online] Available at https://www.brettonwoodsproject.org/2022/12/chad-gets-debt-rescheduling-not-relief-and-is-left-dependent-on-oil-revenues/ (Accessed 4 February 2023)

Buffetrille, K. (2021) Unpublished interview conducted by Pierre-Antoine Donnet, 5 March.

Cabestan, J.-P. (2018) *Demain la Chine: démocratie ou dictature?*, Paris, Gallimard.
(2021) *Demain la Chine: guerre ou paix?*, Paris, Gallimard.
(2019) 'Les nouvelles routes de la soie', *Études*, Cairn. info, December, p. 19 [Online] Available at https://www. cairn.info/revue-etudes-2019-12-page-19.htm (Accessed 25 January 2023)

Cadell, C. (2020) 'Exclusive: China sharply expands mass labor program in Tibet', *Reuters*, 22 September [Online] Available at https://www.reuters.com/article/china-rights-tibet-exclusive-idINKCN26D0G7

Le Canard Enchaîné (2020) 14 October.

CGTN (2020) 'Lawmakers approve law to protect Yangtze River' [Online] Available at http://news.cgtn.com/news/2020-12-27/Lawmakers-approve-law-to-protect-Yangtze-River-WyrnWVfHOw/index.html

Chade, J. (2021) 'Geneva shows the film China wants no one to see', *SWI swissinfo.ch*, 12 March [Online] Available at https://www.swissinfo.ch/eng/business/geneva-shows-the-film-that-china-doesn-t-want-anyone-to-see/46440028 (Accessed 21 February 2023)

Chan, M. (2021) Unpublished interview conducted by Pierre-Antoine Donnet, 8 March.

Chang, K. (2022) 'Scientists Achieve Nuclear Fusion Breakthrough With Blast of 192 Lasers', *The New York*

Times, 13 December [Online] Available at https://www. nytimes.com/2022/12/13/science/nuclear-fusion-energy-breakthrough.html (Accessed 24 January 2023)

Chaponnière, J.-R. (2019) 'Le Cambodge entre sanctions européennes et opportunités chinoises', *Asialyst*, 13 September [Online] https://asialyst.com/fr/2019/09/11/ cambodge-sanctions-europeennes-opportunites-chinoises/ (Accessed 28 January 2023)

Chen, B., Faeste, L., Jacobsen, R., Kong, M.T., Lu, D. and Palme, T. (2020) 'How China Can Achieve Carbon Neutrality by 2060', *Boston Consulting Group*, 14 December [Online] Available at https://www.bcg.com/publications/2020/how-china-can-achieve-carbon-neutrality-by-2060 (Accessed 22 January 2023)

Chen, L. (2020) 'China's ethnic Mongolians protest Mandarin curriculum in schools', *Agence France-Presse*, 1 September [Online] Available at: https://www.aljazeera.com/ news/2020/9/1/chinas-ethnic-mongolians-protest-mandarin-curriculum-in-schools (Accessed 22 January 2023)

Chen, S. (2021) 'Drop by drop, China's Yangtze River is drying up', *South China Morning Post*, 28 February [Online] Available at https://www.scmp.com/news/china/ science/article/3123418/how-drop-drop-chinas-yangtze-river-drying?utm_source=email&utm_medium=share_widget&utm_campaign=3123418 (Accessed 22 January 2023)

Cheng, C.-T. (2021) 'Former Taiwan president admits "one country, two systems is dead"', *Taiwan News*, 12 March

[Online] Available at https://www.taiwannews.com.tw/en/news/4149035 (Accessed 23 January 2023)

Cheng, S. (2022) 'Changes to COVID management policies explained', *China Daily*, 28 December [Online] Available at https://www.chinadaily.com.cn/a/202212/28/WS63ab8dc2a 31057c47eba6825.html (Accessed 16 April 2023)

Cheng, T. (2020) 'China's top chipmaker hires sought-after former TSMC executive', *Nikkei Asia*, 16 December [Online] https://asia.nikkei.com/Business/China-tech/China-s-top-chipmaker-hires-sought-after-former-TSMC-executive (Accessed 23 January 2023)

China International Import Expo (2022) 'CIIE special committee: China's agricultural imports up 13.9 percent y-o-y in 2020', 29 January [Online] Available at https://www.ciie.org/zbh/en/news/exhibition/official/20220129/31685.html (Accessed 22 January 2023)

China-Africa Research Initiative (n.d.) China-Africa Trade [Online] Available at http://www.sais-cari.org/data-china-africa-trade (Accessed 31 January 2023)

Chine Magazine (2020) 'La Chine va construire un barrage hydroélectrique au Tibet', 4 December [Online] Available at https://www.chine-magazine.com/la-chine-va-construire-un-barrage-hydroelectrique-au-tibet/ (Accessed 22 January 2023)

Clover, C. (2020) 'How China's fishermen are impoverishing Africa', *The Spectator*, 9 June [Online] Available at https://www.spectator.co.uk/article/how-china-s-fishermen-are-impoverishing-africa/ (Accessed 22 January 2023)

Collen, V. (2019) 'Gaz: la Chine renforce ses liens avec la Russie', *Les Echos*, 2 December [Online] Available at https://www. lesechos.fr/monde/chine/gaz-la-chine-renforce-ses-liens-avec-la-russie-1153027 (Accessed 22 January 2023)

Combe, M. (2018) 'Pourquoi nous allons bientôt faire face à une pénurie de sable', *Natura Sciences*, 28 November [Online] Available at https://www.natura-sciences.com/ environnement/penurie-sable.html (Accessed 22 January 2023)

Commodity.com (n.d.) China Economy Overview [Online] Available at https://commodity.com/data/china/ (Accessed 22 January 2023)

Commission on the Theft of Intellectual Property (2017) *Update to the IP Commission Report*, Washington, The National Bureau of Asian Research [Online] Available at https:// www.nbr.org/publication/update-to-the-ip-commission-report-february-2017/ (Accessed 18 February 2023)

Complément d'enquête (2021) France2, 25 February.

Corcuff, S. (2021) 'La littérature comme outil d'analyse politique' in Gaffric, G., *Formosana, Histoires de démocratie à Taïwan*, Paris, L'Asiathèque, p. 9.

Coué, P. (2021) '*Chang'E-5* atteint l'orbite lunaire', *L'Astronomie*, January, pp. 32–34.

Council of the EU (2021) 'EU imposes further sanctions over serious violations of human rights around the world', 22 March [Online] Available at https://www.consilium.europa. eu/en/press/press-releases/2021/03/22/eu-imposes-further-sanctions-over-serious-violations-of-human-rights-around-the-world/ (Accessed 21 January 2023)

Crooks, E. (2015) 'China extends lead over US as top green energy backer', *The Financial Times*, 9 January [Online] Available at https://www.ft.com/content/8209e816-97de-11e4-b4be-00144feabdc0 (Accessed 25 January 2023)

CrowdStrike (2019) *HUGE FAN OF YOUR WORK: How TURBINE PANDA and China's Top Spies Enabled Beijing to Cut Corners on the C919 Passenger Jet*, p. 4 [Online] Available at https://passle-net.s3.amazonaws.com (Accessed 24 January 2023)

Defranoux, L. (2021) 'Répression: Fuite en avant sanglante en Birmanie', *Libération*, 16 March [Online] Available at https://www.liberation.fr/international/asie-pacifique/fuite-en-avant-sanglante-en-birmanie-20210316_F4KKVPTOV5CMLK7WLFNPPLWDK4/ (Accessed 28 January 2023)

Delaney, R. and Fromer, J. (2021) '"Quad" summit backs "democratic" Indo-Pacific region, cites Chinese "aggression"', *South China Morning Post*, 13 March [Online] Available at https://www.scmp.com/news/china/diplomacy/article/3125290/us-president-joe-biden-opens-quad-summit-calling-alliance?utm_source=email&utm_medium=share_widget&utm_campaign=3125290 (Accessed 21 February 2023)

Dodwell, D. (2021) 'The myth of China's "debt trap" diplomacy must be put to bed once and for all', *South China Morning Post*, 28 March [Online] Available at https://www.scmp.com/comment/opinion/article/3127314/myth-chinas-debt-trap-diplomacy-must-be-put-bed-once-and-all (Accessed 25 January 2023)

Donnet, P.-A. (2019) *Tibet mort ou vif*, Paris, Gallimard, pp. 321–322.

Drozdiak, N. and Fouquet, H. (2021) 'EU weighs deal with TSMC, Samsung for semiconductor foundry', *Bloomberg*, 11 February [Online] https://www.bloomberg.com/news/articles/2021-02-11/europe-weighs-semiconductor-foundry-to-fix-supply-chain-risk (Accessed 23 January 2023)

Dvilyanski, M. and Gleicher, N. (2021) 'Taking Action Against Hackers in China', 24 March, *Meta* [Online] Available at https://about.fb.com/news/2021/03/taking-action-against-hackers-in-china/ (Accessed 25 January 2023)

Economist Intelligence Unit (2021) *Democracy Index 2020: In sickness and in health?* [Online] Available for download at https://www.eiu.com/n/campaigns/democracy-index-2020/#mktoForm_anchor

El Azzouzi, R. (2020) 'Répression des Ouïghours: "Briser, modeler, puis renvoyer dans la société"', *Mediapart*, 22 November [Online] Available at https://www.mediapart.fr/journal/international/221120/repression-des-ouighours-briser-modeler-puis-renvoyer-dans-la-societe (Accessed 21 January 2023)

The Eurasian Times (2020) 'Is Pakistan "Drowned In Debt" And Losing Its Political & Strategic Autonomy To China?', 30 December [Online] Available at https://eurasiantimes.com/is-pakistan-drowned-in-debt-and-losing-its-political-strategic-autonomy-to-china/

Faligot, R. (2021) Unpublished interview conducted by Pierre-Antoine Donnet, 10 January.

Fallevoz, B. (2021) '"Rescapée du Goulag chinois" par Gulbahar Haitiwaji: le témoignage d'une Ouïghoure de France', *Asialyst*, 12 January [Online] Available at https://asialyst.com/fr/2021/01/12/rescapee-du-goulag-chinois-gulbuhar-haitiwaji-temoignage-livre-ouighours-france/ (Accessed 21 January 2023)

The Financial Times (2020) 'The worrying precedent in China's quarrel with Australia', 26 November [Online] Available at https://www.ft.com/content/ad0b272e-12d4-42f4-9db6-6b5de768f297 (Accessed 4 February 2023)

Fireside Chat with Kathleen Hicks (2022) YouTube video, added by The Aspen Institute [Online] Available at https://www.youtube.com/watch?v=ad1CXKO7LXw (Accessed 28 January 2023)

Fontaine, R. and Ratner, E. (2020) 'The US-China confrontation is not another Cold War. It's something new', *The Washington Post*, 2 July [Online] Available at https://www.washingtonpost.com/opinions/2020/07/02/us-china-confrontation-is-not-another-cold-war-its-something-new/ (Accessed 28 January 2023)

Food and Agricultural Organization of the United Nations (2020) *A Fresh Perspective: Global Forest Resources Assessment 2020* [Online] Available at https://www.fao.org/forest-resources-assessment/2020/en/ (Accessed 22 January 2020)

Fuller, D. (2021) Unpublished interview conducted by Pierre-Antoine Donnet, 5 March.

Futura Sciences (2020) 'Chang'e 5 est de retour sur Terre avec sa cargaison d'échantillons lunaires', 17 December [Online] https://www.futura-sciences.com/sciences/actualites/lune-change-5-retour-terre-cargaison-echantillons-lunaires-54866/

Gehrke J. (2021) '"This genocide is ongoing": Pompeo equates China's Uighur repression with Nazi Holocaust', *Washington Examiner*, 19 January [Online] Available at https://www.washingtonexaminer.com/policy/defense-national-security/pompeo-equates-china-uighur-nazi-holocaust (Accessed 21 January 2023)

Global Forest Watch (n.d.) China [Online] Available at https://www.globalforestwatch.org/dashboards/country/CHN/?category=summary&location=WyJjb3VudHJ5Ii
wiQ0hOIl0%3D&map=eyJjZW50ZXIiOnsibGF0Ijo
zNy45NDU1NDgyMTUwNzYyMTUsImxuZyI6MTA0L
jE2NDYzMDg5MDAwNDA1fSwiem9vbSI6Mi44NTI5OD
I4NzQ3NzA2NDA3LCJjYW5Cb3VuZCI6ZmFsc2UsIm
RhdGFzZXRzIjpbeyJkYXRhc2V0IjoicG9saXRpY2FsLWJ
vdW5kYXJpZXMiLCJsYXllcnMiOlsiZGlzcHV0ZWQtcG
9saXRpY2FsLWJvdW5kYXJpZXMiLCJwb2xpdGljYWwtcGdl
jYWwtYm91bmRhcmllcyJdLCJib3VuZGFyeSI6dHJ1ZSwib
3BhY2l0eSI6MSwidmlzaWJpbGl0eSI6dHJ1ZX0seyJkYXRh
c2V0IjoiTmV0LUNoYW5nZS1TVEVFHSU5HIiwibGF5ZXJzI
jpbImZvcmVzdC1uZXQtY2hhbmdlIl0sIm9wYWNpdHki
OjEsInZpc2liaWxpdHkiOnRydWUsInBhcmFtcyI6eyJ2aXN
pYmlsaXR5Ijp0cnVlLCJhZG1fbGV2ZWwiOiJhZG0wIn19XX
0%3D&showMap=true

Global Times (2021) 'Exclusive: China formulating countermeasures against planned EU sanctions over Xinjiang; no escape for some EU institutions and poorly behaving individuals', 19 March [Online] Available at https://www.globaltimes.cn/page/202103/1218882.shtml (Accessed 21 January 2023)

Glucksmann, R. (2021) 'Les camps de concentration...' 26 February [Facebook] Available at https://www.facebook. com/rglucks1/posts/pfbid02FejwdTocj27H71SDXLPFutPah mxewovYVRhouCXaoGw3dW3Uxy6ERk4zYBuUYNwtl?__ cft__[0]=AZW9QaAVLnWQHwc5m-gWLZQUV-REzyR R9DpUYhJ-poFY37e_vSVJshTja8p2rVgcjaB6M2OX s5qOZ-9bvqFDXzfnV5jzXg2IEYhEoyYte0I2yu_-QLeAi ueC8-5rH1Mk_7_0hsvs0navvLPfmt616laXd4bP7iIhJjoX POT1zuj1KuqSWtMKi8Oih-xkXxp0RvfvwvPRuyVk AB6tz2WOWCOt&__tn__=%2CO%2CP-R
(2021b) 'So I am on the Chinese sanction list: banned from entering China (my family too!), from having contacts with Chinese officials or companies...All of this because I stand for Uyghurs and human rights. Let us be clear: these sanctions are my Medal of Honour. The fight continues!', 22 March [Twitter] Available at https://twitter.com/ rglucks1/status/1374022179105423369?ref_src=twsrc%5Etfw (Accessed 21 January 2023)
(2021c) 'Énième preuve...', 24 March [Facebook] Available at https://www.facebook.com/rglucks1/posts/pfbid024kX ZVLQCx4ShaFgzGmYfqqDpoJARSH3Vp73DKFqxzQR22ei eGPyw73eZPiEgaCQyl?__cft__[0]=AZWerYjsf_ISPfGebw ciq_-iSoPBg73BNxR47RO_rV76xdRjsQomTEC8X_EYty4qB TO5bLDPIx-NA4UGW9vmWZQTz3tky1WxDwzEaW2jQ__ wYKKlKwxLpxRhxfnvtcrgfbFWzpP0ibjgKDH6quHim tiBDHZ9FzAlPLoTjIBEKdN9rCf8DGnzDV5OkrP1Whd CCTH4qlYQ9JBXQPqTMfZYQzOy&__tn__=%2CO%2CP-R (Accessed 28 January 2023)
(2021d) 'Je sors à l'instant...', 26 March [Facebook] Available at https://www.facebook.com/rglucks1/posts/pfbid0PDmet

XVgks2L5HTiJQhUZ6uxoLPrB8ZXp5gbsYp6rfy67xY
t1F7oscw6ZzRttdcbl?__cft__[0]=AZWSG0e-2-F8tI
PYdUdrtvFDhrZCcpC4Bj16r-ocMdCjQm36xT
JVHKVMFhFre-PYH5LABlSxFoLQjuupOM-nEeK
bUt925i_4l667T6oV05cwpjD1wdrQOwg77ymX0jN
L6oemIGB47RGe2-y9GqLH7dyz_6s0mV3MS8VC8o3Hr64q
to-7J90_XRs70m5xq5AH3dqjx10dNSUDbc81h0UtPkmE
WRrMIkV4wMStLIRTR3I_Dg&__tn__=%2CO%2CP-R
(Accessed 28 January 2023)

Godwin, C. (2021) 'Facebook removes accounts of "China-based hackers" targeting Uighurs', *BBC*, 25 March [Online] Available at https://www.bbc.com/news/technology-56518467 (Accessed 25 January 2023)

Goldman, D. (2020) *You Will Be Assimilated: China's Plan to Sino-form the World*, New York, Bombardier Books/Post Hill Press, p. xvi.

Gradt, J.-M. (2019) 'Centrales à charbon: la Chine donne le mauvais exemple', *Les Echos*, 28 March [Online] Available at https://www.lesechos.fr/industrie-services/energie-environnement/centrales-a-charbon-la-chine-donne-le-mauvais-exemple-1004442 (Accessed 22 January 2023)

Greenpeace (2020) 'Biodegradables will not solve China's plastics crisis', 17 December [Online] Available at https://www.greenpeace.org/international/press-release/46066/biodegradables-will-not-solve-chinas-plastics-crisis/ (Accessed 22 January 2023)

Gubert, N. and Baert, P. (2020) 'Céréales: la Chine a eu très faim en 2020', *Agence France-Presse*, 1 December [Online] Available at https://www.latribune.fr/economie/international/cerealesla-chine-a-eu-tres-faim-en-2020-863752.html (Accessed 22 January 2023)

Guillard, O. (2021) 'The "New Silk Roads", China and neo-colonialism in South Asia', *Asialyst*, 22 January [Online] Available at https://asialyst.com/fr/2021/01/22/nouvelles-routes-soie-chine-neocolonialisme-asie-sud-pakistan-birmanie/ (Accessed 25 January 2023)
(2021b) 'Face au créancier chinois, l'Asie du Sud saura-t-elle sortir du "piège de la dette"?', *Asialyst*, 8 January [Online] Available at https://asialyst.com/fr/2021/01/08/face-crenacier-chine-asie-du-sud-sortir-piege-dette/ (Accessed 25 January 2023)

Gunter, J. (2021) 'The cost of speaking up against China', *BBC*, 31 March [Online] Available at https://www.bbc.com/news/world-asia-china-56563449 (Accessed 21 January 2023)

Haitiwaji, G. and Morgat, R. (2021) *Rescapée du goulag chinois: Premier témoignage d'une survivante ouïghoure*, Paris, Equateurs.

Heisbourg, F. (2020) *Le Temps des prédateurs*, Paris, Odile Jacob.

Heritage Foundation (2021) '2021 Index Of Economic Freedom: Global Economic Freedom Remains At All-Time High, U.S. Drops To An All-Time Low', 4 March [Online] Available at https://www.heritage.org/press/2021-index-economic-freedom-global-economic-freedom-remains-all-time-high-us-drops-all-time (Accessed 21 January 2023)

Hill, M., Campanale, D. and Gunter, J. (2021) '"Their goal is to destroy everyone": Uighur camp detainees allege systematic

rape', *BBC*, 2 February [Online] Available at https://www.
bbc.com/news/world-asia-china-55794071.

Ho, K. (2021) 'Beijing approves resolution to overhaul Hong
Kong's elections—candidates to be vetted', *Hong Kong Free
Press*, March 11 [Online] Available at https://hongkongfp.
com/2021/03/11/breaking-beijing-approves-resolution-to-
impose-electoral-overhaul-on-hong-kong/ (Accessed 21
January 2023)

Holzman, M. (2021) Unpublished interview conducted by
Pierre-Antoine Donnet, 5 March.

*Hong Kong Arrests: British Consulate Official Blasts China and the
H.K. Authorities* (2021) YouTube video, added by Bloomberg
Quicktake: Now [Online]. Available at https://www.youtube.
com/watch?v=9NBzUZgkkHo (Accessed 21 January 2023)

Huang, K. (2019) 'Sihanoukville's big gamble: the sleepy beach
town in Cambodia that bet its future on Chinese money', *South
China Morning Post*, 24 September [Online] Available at https://
www.scmp.com/news/china/diplomacy/article/3025262/
sihanoukvilles-big-gamble-sleepy-beach-town-bet-its-
future (Accessed 28 January 2023)

Huang, Y. (2013) 'Choking to Death: Health Consequences of
Air Pollution in China', *The Diplomat*, 6 March [Online]
Available at https://thediplomat.com/2013/03/choking-to-
death-the-health-consequences-of-air-pollution-in-china/
(Accessed 22 January 2023)

Huchet, J.-F. (2016) *La crise environnementale en Chine: Évolutions
et limites des politiques publiques*, Paris, Les Presses de
Sciences Po.

(2021) Unpublished interview conducted by Pierre-Antoine Donnet, 9 January.

IC Insights (2021) *IC Insights Research Bulletin*, 6 January.

Idzko, H. (2014) *Laogaï, le goulag chinois* [Online] Available at https://www.dailymotion.com/video/x577xnl (Accessed 25 February 2023)

indexmundi (n.d.) China Wheat Imports by Year [Online] Available at https://www.indexmundi.com/agriculture/?country=cn&commodity=wheat&graph=imports (Accessed 22 January 2023)

International Energy Agency (2009) *World Energy Outlook 2009* [Online] Available at https://www.iea.org/reports/world-energy-outlook-2009 (Accessed 22 January 2023)

International Monetary Fund (n.d.) Pakistan [Online] Available at https://www.imf.org/en/Countries/PAK (Accessed 25 January 2023)

Izambard, A. (2019) *France-Chine: Les liaisons dangereuses. Espionnage, business… révélations sur une guerre secrète*, Paris, Editions Stock.

Jakobson, L. (2021) 'Why should Australia be concerned about rising tensions in the Taiwan Straits?', *China Matters*, February [Online] Available at https://chinamatters.org.au/policy-brief/policy-brief-february-2021/ (Accessed 23 January 2023)

Kearsley, J., Bagshaw, E. and Galloway, A. (2020) '"If you make China the enemy, China will be the enemy": Beijing's fresh threat to Australia', *The Sydney Morning Herald*, 18 November [Online] Available at https://www.smh.com.au/world/asia/if-you-make-china-the-enemy-china-will-be-the-enemy-beijing-s-fresh-threat-to-australia-20201118-p56fqs.html (Accessed 4 February 2023)

Kliman, D., Doshi, R., Lee, K. and Cooper, Z. (2019) 'Grading China's Belt and Road', 8 April [Online], Washington DC, Center for a New American Security. Available at https://www.cnas.org/publications/reports/beltandroad (Accessed 17 January 2023).

Lau, M. (2021) 'Two sessions: Xi Jinping tells Inner Mongolia's NPC deputies to put Mandarin first in schools', *South China Morning Post*, 6 March [Online] Available at https://www.scmp.com/news/china/politics/article/3124370/two-sessions-xi-jinping-tells-inner-mongolias-npc-deputies-put (Accessed 22 January 2023)

Lausson, J. (2020) 'Le "soleil artificiel" de la Corée du Sud établit un nouveau record en fusion nucléaire', *Numerama*, 28 December [Online] Available at https://www.numerama.com/sciences/678606-le-soleil-artificiel-de-la-coree-du-sud-etablit-un-nouveau-record-en-fusion-nucleaire.html?fbclid=IwAR1-V9ysHaE6M06iiPCrcgoyB4N9rZWOh3oQoxWMbeupNzv1cJwAOQX4Tig (Accessed on 24 January 2023)

Leblanc, C. (2020) 'En Chine, Xi Jinping toujours plus haut devient "dirigeant du peuple"', *L'Opinion*, 6 January [Online] Available at https://www.lopinion.fr/edition/international/en-chine-xi-jinping-toujours-plus-haut-devient-dirigeant-peuple-207682 (Accessed 25 January 2023)

Lee, A. (2020) 'China to curb "chaos" in semiconductor industry and hold bosses accountable for risky, loss-making projects', *South China Morning Post*, 20 October [Online] Available at https://www.scmp.com/economy/china-economy/article/3106307/china-curb-chaos-semiconductor-industry-and-hold-bosses (Accessed 23 January 2023)

Lemaître, F. (2020) 'En Chine, la "pensée Xi Jinping" ne fait pas l'unanimité', *Le Monde*, 16 June [Online] Available at https://www.lemonde.fr/international/article/2020/06/16/en-chine-la-pensee-xi-jinping-ne-fait-pas-l-unanimite_6043030_3210.html (Accessed 25 January 2023)
(2021) '2020, mauvaise année pour les journalistes étrangers en Chine', *Le Monde*, 2 March [Online] Available at https://www.lemonde.fr/actualite-medias/article/2021/03/02/2020-mauvaise-annee-pour-les-journalistes-etrangers-en-chine_6071636_3236.html (Accessed 21 January 2023)

Leng, S. (2020) 'China's semiconductor dream takes a hit as local authority takes over "nightmare" Wuhan factory', *South China Morning Post*, 18 November [Online] Available at https://www.scmp.com/economy/china-economy/article/3110368/chinas-semiconductor-dream-takes-hit-local-authority-takes (Accessed 23 January 2023)

Li, J. (2019) 'Commentary: China pillages Africa's resources? Pure myth!', *Xinhuanet*, 24 April [Online] Available at http://www.xinhuanet.com/english/africa/2019-04/24/c_138004758.htm (Accessed 25 January 2023)

Li, Y. (2021) 'The Great Firewall Cracked, Briefly. A People Shined Through', *The New York Times*, 9 February [Online] Available at: https://www.nytimes.com/2021/02/09/technology/china-clubhouse.html (Accessed 25 January 2023)

Lo, K. (2021) 'China-India relations: Beijing should speed up hydropower project, Tibetan official says', *South China Morning Post*, 10 March [Online] https://www.scmp.com/news/china/diplomacy/article/3124698/china-india-relations-beijing-should-speed-hydropower-project (Accessed 22 January 2023)

Loiseau, N. (2021) Email to Pierre-Antoine Donnet, 14 March.

Lunil (2020) 'Jiuzhang, un ordinateur quantique réaliserait en 3 minutes un calcul qui prendrait 2 milliards d'années à un superordinateur', 8 December [Online] Available at http://www.lunil.com/jiuzhang-ordinateur-quantique-plus-puissant-superordinateur/ (Accessed 23 January 2023)

Mahtani, S. and Yu, T. (2021) 'Hong Kong sentences democracy activists to prison over peaceful protest', *The Washington Post*, 16 April [Online] Available at https://www.washingtonpost.com/world/asia_pacific/hong-kong-democracy-sentence/2021/04/16/d4450258-9c34-11eb-b2f5-7d2f0182750d_story.html

Main, D. (2012) 'A New East Asian Import: Ozone Pollution', Green: Energy, the Environment and the Bottom Line [Blog] Available at https://archive.nytimes.com/green.blogs.nytimes.com/2012/03/06/a-new-east-asian-import-ozone-pollution/ (Accessed 22 January 2023)

Manch, T. (2021) 'New Zealand and Australia "welcome" coordinated sanctions against China, but can't join effort', *Stuff*, 23 March [Online] Available at https://www.stuff.co.nz/national/politics/124624836/new-zealand-and-australia-welcome-coordinated-sanctions-against-china-but-cant-join-effort (Accessed 21 January 2021)

Marmino, M. and Vandenberg, L. (2021) 'The role of political culture in Taiwan's COVID-19 success', *The Diplomat*, 25 January [Online] Available at https://thediplomat.com/2021/01/the-role-of-political-culture-in-taiwans-covid-19-success/ Accessed (25 January 2025)

Mason, J. (2021) 'White House cites "active threat," urges action despite Microsoft patch', *Reuters*, 8 March [Online] Available at https://www.reuters.com/article/usa-cyber-microsoft-idINKBN2B00JT

Mateso, M. (2018) 'La flotte de pêche chinoise, "nouveau pirate des mers" en Afrique de l'Ouest', franceinfo, 16 January [Online] Available at https://www.francetvinfo.fr/monde/afrique/environnement-africain/la-flotte-de-peche-chinoise-nouveau-pirate-des-mers-en-afrique-de-l-ouest_3055631.html (Accessed 22 January 2023)

McCarthy, S. (2021) 'Quad summit: US, India, Australia and Japan counter China's "vaccine diplomacy" with pledge to distribute a billion doses across Indo-Pacific', *South China Morning Post*, 13 March [Online] Available at https://www.scmp.com/news/china/diplomacy/article/3125344/quad-summit-us-india-australia-and-japan-counter-chinas (Accessed 28 January 2023)

McCarthy, S. and Zhuang P. (2020) 'Did half a million people in Wuhan contract the coronavirus?', *South China Morning Post*, 23 December [Online] Available at https://www.scmp.com/news/china/science/article/3115725/did-half-million-people-wuhan-contract-coronavirus (Accessed 21 January 2023)

Menon, P. (2020) 'New Zealand raises concerns with China over Australian soldier image', *Reuters*, 1 December [Online]

Available at https://www.reuters.com/article/us-australia-china-newzealand-idUSKBN28B3E0 (Accessed 28 January 2023)

Metzl, J. (2022) Origins of SARS-CoV-2 [Blog] Available at https://jamiemetzl.com/origins-of-sars-cov-2/ (Accessed 28 January 2023)

Microsoft Threat Intelligence Center (2021) HAFNIUM targeting Exchange Servers with 0-day exploits, 2 March [Blog] Available at https://www.microsoft.com/en-us/security/blog/2021/03/02/hafnium-targeting-exchange-servers/ (Accessed 25 January 2023)

Mihalyi, D., Adam, A. and Hwang, J. (2020) *Resource-Backed Loans: Pitfalls and Potential*, Natural Resource Governance Institute, 27 February [Online] Available at https://resourcegovernance.org/analysis-tools/publications/resource-backed-loans-pitfalls-potential (Accessed 26 January 2023)

Ministère de l'Europe et des Affaires étrangères (2021) *G7 Foreign Ministers' statement (12.03.2021)* [Online] Available at https://www.diplomatie.gouv.fr/en/country-files/china/news/article/g7-foreign-ministers-statement-12-03-2021 (Accessed 21 January 2021)

Ministry of Defense of Japan (2022) National Defense Strategy [Online] Available at https://www.mod.go.jp › strategy › pdf › strategy_en (Accessed 22 February 2023)

Ministry of Foreign Affairs of the People's Republic of China (MFAPRC) (2020) *Foreign Ministry Spokesperson Wang Wenbin's Regular Press Conference on December 15, 2020*

[Online] Available at https://www.fmprc.gov.cn/mfa_eng/xwfw_665399/s2510_665401/2511_665403/202012/t20201215_693534.html (Accessed 21 January 2023)

(2021) *Foreign Ministry Spokesperson Announces Sanctions on Relevant EU Entities and Personnel*, 22 March [Online] Available at https://www.fmprc.gov.cn/mfa_eng/xwfw_665399/s2510_665401/2535_665405/202103/t20210322_9170814.html (Accessed 21 January 2023)

(2021b) *Press Conference by State Councilor and Foreign Minister Wang Yi on March 7, 2021* [Online] Available at http://auckland.china-consulate.gov.cn/eng/gdxw/202103/t20210308_9934042.htm (Accessed 22 January 2023)

Mitchell, T. and Olcott, E. (2023) 'Chinese spy balloon furore puts focus on Xi Jinping's leadership', *The Financial Times*, 7 February [Online] Available at https://www.ft.com/content/73bad3ff-b072-4a64-8edd-7dda6a28c253 (Accessed 13 February 2023)

Mitchell, T., Hale, T., Yu, S. and White, E. (2022) 'The humbling of Xi Jinping', *The Financial Times*, 2 December [Online] Available at https://www.ft.com/content/71bf8a5d-3816-450b-bbfb-ec320b0dba0d

Mu, X. (2017) 'China allocates 8.8 bln yuan for weather modification program', *Xinhuanet*, 21 September [Online] Available at http://www.xinhuanet.com/english/2017-09/21/c_136624811.htm (Accessed 22 January 2023)

Murakami, S. and Baptista, E. (2022) 'Xi, Kishida meet as tensions grow over Taiwan, East China Sea', *Reuters*, 18 November [Online] Available at https://www.reuters.com/world/asia-pacific/japan-pm-says-conveyed-concerns-chinas-xi-about-peace-taiwan-strait-2022-11-17/ (Accessed 22 February 2023)

Nakashima, E. and Lamothe, D. (2023) 'U.S., Japan set to announce shake-up of Marine Corps units to deter China', *The Washington Post*, 11 January [Online] Available at https://www.washingtonpost.com/national-security/2023/01/10/us-japan-set-announce-shake-up-marine-corps-units-deter-china/ (Accessed 22 February 2023)

National Association of Scholars (2022) 'How Many Confucius Institutes Are in the United States?', 19 September [Online] Available at https://www.nas.org/blogs/article/how_many_confucius_institutes_are_in_the_united_states (Accessed 24 January 2023)

National Security Commission on Artificial Intelligence (2021) *Final Report* [Online] Available at https://www.nscai.gov/2021-final-report/ (Accessed 23 January 2023)

New Lines Institute for Strategy and Policy (2021) *The Uyghur Genocide: An Examination of China's Breaches of the 1948 Genocide Convention* [Online] Available at https://newlinesinstitute.org/uyghurs/the-uyghur-genocide-an-examination-of-chinas-breaches-of-the-1948-genocide-convention/ (Accessed 22 January 2023)

Ngũgĩ wa Thiong'o (1994) *Decolonising the Mind*, Harare, Zimbabwe Publishing House, p. 15.

Niquet, N. (2011) 'La Chine et l'arme des terres rares', *Revue internationale et stratégique*, Issue 4.

notre-planete.info (n.d.) 'Déforestation: définition, données, causes, conséquences, solutions' [Online] Available at https://www.notre-planete.info/environnement/deforestation.php

OECD (2007), *OECD Environmental Performance Reviews: China 2007*, OECD Environmental Performance Reviews, OECD Publishing, Paris, https://doi.org/10.1787/9789264031166-en

Office of the United Nations High Commissioner for Human Rights (2021) *China: UN experts deeply concerned by alleged detention, forced labour of Uyghurs*, 29 March [Online] Available at https://www.ohchr.org/en/press-releases/2021/03/china-un-experts-deeply-concerned-alleged-detention-forced-labour-uyghurs (Accessed 25 January 2023)

Pan, C. (2020) 'Beijing's biggest chipmaking champion SMIC faces uncertain future after US blacklisting', *South China Morning Post*, 21 December [Online] Available at https://www.scmp.com/tech/big-tech/article/3114795/beijings-biggest-chipmaking-champion-smic-faces-uncertain-future (Accessed 23 January 2023)

Payette, A. (2021) 'Chine: flatteries à Xi Jinping, "patriotes" à Hong Kong et tensions dans le Parti', *Asialyst*, 25 March [Online] Available at https://asialyst.com/fr/2021/03/25/chine-flatteries-xi-jinping-patriotes-hong-kong-tensions-parti-communiste/ (Accessed 25 January 2023)

Pearl, H. (2020) 'China's coronavirus recovery drives boom in coal plants, casting doubt over commitments to cut fossil fuels', *South China Morning Post*, 21 July [Online] Available at https://www.scmp.com/economy/china-economy/article/3094098/chinas-coronavirus-recovery-drives-boom-coal-plants-casting (Accessed 25 January 2023)

Pedroletti, B. (2020) 'Les Mongols de Chine manifestent pour la défense de leur langue et de leur identité', *Le Monde*, 2 September [Online] Available at https://www.lemonde.

fr/international/article/2020/09/02/les-mongols-de-chine-manifestent-pour-la-defense-de-leur-langue-et-de-leur-identite_6050740_3210.html (Accessed 22 January 2023)

(2021) 'La télévision internationale chinoise privée d'antenne au Royaume-Uni', *Le Monde*, 5 February [Online] Available at https://www.lemonde.fr/international/article/2021/02/05/la-television-internationale-chinoise-privee-d-antenne-au-royaume-uni_6068954_3210.html (Accessed 25 January 2023)

(2021b) 'Au Kirghizistan, l'indésirable présence de la Chine', *Le Monde*, 7 February [Online] Available at https://www.lemonde.fr/international/article/2021/02/05/au-kirghizistan-l-indesirable-presence-chinoise_6068910_3210.html (Accessed 25 January 2023)

Pelosi, N. (2021) *Pelosi Statement on the 62nd Anniversary of Tibetan Uprising Day*, 10 March [Online] Available at https://pelosi.house.gov/news/press-releases/pelosi-statement-on-the-62nd-anniversary-of-tibetan-uprising-day

Pleinchamp (2020) 'Blé, maïs, soja: la Chine a eu très faim en 2020', 3 December [Online] Available at https://www.pleinchamp.com/actualite/ble-mais-soja-la-chine-a-eu-tres-faim-en-2020 (Accessed 22 January 2023)

Pompeo, M. (2020) *Designation of the Confucius Institute U.S. Center as a Foreign Mission of the PRC*, US Department of State, 13 August [Online] Available at https://2017-2021.state.gov/designation-of-the-confucius-institute-u-s-center-as-a-foreign-mission-of-the-prc/index.html (Accessed 24 January 2023)

(2021) *Determination of the Secretary of State on Atrocities in Xinjiang*, US Department of State, 19 January [Online] Available at https://2017-2021.state.gov/determination-of-the-secretary-of-state-on-atrocities-in-xinjiang/index.html (Accessed 21 January 2023)

Power, J. (2021) 'Chinese spying fears revived by security probe into Australian universities', *South China Morning Post*, 11 February [Online] https://www.scmp.com/week-asia/politics/article/3121400/chinese-spying-fears-revived-security-probe-australian (Accessed 24 January 2023)

Radio France Internationale (2020) 'Une loi pour protéger le Yangtsé: le plus grand fleuve de Chine asphyxié par la pollution', 27 December [Online] Available at https://www.rfi.fr/fr/asie-pacifique/20201227-une-loi-pour-prot%C3%A9ger-le-yangts%C3%A9-le-plus-grand-fleuve-de-chine-asphyxi%C3%A9-par-la-pollution

Ramadane, M. (2022) 'Chad agrees debt plan with creditors, including Glencore', *Reuters*, 11 November [Online] Available at https://www.reuters.com/world/africa/chad-agrees-debt-plan-with-creditors-including-glencore-says-minister-2022-11-11/ (Accessed 28 January 2023)

Rédaction Afrique (2017) France Televisions, 20 September.

Reed, J. (2020) 'The Mekong Delta: an unsettling portrait of coastal collapse', *The Financial Times*, 5 January [Online] Available at https://www.ft.com/content/31bf27a4-1c0e-11ea-9186-7348c2f183af (Accessed 22 January 2023)

Renshaw, J. and Holland, S. (2021) 'Biden compares Xi to Putin, Republican voting restriction plans to segregation-era laws', *Reuters*, 25 March [Online] Available at https://www.reuters.com/article/us-usa-biden/biden-compares-xi-to-putin-republican-voting-plans-to-jim-crow-laws-idUSKBN2BH1AY?il=0 (Accessed 25 January 2023)

Reuters (2020) 'Taiwan approves chipmaker TSMC's plan to invest $3.5 bln in new Arizona plant', 22 December [Online] Available at https://www.reuters.com/article/usa-semiconductors-tsmc-idUSL1N2J20UK (Accessed 23 January 2023)

(2020b) 'Factbox: Rare earths projects under development in U.S.', 22 April [Online] Available at https://www.reuters.com/article/us-usa-rareearths-projects-factbox-idUSKCN2241L6 (Accessed 24 January 2023)

(2021) 'Dutch parliament: China's treatment of Uighurs is genocide', 25 February [Online] Available at https://www.reuters.com/article/us-netherlands-china-uighurs-idUSKBN2AP2CI (Accessed 22 January 2023)

(2021b) 'Old H&M comment on "forced labour" in China's Xinjiang raises online storm', 24 March [Online] Available at https://www.reuters.com/article/us-china-xinjiang-cotton/hms-xinjiang-labour-stance-raises-social-media-storm-in-china-idUSKBN2BG1G4 (Accessed 25 January 2023)

(2021c) 'Cambodia's new China-style internet gateway decried as repression tool', 18 February [Online] Available at https://www.reuters.com/article/us-cambodia-internet/cambodias-new-china-style-internet-gateway-decried-as-repression-tool-idUSKBN2AI140 (Accessed 28 January 2023)

(2021d) 'Duterte aide Panelo warns of "unwanted hostilities" over Chinese boats', *Rappler*, 5 April [Online] Available at https://www.rappler.com/nation/duterte-aide-panelo-warns-unwanted-hostilities-chinese-boats/ (Accessed 28 January 2023)

(2023) 'Japan plans to bulk order U.S. Tomahawk missiles by March next year', 14 February [Online] Available

at https://www.reuters.com/business/aerospace-defense/
japan-plans-bulk-order-us-tomahawk-missiles-by-march-
next-year-2023-02-14/ (Accessed 22 February 2023)

Rohde, R. and Muller, R. (2015) *Air Pollution in China: Mapping
of Concentrations and Sources* [Online] Available at http://
berkeleyearth.org/wp-content/uploads/2015/08/China-Air-
Quality-Paper-July-2015.pdf (Accessed 22 January 2023)

Savage, R. and Thomas, L. (2022) 'Test case Zambia exposes
China's rookie status on debt relief—sources', *Reuters*, 31
May [Online] Available at https://www.reuters.com/world/
africa/test-case-zambia-exposes-chinas-rookie-status-debt-
relief-sources-2022-05-31/ (Accessed 26 January 2023)

Scahill, J. (2021) 'Inside China's Police State Tactics Against
Muslims', *The Intercept*, 3 February [Online] Available at
https://theintercept.com/2021/02/03/intercepted-china-
uyghur-muslim-surveillance-police/?fbclid=IwAR0tkdW
aT3sUQFzj72LwVCK-r3eSI9BKD6qVjt5GtlZHUqfx-ruQ-
Ukb9M4 (Accessed 21 January 2023)

Schildt, M. (2018) 'Demain la Chine: démocratie ou dictature?
Entretien avec l'auteur', *Le Petit Journal*, 11 June [Online]
https://lepetitjournal.com/hong-kong/demain-la-chine-
democratie-ou-dictature-entretien-avec-lauteur-232882
(Accessed 25 January 2023)

Senate Hearing 117-45 (2021) *Nomination of Hon. Linda Thomas-
Greenfield to Be United States Representative to the United
Nations*, Congress.gov, 27 January [Online] Available at
https://www.congress.gov/event/117th-congress/senate-
event/LC66932/text (Accessed 26 January)

Shalal, A. (2022) 'World Bank's Malpass criticizes Chad creditors' plan for failing to reduce debt', *Reuters*, 11 November [Online] Available at https://www.reuters.com/article/chad-debt-world-bank-idUKKBN2S1202 (Accessed 28 January 2023)

Singh, T. (2022) 'Zambia's debt crisis a warning for what looms ahead for Global South', *Peoples Dispatch*, 22 September [Online] Available at https://peoplesdispatch.org/2022/09/22/zambias-debt-crisis-a-warning-for-what-looms-ahead-for-global-south/ (Accessed 28 January 2023)

Sintomer, Y. and Gauthier, J. (2014) 'Les types purs de la domination légitime: forces et limites d'une trilogie', *Sociologie*, Vol. 5, 2014/3, pp. 319–333.

Smith, I.D. (2021) 'It's our duty to call out the Chinese Govt's human rights abuse in #HongKong & the genocide of the #Uyghurs. Those of us who live free lives under the rule of law must speak for those who have no voice. If that brings the anger of China down on me, I'll wear that badge of honour.' 26 March [Twitter] Available at https://twitter.com/mpiainds/status/1375252459967418369?lang=en (Accessed 21 January 2023)

Smith, M. (2021) 'Japan says Australia is "not alone" in battling Chinese coercion', *Financial Review*, 9 March [Online] Available at https://www.afr.com/business-summit/japan-says-australia-is-not-alone-in-battling-chinese-coercion-20210309-p5790n (Accessed 28 January 2023)

South China Morning Post (2020) 15 December.

Sputnik News (2020) 16 December [Online] Link no longer available due to Western sanctions.

Sun, H. and Zhao, Y. (2019) 'Most cyber attacks from the US: report', *Global Times*, 10 June [Online] Available at http://www.globaltimes.cn/content/1153777.shtml (Accessed 25 January 2023)

Sureau, D. (2010) 'En Chine, le détournement des eaux du Yangtsé déplace plus de 300 000 personnes', *Radio France Internationale*, 13 August [Online] Available at https://www.rfi.fr/fr/asie-pacifique/20100813-chine-le-detournement-eaux-yangtse-deplace-plus-300-000-personnes
And https://www.jiemian.com/article/5404897.html

Tan, S.-L. (2021) 'China's ban on Australian coal drives diversification, but can it fill the gap?' *South China Morning Post*, 17 January [Online] Available at https://www.scmp.com/economy/china-economy/article/3117908/chinas-ban-australian-coal-drives-diversification-can-it-fill (Accessed 22 January 2023)

Testard, H. (2021) 'Changement climatique: où en est la Chine?', *Asialyst*, 21 January [Online] Available at https://asialyst.com/fr/2021/01/21/changement-climatique-ou-en-est-chine/ (Accessed 22 January 2023)

TV5 Monde (2019) 'Ouïghours: pourquoi le monde musulman ne réagit-il pas face aux persécutions du gouvernement chinois?' 26 May [Online] Available at https://information.tv5monde.com/info/ouighours-pourquoi-le-monde-musulman-ne-reagit-il-pas-face-aux-persecutions-du-gouvernement (Accessed 21 January 2023)

US Department of State (2021) *Joint Statement on Xinjiang*, 22 March [Online] Available at https://www.state.gov/joint-statement-on-xinjiang/ (Accessed 21 January 2023)

(2021b) *Department Press Briefing—February 11, 2021* [Online] Available at https://www.state.gov/briefings/department-press-briefing-february-11-2021/ (Accessed 24 January 2023)

(2021c) *Secretary Blinken's Call with Philippine Secretary of Foreign Affairs Locsin*, 27 January [Online] Available at https://www.state.gov/secretary-blinkens-call-with-philippine-secretary-of-foreign-affairs-locsin/ (Accessed 28 January 2023)

(2021d) *Department Press Briefing—February 19, 2021* [Online] Available at https://www.state.gov/briefings/department-press-briefing-february-19-2021/ (Accessed 4 February 2023)

Valo, M. (2013) 'Comment la pêche chinoise pille les océans de la planète', *Le Monde*, 4 April [Online] Available at https://www.lemonde.fr/planete/article/2013/04/04/comment-la-peche-chinoise-pille-les-oceans-de-la-planete_3154101_3244.html (Accessed 22 January 2023)

Varadarajan, R., Varas, A., Gilbert, M., McAdoo, M., Ruan, F., Wang, G. (2020) *What's at Stake if the US and China Really Decouple*, Boston Consulting Group, 20 October [Online] Available at https://www.bcg.com/publications/2020/high-stakes-of-decoupling-us-and-china (Accessed 23 January 2023)

Varas, A., Varadarajan, R., Goodrich, J. and Yinug, F. (2020) *Government Incentives and US Competitiveness in Semiconductor Manufacturing*, Boston Consulting Group, September [Online] https://web-assets.bcg.com/27/cf/9fa28eeb43649ef8674fe764726d/bcg-government-incentives-and-us-competitiveness-in-semiconductor-manufacturing-sep-2020.pdf (Accessed 23 January 2023)

Vaswani, K. (2021) 'Singapore PM: "Considerable risk" of severe US-China tensions', *BBC*, 11 March [Online] Available at https://www.bbc.com/news/business-56318576 (Accessed 21 February)

Vergara, I. (2021) 'L'ampleur de la cyberattaque contre le logiciel de messagerie Microsoft Exchange inquiète Washington', *Le Figaro*, 8 March [Online] Available at https://www.lefigaro.fr/secteur/high-tech/l-ampleur-de-la-cyberattaque-contre-le-logiciel-de-messagerie-microsoft-exchange-inquiete-washington-20210308 (Accessed 25 January 2023)

Viet, A. (2021) 'Experts worried about impacts of Chinese Red River dams', *vnExpress International*, 1 March [Online] Available at https://e.vnexpress.net/news/news/experts-worried-about-impacts-of-chinese-red-river-dams-4240742.html (Accessed 22 January 2023)

Vincent, E. (2021) 'Tensions entre les Etats-Unis, la Russie et la Chine après deux cyberattaques majeures', *Le Monde*, 13 March [Online] Available at https://www.lemonde.fr/international/article/2021/03/13/tensions-entre-etats-unis-russie-et-chine-apres-la-concomitance-de-deux-cyberattaques-majeures_6072975_3210.html (Accessed 25 January 2023)

Vircoulon, T. (2021) 'Au bout de vingt ans, la "success story" de la Chinafrique a des conséquences qui posent problème,' *Le Monde*, 16 March [Online] Available at https://www.lemonde.fr/afrique/article/2021/03/16/au-bout-de-vingt-ans-la-success-story-de-la-chinafrique-a-des-consequences-qui-posent-probleme_6073324_3212.html (Accessed 25 January 2023)

Vivas, M. (2020) *Ouïghours, pour en finir avec les fake news*, Paris, Éditions La Route de la Soie.

Wang, A. (2021) 'France sends warships to South China Sea ahead of exercise with US and Japan', *South China Morning Post*, 19 February [Online] Available at https://www.scmp. com/news/china/diplomacy/article/3122416/france-sends-warships-south-china-sea-ahead-exercise-us-and (Accessed 28 January 2023)

Wang, A. and Zheng, W. (2021) 'Chinese in fear in Myanmar after attacks on factories', *South China Morning Post*, 15 March [Online] Available at https://www.scmp.com/news/ china/diplomacy/article/3125510/chinese-fear-myanmar-after-attacks-factories (Accessed 28 January 2023)

Wang, K. (2019) 'China's quest for clean, limitless energy heats up', *Agence France-Presse*, 29 April [Online] Available at https://phys.org/news/2019-04-china-quest-limitless-energy.html (Accessed 24 January 2023)

Watts, J. (2011) 'China makes gain in battle against desertification but has long fight ahead', *The Guardian*, 4 January [Online] Available at http://www.theguardian.com/world/2011/ jan/04/china-desertification (Accessed 22 January 2023)

Weill, N. (2021) 'Anne Cheng: "Cela ferait énormément de bien à la Chine de ne plus être cet 'empire du Milieu'"', *Le Monde.fr*, 21 February [Online] Available at https://www. lemonde.fr/livres/article/2021/02/21/anne-cheng-cela-ferait-enormement-de-bien-a-la-chine-de-ne-plus-etre-cet-empire-du-milieu_6070692_3260.html (Accessed 25 January 2023)

White House (2021) *Readout of President Joseph R. Biden, Jr. Call with President Xi Jinping of China*, 10 February [Online] Available at https://www.whitehouse.gov/briefing-room/statements-releases/2021/02/10/readout-of-president-joseph-r-biden-jr-call-with-president-xi-jinping-of-china/ (Accessed 21 January 2023)

Wong, C. (2021) 'Xi Jinping tells China's military "be prepared to respond" in unstable times', *South China Morning Post*, 9 March [Online] Available at https://www.scmp.com/news/china/military/article/3124733/xi-jinping-tells-chinas-military-be-prepared-respond-unstable (Accessed 21 February 2021)

World Bank (n.d.) *WITS World Integrated Trade Solution, China Trade Summary 2019 Data* [Online] Available at https://wits.worldbank.org/CountryProfile/en/Country/CHN/Year/2019/Summary (Accessed 22 January 2023)

World Bank (n.d.) *2022 International Debt Statistics* [Online] Available at https://datatopics.worldbank.org/debt/ids/country/PAK (Accessed 25 January 2023)

World Health Organization (2023) *WHO press conference on global health issues—4 January 2023*, 4 January [Online] Available at https://www.who.int/multi-media/details/who-press-conference-on-global-health-issues---4-january-2023 (Accessed 5 February 2023)

WWF (n.d.) 'Yang-Tsé-Kiang: Fleuve Bleu' [Online] Available at https://www.wwf.fr/espaces-prioritaires/yang-tse-kiang (Accessed 22 January 2023)

Xhie, H., Liu, H., Zhang, X., Huang, J. and Zhang, X. (2013) 'Sip of Death Plagues Cancerous River Villages', *Caixin Global*, 10 September [Online] Available at http://english.caixin.com/2013-10-09/100589447.html (Accessed 22 January 2023)

Xiao, E., Yiu, P. and Beatty, A. (2019) 'Even in death, Uighurs feel long reach of Chinese state', *Agence France-Presse*, 11 October [Online] Available at https://www.bangkokpost.com/world/1768309/even-in-death-uighurs-feel-long-reach-of-chinese-state (Accessed 21 January 2023) An interactive graphic can be seen here: https://graphics.afpforum.com/builds/20190604-xinjiang-mosques/#/?lang=en . The video is available here: https://www.facebook.com/AFPnewsenglish/videos/513247679254740/

Xie, W. and Bai, Y. (2019) 'French professor praises China's de-radicalization measures in Xinjiang', *Global Times*, 10 September [Online] Available at https://www.globaltimes.cn/content/1164175.shtml

Xinhua (2020) 'China's spending on R&D rises to historic high in 2019', 27 August [Online] Available at http://www.xinhuanet.com/english/2020-08/27/c_139321868.htm (Accessed 23 January 2023)

(2021) 'Xi stresses promoting standard spoken, written Chinese language', 5 March [Online] Available at http://www.xinhuanet.com/english/2021-03/05/c_139788095.htm (Accessed 22 January 2023)

Xu, M. and Stanway, D. (2019) 'China's ocean waste surges 27% in 2018: ministry', *Reuters,* 29 October [Online] Available at https://www.reuters.com/article/us-china-polltion-oceans/chinas-ocean-waste-surges-27-in-2018-ministry-idUSKBN1X80FL (Accessed 22 January 2023)

Yan, A. (2020) 'China passes law to protect Yangtze River', *South China Morning Post,* 27 December [Online] Available at https://www.scmp.com/news/china/politics/article/3115431/china-passes-law-protect-river-yangtze (Accessed 22 January 2023)

Yang, J. (2012) *Stèles, La Grande Famine en Chine, 1958–1961* (trans. Vincenolles, L., Gentil, S. and Chen-Andro, C.), Paris, Seuil.

Yuan, J. (2021) 'The Continuing Mystery of the Belt and Road', *The Diplomat,* 6 March [Online] Available at https://thediplomat.com/2021/03/the-continuing-mystery-of-the-belt-and-road/ (Accessed 25 January 2023)

Zenz, A. (2020) 'Xinjiang's System of Militarized Vocational Training Comes to Tibet' [Online] Available at https://jamestown.org/program/jamestown-early-warning-brief-xinjiangs-system-of-militarized-vocational-training-comes-to-tibet/ (Accessed 22 January 2023)
(2021) 'Coercive Labor and Forced Displacement in Xinjiang's Cross-Regional Labor Transfer Program' [Online] Available at https://jamestown.org/product/coercive-labor-and-forced-displacement-in-xinjiangs-cross-regional-labor-transfer-program/ (Accessed 21 January 2023)

Zhang, P. (2021) 'Nomadland director Chloé Zhao's historic Oscars win censored in China, months after she was accused of insulting the country', *South China Morning Post*, 26 April [Online] Available at https://www.scmp.com/lifestyle/entertainment/article/3131131/nomadland-director-chloe-zhaos-historic-oscars-win-censored (Accessed 25 January 2023)

Zheng, S. (2021) 'US-China tensions: Joe Biden signals tougher line on Beijing with key appointments', *South China Morning Post*, 21 February [Online] Available at https://www.scmp.com/news/china/diplomacy/article/3122370/us-china-tensions-joe-biden-signals-tougher-line-beijing-key (Accessed 28 January 2023)

Zheng, W. and Baptista, E. (2021) 'Touchdown for China's Mars rover Zhu Rong after "nine minutes of terror"', *South China Morning Post*, 15 May [Online] Available at https://www.scmp.com/news/china/science/article/3133587/china-successfully-lands-mars-rover-zhu-rong-after-nine-minutes (Accessed 23 July 2023)

Zhou, C. (2020) 'China debt: Beijing may cut belt and road lending due to domestic pressure, to ensure future of project', *South China Morning Post*, 24 November [Online] Available at https://www.scmp.com/economy/china-economy/article/3111052/china-debt-beijing-may-cut-belt-and-road-lending-due-domestic (Accessed 25 January 2023)

Zhou, L. (2021) 'Japan weighs in on South China Sea dispute, adding to pressure on Beijing', *South China Morning Post*, 21 January [Online] Available at https://www.scmp.com/news/china/diplomacy/article/3118717/japan-weighs-south-china-sea-dispute-adding-pressure-beijing (Accessed 28 January 2023)

Zylberman, J. (2021) 'Climat: la Chine peut-elle sortir de ses contradictions?', *Asialyst*, 29 January [Podcast] Available at https://asialyst.com/fr/2021/01/29/podcast-climat-chine-sortir-contradictions/ (Accessed 22 January 2023)

23h (2021), 'Ouïghours: "La Chine remplit tous les critères de définition du génocide"', *France Info*, 13 March [Online] Available at https://www.francetvinfo.fr/monde/chine/ouighours-la-chine-remplit-tous-les-criteres-de-definition-du-genocide_4332709.html?fbclid=IwAR3NqMdBWOpk5tzc2-6SC-y_c5fIvSubOsMv8Gtho4joG46L66H4IBya_R8#xtor=CS2-765-%5Bautres%5D- (Accessed 21 January 2023)

Current Bestsellers from Changemakers Books

Resetting our Future: Am I Too Old to Save the Planet?
A Boomer's Guide to Climate Action
Lawrence MacDonald
Why American boomers are uniquely responsible for the
climate crisis — and what to do about it.

Resetting our Future: Feeding Each Other
Shaping Change in Food Systems through Relationship
Michelle Auerbach and Nicole Civita
Our collective survival depends on making food systems more
relational; this guidebook for shaping change in food systems
offers a way to find both security and pleasure in a more
connected, well-nourished life.

Resetting Our Future: Zero Waste Living, The 80/20 Way
The Busy Person's Guide to a Lighter Footprint
Stephanie J. Miller
Empowering the busy individual to do the easy things that
have a real impact on the climate and waste crises.

The Way of the Rabbit
Mark Hawthorne
An immersion in the world of rabbits: their habitats, evolution
and biology; their role in legend, literature, and popular
culture; and their significance as household companions.